AN EARLY BLUEPRINT FOR ZIONISM

Győző Istóczy's Political Anti–Semitism

by

Andrew Handler

EAST EUROPEAN MONOGRAPHS, BOULDER
DISTRIBUTED BY COLUMBIA UNIVERSITY PRESS, NEW YORK

1989

EAST EUROPEAN MONOGRAPHS, NO. CCLXI

Contents

Preface

The subject of this study, Győző Istóczy (1842–1915), has been lurking in the back of my mind for years, more recently, steadily inching his way to the fore. I was acutely aware of his omniscient, alas malignant, presence when I worked on *Blood Libel of Tiszaeszlár*. When I assembled the mosiac of the childhood of Theodor Herzl, the future founder of Zionism, in *Dori: The Life and Times of Theodor Herzl in Budapest, 1960–1878* I reluctantly found his emergent political philosophy unexpectedly, yet intriguingly relevant.

Győző Istóczy should be a household name with an ominous ring of unwelcome familiarity to anyone interested in the political history of Central Europe in the latter half of the nineteenth century or in modern Jewish history. It is not. Indeed, aside from a vulgar panegyric, *Istóczy Győző élete és küzdelmei [The Life and Battles of Győző Istóczy]*, by Zoltán Bosnyák, a teacher–turned–journalist who was tried and executed by the Communists in 1945 as a war criminal, the interest that Istóczy generated has been insufficient to make him the subject of an independent study.

In Hungary, a small image–conscious country before the Communist takeover in 1948 and a thoroughly ideologized satellite of the Soviet Union since then, individuals who gained—even briefly—international notice through notoriety have been treated with hostile circumspection. For more than a century the name of Győző Istóczy, the founder of political anti–Semitism in Hungary, has erratically bounced like a ball, from hands anxious to throw it away to hands eager to grab it, however briefly. In his lifetime, the very mention of his name evoked contempt and derision from notable people; in the interwar years it was warmly embraced and nurtured by right–wing politicians and the proponents of racism; however, since 1948 it has been treated like a malady. The less it is seen and heard, the better. Outside Hungary it has cropped up occasionally in the writings of fascist émigré writers, tired refrains of a lost cause.

This is a political biography of Győző Istóczy, a man who was consumed by politics much of his adult life. In deference to two excellent studies, Nathaniel Katzburg, *Antishemiyut be–Hungariyah (1867–1914) [Anti–Semitism in Hungary]* and Judit Kubinszky, *Poli-*

tikai antiszemitizmus Magyarországon (1875–1890) [Political Anti-Semitism in Hungary], I chose not to expand, but foray occasionally and briefly, into the general history of political anti–Semitism in Hungary. I undertook this study for three reasons. First, the absence of a scholarly study of Győző Istóczy's political career is a grievous oversight that has been uncorrected long enough. Second, it is generally assumed that the ideology and activism of modern anti–Semitism grew out of the seminal activities of Austro–German politicians, Karl Lüger, Georg von Schönerer and Adolf Stöcker. Documentary evidence, however, indicates a need to reassign chronological precedence. It was Istóczy not his better known ideological comrades–in–arms, who first injected the venomous demagoguery of political anti–Semitism into politics and society. His truculent logic and boisterous demagoguery earned him ephemeral fame in Hungary—he would see it dissipate just as quickly as it appeared—and an enviable measure of international recognition. He was the object of infectious admiration on one hand and of obdurate ridicule and passionate hatred on the other. Third, though no concrete evidence to support this thesis exists, I am convinced that Istóczy's political program, developed in speeches delivered in the old House of Parliament in Pest (and virtually within hearing distance of the building where the teenaged Theodor Herzl lived), had a direct, though perhaps subconscious, influence on the evolution of Herzlian Zionism two decades later.

I would like to express my thanks to a small group of helpers. The late Alexander Scheiber, Director of the Hungarian Rabbinical Seminary, was my teacher and mentor. His death was both a personal and professional loss to me. Although he disapproved of my interest in Istóczy, for emotional reasons, he was a veritable pillar of support, assisting my efforts to secure known sources and calling my attention to ones which otherwise might have eluded me. I derived much satisfaction and profit from the unabating encouragement of my wife and my mother, who also typed the manuscript. Finally, I am indebted to the University of Miami for awarding me a 1986 Max Orovitz Summer Award and thus enabling me to complete weeks of research in the British Library in London.

Chapter I

Youth

If birthplace and upbringing are factors that contribute to the shaping of one's character and the tone and directions of one's career, fate could hardly have assigned a more appropriate congruence of influences to the future founder of political anti–Semitism.

Táplánszentkereszt, a small town where Győző Istóczy was born on 7 November 1842, is in Vas, one of the westernmost counties of Hungary. The cool shadow of the picturesque Austrian Alps, with their abundant rivers and forests, creates an idyllic landscape. Nature, however, is not the area's sole claim to fame and popularity. The area possesses a keen sense of history as well. The principal cities of the region, Szombathely, Kőszeg and Sárvár, situated on a nearly perfect triangle within a distance of thirty miles from one another, proudly proclaim their common origin in Roman antiquity and claim they have been inhabited for nineteen turbulent centuries.

An interesting phenomenon becomes evident to observers of the peoples, culture, and customs of Hungary's westernmost countryside. Since the latter part of the fourteenth century, Pozsony, Sopron and Vas, counties with large and steadily growing population of German–speaking residents, have been constantly exposed to anti–Jewish legislation. Thus, they also were familiar with the resulting prejudice and discrimination felt by exclusivist burghers and xenophobic peasant alike[1] against the members of a religious group whose very physical presence, appearance, and lifestyle were viewed as chronic social and religious irritants.

Favorable and ostensibly relevant influences notwithstanding, no documentable evidence which connects Istóczy's childhood and life-long Judeophobia has come to light. According to his birth certificate, which was preserved in the Roman Catholic rectory of Táplánszent-kereszt, Győző Istóczy was born on 7 November 1842. His parents, Antal and Franciska, née Egerváry, came from similar family backgrounds. Both were Roman Catholic and of noble descent. It is alleged that the paternal family name originated in the town of Istócz, near Kanizsa, a city in neighboring Zala County, and had ceased to exist centuries earlier. The aristocratic forenames, pölöskefői and kürtösi, also stand for localities in Zala. The Istóczy family tradition proudly enshrines 1538 as the year in which the earliest written records about the Istóczys were made and identifies one Lukács Istóczy as the first link to nobility. He received the document of ennoblement from Emperor Maximilian in 1575 and designed the family crest, a griffin standing on a green mound and holding three roses against a background of blue. The maternal line lays claim to an even more impressive genealogy. The Egervárys, whose name derives from Egervár, a small town in the northernmost part of Zala County, trace the identity of their ancestors as far back as 1073. Neither family, however, possesses records indicating the time and circumstances of its settlement in adjacent Vas County, which was to become the land of their union. The inherent advantages of an aristocratic background and individual ambition and initiative on his father's part spared Győző much of the countryside's melancholic uneventfulness, a condition which both Hungarian writers and foreign travelers describe in harshly–worded, albeit true, accounts.[2] Like many heads of gentry families and some of his ancestors, Antal Istóczy had chosen not to dedicate his life to the gentlemanly pursuit of estate management. The family manor near the village of Dömötöri, the centerpiece of an irreversibly shrinking estate no larger than a hundred acres in Győző's boyhood, attested more to a tradition of diverted interest than a legacy of mismanagement. The Istóczys had acquired a reputation of aspiring to positions in county politics and administration. Premature death and the meagerness of biographical data are the principal obstacles to investigating beyond the faint image of Istóczy's father. Antal Istóczy appears to have been a man of learning and ambitions, qualities that in time would enable him to find a respectable position in civil service as a public prosecutor of Vas County. The aforementioned obstacles do not even allow for the presentation of circumstantial or deductive evidence in the attempt to unravel the mystery that engulfed much of his son's youth. What kind of man, husband and father was he? How did he respond to the demands of his position? Did fatherly influence have anything to do with planting the seeds of the son's future Judeophobia? Though such questions challenge the investigating mind they must inevitably leave it unrequited.

An only slightly better fate awaits one who attempts to rescue Győző's mother from oblivion. Inferential data, however, may augment the paucity of information about the former Franciska Egerváry. In a society of rigid customs and traditional values, the conventions of family life bestow upon the father a three–dimensional role of hard working provider, stern moral guide and frequently heavy–handed educator. The premature death of Antal Istóczy created a vacuum which only a determined, strong-willed and perspicacious Franciska could fill successfully. She not only transformed the steadily dwindling and unprofitable estate into a solitary, viable source of income, an unenviable task given the declining fortune of the Istóczys, but she also assumed some responsibility for her son's upbringing and education. Győző's unremitting filial devotion and unusual intellectual versatility would prove that she succeeded on both counts.

Though the particulars of Győző's boyhood and early schooling are lost, apparently irretrievably so, it seems that the absence of the usual, severe paternal discipline did not have adverse effects. One can assume that his early years were happy and carefree. No trace of a traumatic childhood experience, save his father's death, is discernible in any of Istóczy's autobiographical writings. Similarly, the absence of pertinent data prevents any attempt to reconstruct the nature and extent of Győző's earliest educational experience. Did Franciska guide her son's first steps into the realm of learning? Did she hire a private tutor? Or was he enrolled in the elementary school in the village? Again, such questions must go unanswered. Still, retrospection may provide a faint glimpse into that hitherto closed chapter of Győző's life. Whatever the circumstances of his earliest learning experience, the young gentry boy encountered no obstacles in making the often difficult psychological and cultural transition from the placid simplicity of village life to the sights and sounds of a bustling large city. That achievement was due in no small measure to Franciska's good judgment in deciding to provide her son with both the firm foundations of a future career befitting his social origins, and the means to realize it.

In the mid-nineteenth century, Szombathely was the economic and cultural center of not only Vas County but the whole westernmost region of Transdanubia as well. Since the Romans founded it in the middle of the first century A.D., the city, originally called Savaria, had been a commercial and religious center for nearly half a millennium. It fell victim to a devastating earthquake in 455, and to attacks by marauding barbarian tribes. It lay in ruins, deserted and hopelessly desolated it seemed. It was, however, rebuilt and repopulated in the latter half of the ninth century. Subsequently, Szombathely witnessed many battles over the control of the city until it was designated as free in 1407, and as the administrative center of the county in 1578. Its vulnerability was again revealed during the anti-Habsburg wars of István Bocskai (1604-1606) and the revolt of Ferenc Rákóczi II (1703-1711). Fires also severely set back its development. Szombathely's fast-paced restoration and steady rise to one of Hungary's most prestigious cities began in the latter half of the eighteenth century when it became a bishopric and a thriving, guild–run commercial and manufacturing center. János Szily (1735–1799), who in 1777 became its first bishop, was a patron of architects and men of letters. He was the inspirational and driving force behind the construction of Szombathely's imposing cathedral, bishop's palace and seminary. A discriminating and learned bibliophile whose famous library was an object of envy and admiration among the literati, Bishop Szily was also the founder of a printing press. The lyceum, established in 1793, was one of the treasured educational institutions of the city. This progressive attitude attracted the sons of wealthy and socially prominent families, including István Széchenyi, destined to become one of Hungary's greatest politicians. Before Szombathely could fully utilize the opportunities the Industrial Revolution provided, it had to overcome the effects of the 110–day occupation of Napoleon's army (1809) and a devastating fire (1817).[3]

Such was the city that received the young gentry boy from the quiet countryside. It provided an introduction to the sophisticated urban lifestyle that would, with rare interruptions, captivate Istóczy to the end of his life. He would give his mother no reason to regret her decision to educate him in Szombathely. Győző is said to have been an outstanding student, his talents more evident in writing and music. He was the editor of a student newspaper in which he published his earliest writings. His instrument is yet to be identified, but he was sufficiently proficient in music to give public concerts. Though none of his works are extant, Győző was also credited with an unmistakable flair in painting. Finally, his talents were not limited to the realm of the cerebral. He excelled in sports and was a member of the county's gymnastic association. Small wonder that a young man of an acceptable social standing and an unusual combination of achievements should find none of the doors of the houses of Szombathely's well–to–do and socially prominent citizens closed.

In regard to Istóczy's hatred for Jews, an obsession that was to consume much of his adult life, one is tempted to search for early clues. Not one has ever been found. Theoretically, in the first ten years of his life Győző could hardly have been familiar with the future objects of his implacable wrath. The list of Jewish communities in Vas County in the nineteenth century does not include the place of his birth.[4] Still, the possibility of his sighting itinerant Jewish peddlers or Jewish merchants traveling through his hometown is a reasonable conjecture. Dömötöri was situated midway between Rohonc, the city with the oldest and once the largest Jewish community in Vas County, and Vasvár,[5] a town in the southeastern region of the county where

Jews had settled in the early 1800s.

No documentary evidence can be cited in response to the hypothetical question of whether Istóczy, an intelligent, inquisitive and impressionable young man could spend eight years in a city with an established Jewish community and remain oblivious to its members. Jews had lived in Szombathely since the late seventeenth century. For nearly a century and a half their community was a branch of the Jews of Rohonc. In 1830 the community became independent and elected the merchant–turned–rabbi Lajos Königsberger its first spiritual leader. By then a permanent synagogue had been built. The *Chevra Kaddisha* (burial society) was established in 1828, and a Jewish school opened its doors in 1842. The Jews of Szombathely took an active part in the thriving economy of the city and extended their operations into the adjacent countryside.[6] Győző would leave the city apparently without the Jews having left an indelible impression on him in one way or another. His anti–Jewish harangues contain no mention of the Jews of Szombathely.

It could be expected that a young boy at the threshold of adulthood would consider the practicality of returning home and helping his widowed mother manage the family estate in preparation of running it himself in the not too distant future. Yet the multitalented Győző's unmistakable display of intellectual prowess and creative energy would point to a more reasonable, though less pragmatic, alternative. His decision to continue his pursuit of intellectual goals must have come from a maternal recognition of such virtues and from her obligation to ensure the continuation of the family tradition in public service. A decision to have Győző return home would have ill–served either consideration.

Preparation for a career in public service or simply creating a convenient subterfuge to extend the pleasures of carefree student life—it is not known if Győző had already shown preference for a profession—was thought best served by enrolling in the law school of one of Hungary's two universities. Neither institution had earned the respect usually accorded facilities of higher learning. According to the pundits, the faculty of law in both universities was a "doctor factory" which conferred with alarming indiscrimination the prestigious title on outstanding lawyers as well as undeserving youths who passed the examinations only because of their social status and influence.[7] Sheer distance and the prolonged inconveniences of travel and communication—it was located in the other extremity of the country—may have ruled out the University of Kolozsvár for Győző. He then made the decision in favor of the bustling capital: Pest–Buda. No matter how demanding a nearly 200–kilometer bumpy ride in a horse–drawn carriage may have been, the tired passenger could hardly remain unimpressed by the unfolding spectacle of sights and the cacophony of sounds as he was nearing his destination.

It would take but a short time for the newcomer to learn to appreciate the natural beauty of the city. When approached from the west, arguably the best angle from which to see the whole city, the mountains of Buda come into view. One of the most picturesque of European capitals, the city cradles the Danube as if the river belonged to no one else. Buda, on the right, stood as a tranquil monument to Hungary's rich legacy with its cheerfully unassuming small houses and huts which followed the gentle flow of the hills; its ornate Gothic churches and majestically solemn royal palace; and quaint suburbs. The sole dissonant feature may have been the frequency with which one could hear German spoken among its 60,000 residents. Pest then was linked only by the famous Lánchíd (Chain Bridge) and a tunnel to its older and smaller counterpart. No link could, however, narrow the gap between the differences in appearance and character. Resting on an expansive plain which facilitated its rapid urban growth and industrial development, Pest, with its wide tree–lined thoroughfares, imposing public buildings and large apartment houses, and proliferating factories, exuded the confident spirit of incipient capitalism and industrialization. Ironically, modern Pest rather than historic Buda emitted sounds more soothing and familiar to the visitor accustomed to hearing and speaking the national tongue. The majority of its population of 120,000, especially in the bustling, elegant inner district, spoke mostly Hungarian. Once there, those who came in search of knowledge headed in the direction of the light green building of the university.[8]

The newcomer could hardly have chosen a more propitious time to arrive in Pest–Buda than the early 1860s. The painful memories of the Hungarians' heroic but ill–fated revolution against the Habsburgs had eased somewhat and the decade–long Austrian absolutism, the Bach System, that followed it had been dismantled in the aftermath of the Austrians' surprisingly poor performance against the armies of France and Piedmont–Sardinia. The Treaty of Villafranca (11 July 1859) and the Peace of Zürich (10 November 1859) exposed the manifold weaknesses of the Habsburg empire and left its absolutist ruler, Francis Joseph, stunned and shaken. The Hungarians were quick to take advantage of the situation. Rallying around Ferenc Deák, the venerable "Sage of the Nation," whose pragmatic philosophy departed from the revolutionary fervor of Lajos Kossuth, the implacably Austrophobic leader of the 1848 Revolution, the Hungarians sought a secured position of partnership with the Austrians within the framework of the imperial system. The promulgation of the so–called October Diploma (20 October 1860), which eased many of the most offensive features of Austrian absolutism in Hungary, was a belated sign of Francis Joseph's recognition of the realities of his changed position.

The majority of the people of the countryside kept disdainfully aloof from the middle class lifestyle. Both the tradition–bound peasantry, viewed as the true upholders of the Magyar soul and culture, and the haughtily exclusivist landed aristocracy and gentry looked to Pest–Buda as the reprehensible stronghold of German burghers and Jewish merchants. Yet the big city showed unmistakable sounds and sights of unabashed patriotism. Any gathering of people, planned or accidental, led to a spirited singing of nationalistic songs or chanting of political slogans. Distinctively Hungarian attires worn even over clerical garbs could be seen with increased frequency especially in the central districts. In cafés, restaurants, and bookstores, in the immensely popular Városliget, an expansive meadow in the outskirts of Pest, and in the abundantly green hills of Buda, carefree crowds basked in the sunshine of pretended freedom, making plans for an even brighter future.[9]

If the reputation of the Faculty of Law of the University of Pest left a great deal to be desired, its facilities were even less inviting. Founded by Péter Pázmány (1570–1637), the cardinal archbishop of Esztergom and the leader of the Counter–Reformation in Hungary, in 1635 and located in the northeastern city of Nagyszombat, the university was moved to Buda in 1777 and subsequently to the central district of Pest. There it was set up in a building that had previously housed the monks of the Order of St. Paul and until 1783 the *Kúria* (High Court). The school of law was assigned three lecture halls and a faculty lounge. The halls with low ceilings, small windows and forbiddingly spartan seating could accommodate no more than two–thirds of the students at any given time. By the early 1860s the number of law students exceeded a thousand, yet the law faculty consisted of less than a dozen regular members. Still, excellence of the faculty offered a measure of compensation for their insufficient number. Among the professors were such luminaries as Ágost Karvasy, an expert in political science and commercial law; János Baintner, who taught civil law and authored well–received works on Austrian civil law; Tivadar Pauler, whose *Penal Law* raised Hungarian jurisprudence near the western European standard and made him one of the most celebrated legal experts of his time, and who in the 1870s would serve consecutively as minister of cults and public education and minister of justice; and Gusztáv Wenzel, a much–respected expert and prolific author on the history of law upon whom the Emperor Francis Joseph would confer a noble title in 1879 in recognition of his lifelong service. Furthermore, many of the pains of pedagogical regimentation—students were required to listen to 20 hours a week of legal instruction as well as three series of lectures (philosophy, history, and an elective) in the faculty of philosophy—were eased by awards of partial or full scholarships, useful handbooks distributed by the professors, and last but not least, the proximity of Pest's entertaining and fashionable central district that could temporarily free even the most studious mind from the anguish and rigor of academic discipline.[10]

Istóczy would give the admissions officials of the university no cause to regret their decision to accept him as a regular student. He thrived in Pest. No unpleasant memories, save one with regard to acquiring the title of *doctor juris*, would cloud his memories of his years as a law student. He passed his examinations with distinction. For reasons never explained, Istóczy decided to continue his studies in Vienna. Perhaps his decision was prompted by a need to utilize his uncommon facility in foreign languages or by a combination of curiosity and restiveness, traits that would soon lead to extensive travels abroad. His stay in the imperial city remains among the most cryptic experiences of his youth. It also went against all reasonable considerations. In view of the Hungarians' defiant flaunting of their nationalist feelings and their virtually uniform rejection of everything Austrian, a person seeking a career in the civil service or politics could well do without such associations. Istóczy's only unsavory memory of his student years bears out that conclusion. In the 1865–1866 academic year, following his return from Vienna, the strenuous preparations for three qualifying examinations nearly cost him his health. However, he did not seek to have the title of *doctor juris* conferred on him. Due to the unpopularity of the increasing numbers of Austrian *doctors juris* in Hungary—the title itself was viewed as a hated symbol of the absolutist Bach System—many graduates of the two Hungarian law schools declined to become its bearers. He would regret that decision years later; however, he obtained a diploma attesting his qualification to practice civil and exchange law.

Contrary to his mother's designs and expectations, Istóczy displayed no inclination to return permanently to the family estate and assume its management. She should have known better. During his periodic visits home he did chores his mother asked of him, more out of filial love than a burgeoning interest in agriculture. Soon, however, he would be found absorbed in one of his ubiquitous books. That proclivity for studiousness was one of his most durable and observable traits. Even after the completion of his legal studies he chose to broaden and enrich his experiences. He embarked on an extended journey—no doubt with his mother's support—during which he visited Austria, Switzerland, Germany, France, and England. His proficiency in the languages spoken in these countries made the experience all the more enjoyable and rewarding. It is said that he also knew Latin, a not altogether surprising attribute of intellectuals of his time, and Hebrew, an extraordinary achievement.[11]

The quest for early influences that would inevitably contribute to the evolution of Istóczy's implacable Judeophobia reveals two avenues leading to obvious sources. The first involved the university itself. No Jew had ever sat among its students, a tradition that started in Nagyszombat. Technically, Jews were not prohibited by law to seek admission. However, by the time the university was established in 1635, nearly a hundred years had passed since the Emperor Ferdinand had expelled them from the city. Only by complying with the precondition, subsequently laid down, that he convert to Roman Catholicism could a Jew hope to gain entry to the university. Thus, until it was relocated in Pest, the university was not confronted with the challenge of admitting students of the Jewish faith.[12] Notwithstanding a gubernatorial rescript, issued on 6 March 1827, that provided assurances to qualified Jewish students that they would be admitted to the law faculty of universities and provided means to pursue and complete their legal studies, the admission records at the University of Pest as late as 1840 showed not a single application for admission submitted by a student of the Jewish faith.

The first Jew to test the practicality of the rescript was one József Basch, a merchant in Szeged, who in 1840 attempted to have his son, Móric, enrolled in the faculty of law in Pest. However, Dean Ferenc Vizkelety, an expert in canon law and a vocal proponent of the retention of German as the official language of instruction, turned down Basch's application. In a complaint submitted to the council of the governor–general, the elder Basch stated that his son had been admitted but other students prevented him from attending the lectures. The council agreed and instructed Vizkelety to comply with the rescript. The dean, however, remained defiant. There were three reasons, he argued, that prompted him to reject the application. First, the younger Basch, in the presence of several eyewitnesses, committed a deceitful act in connection with the payment of tuition. He had paid an insufficient sum (1 forint and 40 krajcárs), but after he was prevented from entering the classroom, he demanded the refund of the full tuition (3 forints). Thirdly, Jews had not pursued legal studies at Hungarian universities since time immemorial. In addition, Vizkelety reasoned, the rescript had been issued upon the request of one Ábrahám Fleischer, a Jew who was preparing to convert which he subsequently in fact did; at no point was the rescript implemented.[13] He also cited the threat of violent reaction by law students to the presence of a Jew, a situation that would disturb order and discipline. He blamed the younger Basch for willfully causing unnecessary disturbance by insisting upon being seated in the classroom of first–year law students, even though his application for admission had been turned down. The other students had removed him by force.[14] The embarrassing incident was forgotten with the young Basch's departure. The law school, however, remained tainted with the stigma of anti–Semitism for decades. Future generations of students—many would be political and judicial luminaries—were exposed to the unsavory atmosphere which the Basch affair and its legacy only exacerbated.

The other source of anti–Semitic impulses Istóczy inevitably absorbed was Tivadar Pauler. One of Hungary's leading criminalists, Pauler deservedly earned a reputation that kept him on a course of steady progress to the highest positions in academic life and of juridical and ministerial responsibility. He was professor of penal law (1852–1878) and rector (1861–1862) at the University of Pest. Istóczy's complimentary remarks about him in his later writings demonstrate convincingly that of all his law professors Pauler had left an indelible impression on him. On first consideration, Istóczy's association with the faculty of law at the University of Pest could be cited as proof that the prevailing anti–Semitic atmosphere at the university caused him no pangs of conscience. But an event that took place nearly twenty years after Istóczy completed his legal studies makes retrospective confirmation of a suspicion a worthwhile undertaking. In the course of the infamous blood libel of Tiszaeszlár,[15] the greatest obstacle to quickly resolving the case that turned into a major embarrassment for the government of Kálmán Tisza proved to be the unmistakably obstructionist stance struck by Pauler, then the minister of justice. It became clear that he had taken great pains to conceal the Judeophobia which would have been an impediment to his brilliant career had it been public knowledge.

Ironically, Istóczy's legal studies at the University of Pest coincided with the appearance of the first generation of Jewish law students of significant numbers. Between 1861 and 1864, four Jewish *doctors juris*—Simon Goldstein, Ármin Schönberger, a former rabbi of Eperjes named Beck, and Mór Mezei, soon to become one of the most distinguished leaders of Hungarian Jewry—passed the bar.[16] No trace of predisposition to anti–Semitism during his early years in Pest can be discerned in Istóczy's later writings; no record of his coming face to face with a Jewish law student has come to light. Similarly, despite his interest in Hebrew—there in fact is no way to determine when he actually started studying it or reached his proficiency in it. His knowledge of it would presuppose a modicum of interest in the people whose sacred language it was, but his proximity at the university to Józsefváros and Ferencváros, the two districts of Pest most densely populated by Jews, seems inconsequential. He was seemingly oblivious to the conspicuous, magyarizing and patriotic Jews in Pest who were rapidly forsaking the petrified stereotypic images for assimilation.[17] Clustered around the Dohány–Street Synagogue, the recently (1859) completed pseudo–Moorish edifice, these truly progressive Jews were led by their indefatigable president, Dr. Ignác Hirschler, a prominent opthalmologist with useful ties to many of Hungary's political and cultural notables. They were enthusiastic practitioners of Magyarization, pragmatic contributors to, and grateful beneficiaries of social, economic and cultural endeavors aimed at transforming Hungary into a modern nation.[18] None of the manifestations of these anti–Semitic characteristics in his environment left a lasting impression on Istóczy. Whatever the extent of his familiarity with the lifestyle of the Jews of Pest in the 1860s, it would not influence his emergent anti–Semitic political and social philosophy. Instead the Jews of the countryside and the new immigrant Jews—with whom he was considerably less familiar—would become the principal targets of his venomous remarks and political philosophy based on demagoguery.[19] Predictably, Pest's progressive Jewry would ill–serve his anachronistic world view and largely inaccurate generalizations. The mythical figure of the wandering Jew was awaiting its newest animator.

Chapter II

In Search of a Springboard

For a young man of twenty–four, the transition from the life of a student to the adult world of uncertainties and decisions can result in his becoming extremely introverted. A student experiences prolonged periods of anguished preparation followed by brief exhilarating moments over high marks on examinations. All external occurrences are reduced to inconsequentia in a mind absorbed in fulfilling personal priorities. "Studying, of which I did so much, nearly cost me my health," recalled Istóczy about his last months as a law student.[1] In doing just that, he would have remained oblivious to the unfolding of one of the most momentous sequences of events in the history of modern Hungary, even though he was in the enviable position of being a virtual eyewitness to it. Luckily he passed his qualifying examinations by the end of 1866. With his lawyer's diploma in his pocket, he was free to reflect, observe and plan ahead. He could not witness the glittering climax that capped numerous rounds of parliamentary tugs–of–war: Austria's humiliation at Königgrätz (3 July 1866), Francis Joseph's Waterloo; two rounds of negotiation in Budapest and Vienna between Hungarian and Austrian ministerial delegations, led by Count Gyula Andrássy and Foreign Minister Baron Friedrich Ferdinand Breust, respectively; and the somber, contested ratification in Hungary's divided Parliament. The *Ausgleich* that transformed the Habsburg empire into the Dual Monarchy was for Hungary both a pragmatic solution to a multiplicity of grievances and inequities and a compromised fulfillment of the ideals and aspirations of 1848.

On 18 February 1867 Francis Joseph restored the constitution. Hungarians all over the country celebrated and held torch–lit parades. The streets of Pest–Buda were filled with people greeting the dawn of a new age by the light of hundreds of candles on the broad façade of the National Museum that spelled out the word *Ministerium.* On 8 June, amid the solemn notes of Liszt's Coronation Mass in Buda's historic Mátyás Church, Prime Minister Count Gyula Andrássy, with the help of the archbishops of Esztergom and Kalocsa, placed the crown of St. István on the head of Francis Joseph, proclaiming him king of Hungary. Heading an elaborately gowned procession of nobles and church dignitaries and surrounded by a mounted escort bearing standards, the newly crowned king of Hungary was greeted by excited throngs. The nostalgic recreation of medieval pomp and ritual befitted the transformation of the thoroughly Austrian emperor into a much–beloved national king and, with Hungary's help, propped up of his tottering state system and created an illusion of quasi–independence.[2] Much of that illusion rested on both the fragile shoulders of the immensely popular Empress Elizabeth, viewed by Hungarians as a true friend and tactful intermediary, and on an incorrigible press known for manipulating public opinion.[3] Settling into a half century of uneasy coexistence, Hungarians would soon discover that the real obstacle to the fulfillment of their national aspirations was the obdurant monarch himself whose heavily accented, halting Hungarian could barely conceal a genuine antipathy toward its native speakers.

Two options awaited Istóczy in his virtually preordained way of life. He could accede to the wish his mother had nurtured for so long. By returning to the family estate and attempting to reverse its slow but steady deterioration, he would simultaneously fulfill his filial obligation and enter the ranks of the thousands in his social class whose estates suffered from their bad management and pursuit of a care-free, extravagant lifestyle. Clearly, neither temperament nor business acumen drew him in that direction. His sporadic visits to the estate were more a thoughtful gesture than a declaration of intent. Not even motherly forbearance overlooked his indifferent attitude indefinitely. "I can't use this Győző for anything," she would at last say with a mixture of regret and forgiveness.[4] By the time he completed his legal studies the decision not to bind himself to the family estate was a foregone conclusion.

He found the second option far more appealing. Clinging to the illusions of the bygone days of their privileged status, young lawyers of gentry background acquired positions in county administrations as a means to ensconce themselves in the life their ancestors had sought to perpetuate. Or, they used these positions as a training ground for a career in county or national politics. For the latter, four prerequisites were considered indispensable: suitable qualifications, such as professional, preferably legal, training; some administrative or juridical experience; the ability to make promises and keep them; and an impressionable and supportive constituency. In 1867 Istóczy possessed none of them, but within five years he would return to Pest and take his place among elected representatives in the Diet.

For a young man of Istóczy's social background and professional preparation, acquiring the first prerequisite took little more than making the decision to do it and working at it. Soon after his return from

Pest in 1867 and his short–lived and unfulfilling attempt at private practice, Istóczy entered public service. The initial results were auspicious. In the same year he was elected deputy clerk of Vas County, an impressive achievement considering his lack of experience and narrow base of operation and support. By his own account, he "took a very active part in the public affairs of Vas County,"[5] yet during the brief tenure of his first elective position there was only one event he deemed worthy of recalling. Though the event itself was odd and unexpected, it is Istóczy's description of the circumstances surrounding it that makes it a matter of considerable significance. Current knowledge about the event and Istóczy's observation of it reveal details regarding Istóczy and Vas County. Thus, significant implications previously based solely on circumstantial evidence can be fully corroborated for the first time.

In 1867, using whatever personal and political influence he might have exerted as deputy county clerk, Istóczy campaigned hard for a former law–school classmate who was running for the elective post of county venireman. The unnamed candidate was a Jew. Istóczy took credit for getting his classmate elected, noting that he then was not an anti–Semite—though he had plenty of personal reasons to be one—and many of his prospective supporters, prominent and influential in county politics, even took offense at his activities in behalf of the Jewish candidate.[6] No direct evidence has been found to substantiate the statement concerning his feelings about Jews. Again more questions can be posed than answers found. Was he referring to childhood experiences? Could he have meant impressions he formed of Jews while studying in Szombathely, Pest or Vienna? Was the statement a reflection on something he witnessed during his travels abroad following his final examinations in law school? It is easier to ascertain the validity of the concluding portion of his description.

The manifestation of an anti–Semitic attitude among some politically active individuals may indeed have been triggered by Istóczy's public support of a Jewish candidate. However, anti–Semitism in Vas County had evolved as predictably and inevitably as in any other county of Hungary, although it is more difficult to logically justify its development there. Less than three decades earlier, delegates to the 1839–1840 Diet were engaged in a series of debates concerning the desirability of granting Hungary's Jewry civil equality. The courageous man who made the motion that "Jews be granted all the rights nobles possess" was the delegate from Vas County.[7] Simon Dubravitzy, the delegate from Pest County, seconded, and even amended the motion so that it would also contain certain provisions "making Judaism an accepted religion, granting civil equality, and making them eligible, if deserving, to receive titles of nobility."[8] The ensuing vote in the Lower House recommending passage of the motion was struck down by the Upper House of Magnates despite the passionate pleas of some of its most progressive members. The majority favored a gradual extension of civil rights. They voted to repeal the toleration tax, one of the more humiliating vestiges of medieval anti–Jewish legislation, and permit Jews to acquire urban real estate and become guild members.[9]

The growing recognition and appreciation of the socioeconomic utility of the Jews were firmly rooted, particularly in Vas County. Scattered among its population of 262,592 were 4,247 Jews who had been allowed to settle on estates belonging to nobles and bishops.[10] They were hardworking people who lived modestly and frugally, meeting with quiet determination the constant challenge which the payments of rent and taxes created. They were preoccupied with their children, hiring tutors, maintaining roving schools, and making joyous preparations for the impending holy days when they journeyed to the nearest large town with a permanent synagogue. Still, theirs was not a life of mysterious aloofness from non–Jews. In addition to their indispensable role in the rural economy, Jews in the many communities, especially in the areas of Vas County dominated by people of pure Magyar stock, spoke Hungarian fluently, "knew German about as well as they knew Chinese," and sang Hungarian songs and played Hungarian music at betrothals and weddings.[11] Such people would not give men like Istóczy cause for "many personal reasons to be an anti–Semite."

Reactions to his campaigning for the election of a Jewish candidate had no adverse effect on Istóczy's budding career. None of his prospective supporters remained resentful for long; he was in no danger of acquiring the reputation of being a Judeophile. In fact, he could hardly have advanced more rapidly even if he had allowed those unspecified personal reasons to take control of his political senses and voiced anti–Semitic views in public, an activity not commonly regarded as an impediment to political careers in the history of modern Hungary. In 1868, within a year of becoming deputy county clerk, Istóczy was appointed judge. In February 1867, the Diet passed a bill, a request of the ministry of justice, instructing the lord lieutenants of counties "to appoint suitable individuals, especially to judgeships, those knowledgeable of the law."[12] The appointment may indicate the twenty–six–year–old Istóczy's growing reputation in county administration. The virtual absence of corroborating evidence, however, creates an atmosphere of uncertainty and doubt regarding the motives behind his being appointed.

Had Istóczy displayed convincing proof of his expertise in law

within two years of his graduation from law school even after serving
a year in a position that did not offer him the opportunity to acquire
legal experience? Or was he appointed merely because he possessed a
law diploma and was at home in the backwater politics where a personal favorite was allowed an indiscretion, such as supporting a Jewish
candidate for a county post? Istóczy himself promoted the lingering
suspicion regarding his appointment. Never one to be accused of
modesty, oddly enough his recollection of his three years of juridical
service is limited to one case which shows him in an unfavorable light.
In the late 1860s authorities were embarrassed over the rapid proliferation of rural crimes attributed to virtually uncontrollable gangs
of rowdy highwaymen. Terrorized or adulating village folk protected
many of the highwaymen from inept Austrian gendarmes, unfamiliar
with the language and traditions of rural Hungarian society.[13] That
Istóczy had so few memories of such an area of jurisdiction brings his
legal expertise and recollective powers into question.

The case in question, a routine civil court proceeding, is remembered not for testing Istóczy's juridical qualities but for triggering
the release of a torrent of unsubstantiated suspicions and hateful
convictions—his first anti–Semitic salvos. The few details that may
be extracted from the meager sources of information portray him as
a man of uncontrolled emotions.[14] Istóczy was appointed supervi-
sor of an auction involving a sizeable estate located in Baltavár. The
bidding was unspectacular. However, soon thereafter Istóczy was con-
tacted by a wealthy Jew, a resident of the county, who claimed that his
son had used his name in making bids without written authorization.
The man wished to have the proceedings ruled void. A representative of the estate's creditors, "wealthy Viennese Jewish capitalists,"
attempted to dissuade Istóczy from reviewing the contested particulars and thus uphold the results of the auction. Caught between
conflicting Jewish interests, Istóczy ruled in favor of the plaintiff. A
new auction was held. The final bid, however, yielded 45,000 forints
less than that of the voided proceedings.[15] The angry creditors sued
Istóczy in an effort to recover the difference between the two final
bids. In turn, Istóczy sued the son of the wealthy Jew for the unau-
thorized use of his father's name. That move, however, resulted in a
sequence of events which Istóczy believed instigated an intercounty
"conspiracy of Jews" which targeted him as its victim. When the action of the "*kahal* of Szombathely" failed to have a mitigating effect
on him, the whole of the county's Jewry closed ranks in a display of
solidarity.[16]

The affair hovered like an oppressive cloud over his career but
did not jeopardize it. As he successfully weathered the controversy

which his support of a Jewish candidate had stirred up, his career in county administration suffered no visible setback as a result of the pending suit against him. The Baltaház affair dragged on for four years. In 1874 a lower court acquitted the defendant in Istóczy's suit and found Istóczy guilty of juridical misconduct. He was ordered to make full restitution to the Jewish creditors of the estate in the amount of 45,000 forints. Istóczy appealed the verdict and the *Kúria* overturned it. He was vindicated, financially and morally. His accuser was found guilty and ordered to pay the contested sum in full.

Even before his case was tried in court Istóczy had second thoughts about picking up the shattered pieces of his juridical career. He was convinced that the suit pending against him was manipulated by the "Pest *kahal*" after the machinations of its counterpart in Vas County had proved ineffective. He also suffered another recurring bout of anguish over his decision to not earn the title of *doctor juris*, a miscalculation, however patriotically motivated, that he regretted and viewed as a liability in his legal career. In 1871, in the course of the reorganization of the court system, he declined reappointment to the judgeship and arranged to be appointed *főszolgabíró* (chief magistrate) of the district of Vasvár, situated in southeastern Vas County. His designs on the new position turned out to be a convenient subterfuge, however, not an attempt to validate his somewhat tattered qualifications. "I went to Vasvár to become *főszolgabíró* with the assumption I would have myself elected its representative [in the Diet]," Istóczy recalled.[17] This time his calculations proved him right.

Putting some distance between himself and Szombathely, the city where the embarrassing incident had taken place and whose sizeable Jewry may have proved an obstacle to his political aspirations, seemed like a reasonable way out of his predicament. Vasvár, a picturesque hillside town whose archeologically traceable origins go back to Roman times when it was an important fortified settlement called Castrum Ferreum, provided Istóczy with suitably tranquil surroundings to regain his composure and plan his entry into national politics. The title of *főszolgabíró* and an enlarged jurisdiction would be additional feathers in his new political cap. He would also be less than likely to run into early opposition. The Jews of Vasvár were relative newcomers—the imperial decree allowing them to settle in the city and purchase real estate was issued in 1860—and more interested in laying firm community foundations and developing their spiritual and educational institutions than obstructing the political aspirations of the new *főszolgabíró*.

Although the tenure of his last post in county administration was brief and uneventful—no information concerning the quality and

details of his activities have come to light nor do Istóczy's subsequent writings contain clues—they are filled with puzzling inconsistencies. In twentieth–century right–wing hagiographies, the young
Istóczy's majestic rise to political prominence is strewn with pearls of
precocious wisdom. From a rural background of bureaucratic pet-
tiness, a young, talented politician arises with a humanistic program of national significance aimed at transforming the newly "self–
conscious masses into a massive political power."[18] A no less venerated political sage than Ferenc Deák serves as Istóczy's political
godfather. Upon recognizing Istóczy's outstanding qualities and political promise, Deák persuades him to enter the turbulent world of
politics and arranges an audience for him with the kind–hearted, Hun-
garophile Empress Elizabeth.[19] One can hardly resist imagining a
smirking Istóczy perusing such accounts of himself with benign incredulity. Not even he, who later mastered the art of making lies and
accusations, could have done it better. Yet the person responsible for
such flagrant distortions of historical truths was, to be sure, Istóczy
himself. His visceral description of the circumstances of his initial for-
ays into the political battlefield is a true presage of the obsession that
would engulf his career from start to finish. Through the deceiving
haze of more than thirty years, he managed to salvage some details
intact and infuse modest though ill–conceived personal motives with
the false ring of self–aggrandizement, Istóczy saw himself as a heroic
victim of his own convictions, struggling mightily and nearly going
bankrupt, to cast off the shackles of a nationwide Jewish conspiracy.[20]

It is difficult to gauge the degree of unsavoriness with which
the Baltaház affair tainted Istóczy's reputation. Prior to 1867, anti–
Jewish statements of varying intensity in local and national politics
had been uttered with impunity by some of Hungary's most respected
politicians. Many such statements were made out of heartfelt, though
ill–founded, concerns for the good of the nation.[21] Istóczy's incipient
Judeophobia, however, was a self–serving preoccupation with personal vengeance. To use it as the principal vehicle of a political election campaign would have assured his political suicide. However, by
the early 1870s Hungarian politics bore little resemblance to the pre–
1848 pervasive tension that existed during the desperate struggle for
freedom and independence or to the dismal aftermath of the revolution. The pragmatic philosophy of the early 1860s of striving for
attainable objectives continued in the post–*Ausgleich* era. By 1872,
the emancipation of the Jews had been a *fait accompli* for five years,
seemingly justified by Jewish contributions to Hungary's progressive
self–image and economic progress. Hungary's most respected politicians would not consider the espousal of a patently anachronistic and

unsound ideological platform which catered to the basest emotions as deserving of their support. Istóczy's preposterous assertion that his clearly anti–Semitic political and socioeconomic views attracted the support of Ferenc Deák and won him a seat in the Diet presumes his readers incompetent or naive. The Baltaház case, an incident of limited sensationalist value, was put in temporary cold storage due to Istóczy's pending countersuit. As he managed to keep his "personal reasons for becoming an anti–Semite" under control earlier, Istóczy, having already demonstrated a flair for the art of political survival, resisted attempting to win his first political election with speeches containing strong doses of anti–Semitism.

There is no record in Istóczy's subsequent writings of any such public utterance in connection with his initial campaign. The first record of an anti–Semitic speech took place three years later. The qualities that earned him the attention he had sought were more of a credible rather than controversial sort. By the early 1870s Istóczy had made a name for himself. He possessed enviable intellectual accomplishments, not inconsiderable social graces, and the skills of an artful survivalist in the often puzzling maze of county politics. Indeed, such were virtues to attract the attention of seasoned national party politicians in search of young talent.

Istóczy planned to represent the district of Rum in the Diet, a district encompassing the town of the same name and located to the north of Vasvár. He campaigned with his customary dogged determination, aligning himself with the political program associated with one of the country's most respected politicians: Ferenc Deák. The beloved "Sage of the Nation" was, Istóczy allegedly declared, his mentor.[22] Deák, with his demeanor and pragmatic views, both distinctive traits of his policy of passive resistance, was largely credited with initiating and implementing the Compromise (1865–1867) that cushioned the dramatic impact of the Austro–Prussian War and encouraged the imperious Francis Joseph to reconcile himself to the inevitable overhaul of his realm, agreeing with dignity to the establishment of a dual monarchy. With the backing of such a political guardian angel, Istóczy could not lose. Among the people of the Hungarian countryside, the veneration of Deák was a shibboleth. Still, running on the Deák Party ticket in 1872 was similar to beginning a sea journey on a sinking ship. Founded in 1865 and representing the vested interests of the gentry who constituted the bulk of its membership, the party was by then well on its way to dissolution.[23] Its demise took place in 1875. Its newer members, like Istóczy, would soon be faced with an important choice: to join the Liberals who stood for the preservation of the compromise system, or switch to the opposition Independence Party.

Although franchise was a preciously rare commodity—less than 7 percent of the population were eligible to vote—preparations for elections were festive, happy occasions. Party committees saw to it that every town and village had sufficient visual reminders—slogans, banners, and cockades—of their candidates. The real footsoldiers, however, were the *kortesek* (party functionaries). Traveling from place to place, they rustled up enthusiasm and made lists of voters whom they treated to drinks in the local inns.[24]

The *kortesek* were also mudslingers, throwing themselves—often with relish—into the inevitable political dirty work that ranged from slandering the opposition candidates to buying votes. Voting was often marred by irregularities; individuals suspected of being sympathetic to the opposition were harassed and intimidated or frustrated by subtle delay tactics. Hungary's peculiar structure of public administration, which allowed the counties to retain virtual autonomy in the maintenance of law and order, was badly in need of sweeping reforms. To those who idealized the traditional practice of titled families controlling the rural areas, the counties were "the bastions of the constitution"; the critics lamented the "almost Asiatic conditions" prevailing in them.[25]

Istóczy came through the ordeal of his first major political election somewhat rumpled, financially exhausted, yet a winner. The district of Rum remained his political base throughout his career and kept him in the Diet for nearly two decades. The district was ideally suited for keeping his still well–concealed program of vituperative anti–Semitism. Why would anyone suspect the new parliamentary delegate, a man of pleasant manners and considerable cultural polish—and who had even learned the language of the Old Testament—of harboring such implacable hatred? If anyone did, no one talked. Unlike Szombathely and Vasvár, Rum, which the weary traveler would recall only because of its sixteenth–century Gothic Roman Catholic church, had no Jewish community.[26] Judging from the steadfast support his stolid constituents would give him even after his malconduct in the Diet earned him much derision and nationwide notoriety, the district in which Istóczy made his first stand was political *terra firma.*

Chapter III

The Opening Salvo

A city on the threshold of becoming one of Europe's newest—and in many ways most beautiful—metropolises greeted the newly elected delegate from Vas County. Pest–Buda faced an arresting multiplicity of problems, some inherited and others of recent origin, which the city fathers tried to address in a variety of ways. Some problems were being resolved, others tolerated, and still others simply were ignored. Growth and progress created peculiar sets of dreams and nightmares, and virtues and vices for Pest–Buda. These conditions were reminiscent of the ones that had ravaged the industrial cities of western Europe a generation earlier.

Numerous health hazards plagued the city. Critics lambasted the chronic inability of the city government—Pest's in particular—to provide proper safety measures against the centuries–old scourge and flood, that had caused extensive damage as late as 1838. Water was in short supply and at times was in danger of being contaminated by the network of often clogged or overflown sewage canals. The stench rising from them attested to this alarming threat of public health and safety. The city's only hospital, Rókus, was hopelessly overcrowded. Only the well–to–do could afford treatment in the few private sanitariums. Less than 600 physicians met the multiplicity of medical challenges that the rapidly growing population was creating. Observing everyday conditions and practices, one may have thought that health inspection and public sanitation were yet to be invented. Foodstuffs, always unwashed, and often contaminated, changed hands from peasant producers to merchants and consumers. The streets were dusty, litter accumulated in layers, and garbage collection was at best sporadic. No less distressing was the profound shortage of housing. An average of three persons lived in each of the city's inhabitable rooms, of which there were fewer than one hundred thousand in fewer than ten thousand buildings.

Like the flood, cholera was a frequent visitor. In 1872–1873 more than half of those who fell ill with it died. Only slightly less severe was the outbreak of typhus in 1871–1872.[1] It is no surprise that such conditions invited disaster. And the day's end brought only partial

respite, the quiet bliss of darkness often shattered by the denizens of
the night. The constables of Captain Elek Thaisz, the unchallenged
guardian of law and order between 1861 and 1884, had their hands
full with sensational, often unsolved murders; secretly arranged duels;
the suicides of political and business failures; and the ever–increasing
legions of prostitutes who virtually ruled the darkened streets and
rowdy bars of Terézváros, one of Pest's crowded districts.[2]

An almost eerie yet intriguing mixture of blights and blessings
coexisted in the capitalist system. Impressive achievements competed
for recognition against the visual horrors of poverty, neglect and mismanagement in the city. For the more optimistic soul, tranquil, historic Pest–Buda offered a bewildering variety of sights, sounds and
tastes to both residents and visitors alike. The newly built funicular
took its riders to the top of the Várhegy in minutes for a spectacu-
lar panorama of the whole city. One never tired of a leisurely stroll
through the picturesque streets which wound by elegant mansions and
solemn churches and led to the grounds of the imposing royal palace.

For those more impressed with the hubbub of modernity, the
inevitable destination was Pest, the unrivaled center of capitalism
in Hungary. At first glance, Pest revealed the sights and sounds of
dynamic progress with rampant construction, a telltale sign of its
growth. Streets, huge apartment buildings, elegant mansions of the
nobility and the well–to–do, public buildings, institutions of education
and the arts, and graceful parks created an ambiance of reassuring
permanence and wealth. Massive churches and the new synagogue
of the Progressive Jews, thought by some to be, architecturally, the
most beautiful edifice in Hungary, softened the unyielding visual images of fast–paced materialism. With its horse–drawn carriages and
buses, new stores and hotels, romantic cafés, gourmet restaurants,
and multi–lingual atmosphere–more languages were spoken in Pest
than anywhere else in Europe—Pest exuded the bustling energy that
made it look and sound so unlike its placid counterpart on the other
side of the Danube.[3]

In 1873, an administrative reorganization fused Pest, Buda, and
Óbuda, an ancient settlement of small quaint houses and dockyard
chimneys to the north of Buda. Christened Budapest on October 9,
the name's components inverted and dehyphenated, signaled the end
of the laborious process of unification.[4] The year of Budapest's official
birthday witnessed the passing of many inauspicious crises, the raging
cholera epidemic and labor unrest. Still, the new city government of
the "three Charleses," Ráth, the lord mayor, Kamermayer, the mayor,
and Gerlóczy, the vice mayor, looked with confidence and optimism
to the last quarter of the century.

Within a stone's throw of one another in Budapest's central district stood the two buildings that were the terminuses of Győző Istóczy's political career. In one of the corners of the Friars' Square, named for the Franciscan church and which had been the center of Istóczy's intellectual world during his first extended stay in Pest, stood a building that until 1783, when it was moved to Buda, housed the *Kúria*. It was subsequently shared by the schools of arts and law of the University of Pest. The square was separated by the Museum Road, a portion of the *Körút* (Circular Road) that slices across the edge of the central district like a scimitar, from the eastern end of Sándor Street which in turn runs along the splendid garden of the National Museum.

Past the northern gate of the garden, which embraced not only the principal repository of Hungary's treasured masterpieces, but also the proud assembly of its notables—the hereditary House of Magnates had found temporary haven in the ceremonial hall of the museum— lay the Diet (House of Representatives), a modest, hastily constructed single–story Gothic building nestled in the midst of ornate palaces and mansions owned by some of the country's most aristocratic and wealthy families.

The consequences of apparently irreparable technical flaws annoyed generations of its inhabitants. Because of hasty and careless construction, the walls did not dry for years, causing the representatives in the chamber to shiver in the dampness of the winter and perspire in the oppressive heat and humidity in the summer. Soon another flaw was discovered much to the anguish of the representatives, whose very reason for being there was to make speeches and be heard: speakers could not be heard. For unknown reasons, the deplorable acoustics of the chamber defied correction. Numerous attempts at improving the acoustics merely succeeded in upgrading them from unsatisfactory to bad. Still, the situation was not altogether disadvantageous. Some representatives could now steal brief naps during lengthy or confusing speeches, while others chose to openly violate parliamentary manners by engaging in loud, heated arguments. Only the president's bell or stentorian voice could wake the slumberers or quiet the noisemakers.[5]

The perplexing *mala in se* notwithstanding, the Diet commanded nationwide reverence as the presumed fount of political wisdom. Visitors gaped at it as "Muhammedans gape at the Kaába." The everpresent doorman, wearing a livery resplendent with gold and silver-braid stripes and holding a huge gold–tipped staff as he greeted the representatives, was the most visible manifestation of that national reverence. Like the edifice in which they made speeches, debated and legislated, the legislators' performance fell considerably short of the efficiency, perseverance, wisdom and decorum with which the myth-makers credited them. Less than 10 percent of the 315 representatives truly justified the confidence of their constituents, one acid-tongued critic noted. Perhaps his figures were exaggerated, though his motives well-intentioned.

Many representatives viewed their parliamentary responsibilities as a decorative appendage to the social graces and obligations expected of them. They received a daily allowance of 5 forints and 25 krajcárs and an increment of 800 forints to cover the high rents in apartment-deficient Budapest. They were expected to respond to an endless variety of their constituents' requests and complaints and participate efficaciously in parliamentary proceedings which required considerable discipline. Cabinet ministers and representatives followed one another in delivering eloquent speeches without limitations on the number or length of their presentations. However, speakers were prohibited from using notes and were required to speak in a carefully prescribed style. Older representatives who were graduates of schools of antiquated oratory often spun words and thoughts so elaborately that no one could—or cared to—recall the speakers' point. The younger representatives were prone to resort to modern, sharply worded expressions and emotional gestures. Some representatives were also skilled in the art of filibustering, often turning their obstructionist talent, given the chamber's climatic and acoustical liabilities, into a nerve-wracking and physically exacting assault on the patience and senses of their audience.[6]

By the early 1870s, the post-1818 configuration of the political system began to wane, giving way to a new spectrum of political associations. Dominating the rows on the right side of the chancel-structured chamber sat the members of Ferenc Deák's party. His pro-*Ausgleich*, pro-government stance revealed signs of the often conflicting or competing interests of fratricidal groups and the impassioned criticism of the Forty-Eighters who, hoping to keep the spirit of revolt and freedom alive, were sustained and nurtured by the implacable pronouncements of the exiled Lajos Kossuth. More assaults came from the Conservative Party, whose members sat even farther to the right. Seated across the aisle from Deák's party, in the left section, were the representatives of the Left Center, clustered around their leader, Kálmán Tisza (1830–1902), an aristocrat turned title-shy politician. He had gained popularity as an opponent of the *Ausgleich* and won the support of a number of Forty-Eighters as well, by demanding the establishment of an independent Hungarian army and separate ministries of finance and commerce.[7] Tisza's skillful manipulation of political emotions, including his own, in a subsequent quest for the premiership, significantly retarded the development of factions leaning toward the extreme left. This party of persistent opposition to the 1867 system was willing to compromise its political conviction on one count only: the shared person of the emperor.

Many former participants in the 1848 Revolution, having returned from exile in the wake of the general amnesty granted by Francis Joseph in 1869, supported the party's program.[8] Much of its steam, however, dissipated as the party struggled to gain a readily discernible identity in the shadow of Tisza's growing personal leadership and deepening political influence. Except for the verifiable fact that he sat among the representatives of the Deák party, no record of Istóczy's political activity removes the veil of obscurity from his years of political apprenticeship (1872–1875) in the Diet.

Although he was an indefatigable practitioner of the art of self–promotion, Istóczy later chose to shed no light on this initial phase of his political career or the relevant details of his personal life. However, Istóczy's inexplicable reticence does not yield a *tabula rasa*. Three narrow gaps afford rare, obstructed glimpses into Istóczy's phase of patient preparation for hurling himself into the political limelight. Retrospection on his early political career gives the first insight into Istóczy's carefully laid plan. In 1875 Istóczy was reelected by the voters of the district of Rum. He had run an uneventful campaign; his victory was a foregone conclusion. He had succeeded in earning the confidence of his constituents and building a firm political base that was to prove remarkably durable, supporting and protecting him even in the most tumultuous of times. Bosnyák's undocumented assertion that Istóczy took his new position seriously , divided his time between discharging parliamentary responsibilities and fulfilling duties to constituents, and maintaining close ties with them by holding weekly party days[9] has a ring of truth undisputed by evidence to the contrary.

Through the second gap, one can glimpse the setting of the stage for the gradual transference of his anti–Semitism spawned by personal problems into the realm of national politics. The disconcerting Baltaház case that had haunted him during two of his first three years in the Diet was finally resolved after a four–year legal tangle. In 1874 the *Kúria* reversed the decision of the lower court and acquitted Istóczy. Had the decision stood, it would have left him bankrupt, forced him into a lifelong debt, and ruined his budding political career. The verdict had a twofold effect on Istóczy. He obviously heaved a deep sigh of relief as the oppressive cloud dissipated; however, it left a residue, an indelible psychological imprint. Istóczy became convinced that he had been made the sole target of a nationwide Jewish conspiracy, organized by the influential and wealthy Jews of Pest. The imagined conspiracy and its ominous implications for the people of Hungary suddenly emerged as a twofold menace to Istóczy; he now felt compelled to put it before the nation and dedicate his political career to destroying it.

The third privileged glimpse into Istóczy's career is a natural consequence of the second. Strong emotions and firm commitment alone could not turn him into an effective anti–Semite overnight. His vindicitive personal crusade could only be achieved by laying an adequate intellectual foundation and developing a perspective ruled by emotion. Thus, before he could hope to impress on and solicit support from his audience in the Diet, Istóczy had to expand the crude, street–smart demagoguery in which he excelled and with which he won much of the respect of his supporters in Rum into a historically justifiable panorama of anti–Semitism. Before he embarked on that undertaking he had to become familiar with the modern versions, slogans, and principal proponents of anti–Semitism. He had to acquire a fluid proficiency in the jingoistic expressions and other linguistic particulars by which anti–Semitism concealed its fallacies and contradictions and magnified the Jews' threat to the Christian way of life. It was to these ends that Istóczy decided to translate into Hungarian Chapters IX and XII of Du Mesnil–Marigny's popular *Histoire de l'économie politique des anciens peuples, de l'Inde, de l'Egypte, de la Judée et de la Grece* devoted to Judea. In 1875 he published it under a separate title[10] not unintentionally just one month before his first major anti–Semitic speech on record. The translator's motivation is clear before it is actually declared.

Under his name the words, "Parliamentary Representative of Vas County's Rum District," read like a defiant espousal of a political theme whose age is about to dawn. "Let us rack our brains concerning our miseries and their cause," Istóczy exclaims in the preface.

> It will not be harmful if our attention, hitherto carefully diverted in other directions, extends at long last to an area that is still intended to remain *terra incognita.*[11]

Istóczy could hardly have chosen a more suitable training ground. Du Mesnil–Marigny's sweeping account of the history of the Jews from ancient times to his own features a carefully selected melange of all too transparent ingredients, interspersed with sufficient vituperative remarks. Du Mesnil–Marigny enumerated the forbidding characteristics of an irreversible *fait accompli*: the Jews' seemingly inherent talent for numerical increase, a characteristic corroborated by many

an ancient sage, despite their killing of the Savior; their steadily evolv-
ing commercial talents by which the Jews establish their worldwide
monopoly and pursue their exploitive interests; the rising emotions
of hatred and envy aroused by the Jews' usurious and self–serving
practices; a country–by–country estimate of the Jewish population;
and the increasing Jewish influence in the intellectual facets of society. Istóczy proved to be not only a capable translator, but a quick
learner as well. Du Mesnil–Marigny's hate–filled observations found
a direct passage into Istóczy's expanding storehouse of political material. Only a suitable opportunity to empty it was wanting.

Chapter IV

The Evolution of a Cassandra

Any description or analysis of anti–Semitism, ranging from the objective to the critical, inevitably contains a number of detracting adjectives, such as illogical, unreasonable, immoral, unoriginal, inaccurate, undisciplined, disruptive, and the like. The elemental force and sweeping perspective with which Istóczy burst on the scene of national politics on 8 April 1875 transformed him virtually within hours from a provincial unknown into a highly visible person at the center of impassioned controversy. Thus, the word, unpredictable, is added to the list of adjectives due to the surprisingly broad panorama of Istóczy's assaults, the unshakable consistency of his arguments, and polished quality of his expressions that one would expect to have evolved only after years of trial and error. However, it was inevitable that someone like Istóczy would emerge in reaction to certain political, social and economic changes.

Rarely in the post–*Ausgleich* history of Hungary did the coalescence of circumstances prepare so well for a successful promotion of the anti–Semitic propaganda as in the mid–1870s. The political structure and its corresponding party alignment in the Diet underwent major changes, creating uncertainty as many personal commitments were redeployed. The dissolution of the Deák Party had a particularly disruptive centrifugal impact on its former members. The leftists formed the Independence Party; right–wing extremists had a frustrating experience. The short–lived Conservative Party was led by the haughty, unpopular "Black Baron," Pál Sennyei (1824–1888). An aristocrat whose not inconsiderable political and administrative talents and versatility virtually foretold a brilliant career,[1] Sennyei served as a representative in the Diet (1872–1881), was president of the House of Magnates (1865–1867, 1884–1888) and was appointed President of the *Kúria* (1884). After three years, the Conservative Party's thirty–eight members voted to join the United, or Moderate, Opposition, a new aggregation of widely disparate elements which quickly became a much–ridiculed target of acid–tongued political observers.

The most successful and enduring group that emerged from the process of political realignment in 1875 was the Liberal Party. Its membership— composed of former left–centrists, frustrated by years of stymied activity within an opposition warp, and Deákists, chagrinned by the disintegration of their ruling party—demonstrated remarkable resilience in putting ideological differences aside and joined forces in an effort to make their new party the dominant power in the Diet. With a display of strict discipline rarely seen in party politics, the Liberals closed ranks behind their leader, Kálmán Tisza, whose notable turnabout from outspoken opponent of the *Ausgleich* to upholder of the dualist system, symbolized their spirited and pragmatic quest for power. As minister of interior (2 March–20 October 1875) in the government of Prime Minister Baron Béla Wenckheim (1811–1879), a much–respected patriot—he took part in the 1848 Revolution and spent some years in exile—an experienced politician, Tisza took a careful aim at the premiership, a target he doggedly pursued with well–earned success. On 20 October 1875 he was appointed prime minister and, with the resolute support of the Liberal Party, for the next quarter of a century created an impression of stability and durability which the rapid succession of preceding governments— (Count Gyula Andrássy, 1867–1871; Count Menyhért Lónyai, 1871–1873; József Szlávy, 1873–1874; István Bittó, 1874–1875; and Wenckheim, 1875)—only accentuated.

The second set of circumstances that created an atmosphere of tolerance and considerable, although partial, justification of political anti–Semitism originated in the events which made 1873 a year of national tragedies. A six–year era of progress that witnessed encouraging phenomena, such as a healthy growth in population (0.93 percent in 1870), the development of a modern banking system, the building of an extensive railway system, and qualitative and quantitative increases in agricultural and industrial production, suffered a dramatic, albeit short–lived, setback as a result of the crash of the Vienna Stock Exchange on 9 May 1873. The devastating event pounded Hungary's national economy until nearly the end of the decade.[2]

That of the five large banks that dominated Hungary's post–*Ausgleich* financial system only the Austrian Rothchild–controlled Credit Bank rode out the crisis had ominous, unmistakable implications. The social instability of Budapest's steadily growing proletariat, mostly illiterate, poorly paid refugees from the oppressed agrarian sector and Austrian and Czech immigrants, created a dangerous and tense situation in which the public whipping of an all too accessible scapegoat would seem justified. Adding to the economic woes were a devastating cholera epidemic, which caused over 2,500 deaths among the many thousands who had been taken ill,[3] and an outbreak of philoxeria in 1875, which paralyzed the country's thriving wine industry. Industrial Pest, where the cholera raged between October 1872 and November 1873, was particularly affected. Considering the tendency of irresponsible and misguided fanatics who held Jews culpable in times of plagues and epidemics, the insidious and scandal–ridden blood libel of Tiszaeszlár ten years later would, oddly enough, confirm the persistent legacy of medieval superstitions. The objects of suspicions and accusations did not remain unidentified for long.

The regression caused by the socioeconomic woes of 1873 and the belief that the political realignment of 1875 was by nature transitory proved useful to Istóczy's emergent logistics. To place his truculent political message, an almost monotonously unswerving diatribe, on firm foundations and infuse it with a ring of permanent validity, he wasted no time in institutionalizing the anathemization of Hungary's Jewry. He discovered a convenient vehicle for self–aggrandizement, a platform compatible with his views, and a ready–made nationwide audience whose favorable disposition he hoped to assure by piercing the fragile veneer that concealed a century–long tradition of prejudice and discrimination. Viewed in retrospect, Istóczy's timing was correct and his perceptions accurate. Istóczy's decision to unfurl the banner of political anti–Semitism in Hungary looks more like the official beginning of a circumspect movement than a claptrap plot. He wedged his movements between the disquieting reports of sporadic manifestations of anti–Semitism in the early 1860s and the outbreak of serious anti–Semitic disturbances during the infamous trial of the accused Jews of Tiszaeszlár and in its turbulent aftermath. Against such a forbidding backdrop, the manifold attempts of Jews to demonstrate their firm commitment to Magyarization and assimilation proved futile.[4]

In 1875 Hungary's twice–emancipated Jewry projected an anomalous self–image.[5] For over a quarter century the Progressive Jews subscribed to "the effort of Hungarian political leaders to build a Magyar nation state by integrating Jews into Magyardom."[6] Under the guidance of such respected and enlightened leaders as Ignác Hirschler (1823–1891), a famous ophthalmologist and president of Pest's Jewish community, Lipót Löw (1811–1875), rabbi of Szeged and an indefatigable proponent of Magyarization and the emancipation, and Ferenc Chorin, Sr. (1842–1925), a prominent lawyer–editor and politician–industrialist, the Progressive Jews gradually established themselves as the nation's indispensable "substitute middle class"[7] and became firmly ensconsed in virtually all sectors of social and cultural life. They, however, represented only a portion of the whole. Except for a negligible, well–educated faction that "was more fervently Magyar than the Magyars themselves,"[8] the masses of Orthodox Jews held fast to their self–imposed exclusivity and autonomy as God's chosen people awaiting the arrival of the Messiah. Led by such famous rabbis as the saintly and learned Mózes Teitelbaum (1759–1841) of Sátoraljaújhely, and Hillel Lichtenstein (1815–1891), an implacable opponent of modernization and assimilation,[9] the Orthodox were easy targets of the anti–Semites who viewed them as harmful aliens incapable of assimilation.

No faction of the Orthodoxy earned the hatred of the people of the countryside more quickly, retained it longer, or was attributed with more odious characteristics by the standard bearers of political anti–Semitism than the Polish Jews who had been settling in large numbers in Hungary's northeastern counties since the last decades of the eighteenth century. In 1772, as a result of the first partitioning of Poland, the Habsburgs took control of Galicia, a province densely populated by Jews. The consequent political, communal and economic exigencies triggered a steady flow of emigration toward regions of greater promise in the empire. Unlike their coreligionists who settled in Hungary in two major waves of immigration, Austrian–German Jews in the seventeenth century and Moravian–Bohemian Jews in the eighteenth century, the Galician Jews were poverty–stricken, separatist and traditionalist perpetuators of a closed, God–centered, communal lifestyle dominated by powerful spiritual leaders who developed new ways to reconcile the conflicting traditions and practices of rabbinism and Hasidism. The former had become not only the affluent beneficiaries and innovative pioneers of Hungary's burgeoning age of capitalist enterprise and Magyarization, but also the champions of enlightenment and assimilation. To many observers, Jews and non–Jews alike, the Galicians were the very antitheses of Hungary's Progressive Jewry. Those who gave credence to the warning of alarmists embraced statistics with, for them, ominous implications. Hungarian economy and culture were not only controlled by Jews but by Jews who would soon consist primarily of the hated Galicians, and form the dominant majority.[10] Even though Magyarized and integrated, the Jews of Pest, the critics claimed, made the capital appear to deserve the callous sobriquet "Jewpest"; the critics subscribed to the view, "Let Budapest have her fun; Budapest is not, after all, the country."[11] The pervasive Jewish threat was real. It had to be contained and its perpetrators removed, the sooner the better.

Still, Istóczy could hardly lose sight of two of the most visible obstacles to his becoming the political redeemer of a de–Judaized Hungarian nation: by 1875 nearly twenty Jews had received aristocratic forenames, and four of them received the title of baron as well, for a variety of services rendered in the national interest;[12] and a small group of his fellow representatives in the Diet—Mór Wahrmann, Ferenc Chorin, Ede Horn and Ignác Helfy—would surely be among his first opponents, possibly attempting to keep him insulated and make him a political pariah.

Istóczy chose to make his first public speech in the Diet attacking the Jews amidst a controversial situation which easily aroused emotions and provoked impassioned arguments. For seven years the Orthodox and Progressive communities had been locked in an acrimonious tu–of–war which began when the representatives of both factions met at a council, sponsored by Baron József Eötvös (1813–1871). Eötvös was then minister of cults and public education and one of the most resolved proponents of the emancipation of Hungarian Jewry. The Orthodox leaders opposed the establishment of the National Rabbinical Seminary—one of the stipulations of the 1850 School Fund[13] was the establishment of the National Rabbinical Seminary, a stipulation which the emperor approved on 29 April 1873 on the ground that its religious orientation and pedagogical philosophy clashed with the traditional rabbinical training. Orthodox leaders who opposed the establishment of the seminary petitioned the Diet, protested the *fait accompli*, and requested the distribution of the Fund for the establishment of a network of Talmud Torah schools instead. However, both the Progressives and the secular authorities viewed the schools' curriculum with suspicion. The Diet agreed to consider the petition and seek resolution of the controversy. Thus, this tense and confrontational intra–Jewish affair was given national exposure.

On 4 July 1874, in response to a request for information and classification, Ágoston Trefort (1817–1888), Eötvös's successor as minister of culture and public education, presented the government's position and recommendations. Trefort upheld the specifics and goals of the charter of the School Fund. The Fund would remain undivided and the interest it generated would finance the establishment of a teachers' institute, an institute for the blind, and the National Rabbinical Seminary. The unspent portion of the interest would be turned over to the Orthodox leaders to cover the needs of the Talmud Torah schools. Despite a number of spirited speeches that yielded no less than eight motions, the Diet voted down both the motions and Trefort's recommendations, and, upon Prime Minister István Bittó's motion, the matter was tabled. The Orthodox leaders were dismayed. The construction of the building that would house the National Rabbinical Seminary was completed four years later.[14]

Although the fate of the Orthodoxy's petition was left in a legislative limbo, the bellicose condition that had spawned it cast an unexpectedly bright light on the sharply drawn features of the heterogeneous Hungarian Jewry and exposed a vulnerable area, a target which Istóczy then struck.

"On 8 April 1878 I made my first anti–Semitic speech," Istóczy recalled wistfully, "the first anti–Semitic speech heard in [the Hungarian] parliament. The first in a European parliament."[15] After having seen his career eclipse many years before, he was justifiably proud. Unlike the preceding ideologically sophisticated manifestations of anti–Semitism outside Hungary[16]—incendiary, anti–Jewish articles that appeared in newspapers, such as the *Germania* in Berlin and the Viennese *Vaterland*, or the virulent anti–Semitic propaganda in Romania in the 1860s and 1870s which produced an outbreak of atrocities—Istóczy was a one–member movement without a sympathetic press or even a group of like–minded companions. That dissimilarity, however, turned out to be an advantage, not a liability. He set the time and course of his speeches as he saw fit, owed allegiance to no one, was unhindered by fratricidal challenge, and spoke his mind—within parliamentary reason—without regard to conventions or the sensitivities of others. The firm, consistent, and uncritical support of his constituents allowed him the rare luxury of expressing himself in complete freedom. The most important tactical advantage, however, was the element of surprise. As he rose from his seat none of his fellow legislators apparently had the slightest inkling of what they were about to hear. Still, it is difficult to dismiss altogether the lingering suspicion that the Mecca of Hungarian politics had not cleansed itself completely of the taint of anti–Semitism and that it passed it on to other generations of legislators. "One man could not have set a whole country afire," lamented Lajos Venetianer (1867–1922), a prominent rabbi and one of the most erudite of the historians of Hungarian Jewry, "had the firewood not already been piled up."[17]

Technically, the topic of Istóczy's speech was not relevant to the ongoing debate,[18] but making his point always took priority over sticking to the subject at hand. Nor was his a speech in the accustomed meaning of the word, but essentially a brief point addressed to Prime Minister Wenckheim and expanded into an hour–long tirade; however, the speech's positive traits were quickly discernible. He gave no formal introduction laden with theoretical sophistry, and despite the occasionally disconcerting circuity of words the caustic intent came into full view. Istóczy plunged into the untested waters of political infamy, brushing aside both Trefort's remarks of the influential role played by Hungarian Jews and an equally commendatory speech by Ferenc Pulszky (1814–1897), an undersecretary of finance in the short–lived revolutionary government of 1848–1849, one of Kossuth's close associates in exile and a much-respected former Deák party representative. Istóczy's technique of delivering his rapidly and indiscriminately fired salvos, consisting of repetitive, harshly-worded, unsubstantiated and mostly insupportable accusations softened periodically by brief, salutory remarks, would be imitated by all subsequent practitioners of political anti-Semitism.

The Jews' rapid increase in population and almost dictatorial economic power, Istóczy charged, "threaten not only to eclipse us, a condition that has already come to pass, but to subjugate us as well." The Jews, an exclusivist, almost aristocratic social caste insulated by blood brotherhood, ancient traditions, common interest, and religious fanaticism, view all non-Jews as inferior and exploitable objects. The Jews lack a living national tongue. Under the guise of liberalism they profess the most conservative of views. In their unrelenting quest for economic domination of the world, they conspire to undermine and destroy the institutions of non-Jews. Their control of the press allows them to stress their martyrdom whenever they are criticized or attacked. Still, the proponents of the mystifying nature and tendencies of Judaism succeeded in creating the impression that "this element, possessing great talent and capabilities, stubborn persistence and preponderant financial power," would, through intermarriage, fuse with the people around them, their threat thereby dissipated. "Never!" Istóczy thundered:

> To expect a race that for four and a half millenia preserved its total isolation, purity of blood, indigenous way of thinking and life and customs, which since the emancipation strengthened even more, is nothing but a naive *pium desiderium* or an absurd utopia.

Nor, according to Istóczy, would there be, as the optimist hopes, a mutual weakening and ultimate self-destruction caused by the Orthodox-Progressive controversy.

> They are like the cutting edges of a pair of scissors sharing a common point of origin and a goal. The more they seem to move against each other the more our necks feel their sharpness. The Orthodox strive to preserve Judaism in its original form and the purity of their blood, forming an impenetrable phalanx which will provide a haven to the Progressives if forced to retreat. The Progressives abandon customs that outlived their utility and lost their relevance in the pursuit of goals which they intend to realize, if need be, by using the services of strangers and even resorting to intermarriage.[19]

Suddenly, the president of the Diet, Kálmán Ghyczy, intervened.[20] Citing the indistinct rule regulating the length of interpellations, an obviously chagrined and long-suffering Ghyczy issued a gentlemanly reminder to Istóczy, with which the representatives concurred, that the discussion of important bills was still awaiting the attention of the Diet.[21] The subtle expression of impatience notwithstanding, Istóczy would not yield the floor. Nor would he give an indication that the end of the preface to his interpellation was nearing. He had grasped a personally historic moment and was resolved to exploit it to the fullest. "I am not one of those representatives who lay frequent claim to the attention of the House," Istóczy replied, eliciting rumbles of assent. "I have not wasted the precious time of the House so far, for the topic at hand cannot be resolved in a few words."

Istóczy continued:

> Although Jews liken themselves to the fermenting leaven of civilized society, they are more like the *cuscuta*, that parasitic plant. The attacking forces of Pan–Judaism advance in the disunited society of non–Jews, torn asunder by thousands of contradictions, gain control in financially beleaguered nations, create legions of proletarians and thus threaten social and national catastrophes in the not too distant future.

Non–Jews, he advised, should acquire the positive traits of Jews, and thus strengthened, not only engage them in peaceful competition but reoccupy positions lost to them.[22]

Such were the reasons that paved the circuitous path to the long–awaited concluding questions to the prime minister. Those who heaved a deep sigh of relief were, however, soon made aware of the nature of their premature optimism. They were further chastised in six long–winded recapitulations, each prefaced by the words, "in view of," for dramatic effect. At long last, even Istóczy had exhausted his seemingly bottomless well of oratorical tricks, unusual for a politician of such limited exposure and experience as a public speaker. Even when dwarfed by the sheer magnitude of the preliminaries, the three–question interpellation was ominous. First, did the government intend to prevent the naturalization of foreign Jews that had invaded the country? Second, would the government attempt to thwart the evolution of a powerful movement of self–defense by non–Jews against this attacking caste? Third, did the government expect to take a decisive position in this matter, though continuing in all other respects, its policy of neutrality and indifference unjustified by occurrences since the implementation of the laws of emancipation?[23]

It took the government less than two weeks to organize the rescripts from the ministries to which copies of the text of the interpellation had been sent. On April 21, Prime Minister Wenckheim presented the official response in the Diet. The government did intend to regulate immigration by implementing the naturalization laws, though not for the reasons the interpellation had cited. The government would approve and encourage the development of any well-intentioned social movement, but would take a hostile position against any movement that intended to disturb the peaceful and respectful relations among religious associations and citizens affiliated with them. In view of the Law 1867: XVII that declared the civil equality of the Jews, the government did not and could not recognize the existence of a Jewish Question and thus could not take a position regarding it.[24]

The Prime Minister's firm statement elicited outbursts of approval from the representatives. Baron Wenckheim, a man of considerable political experience and influence despite the brevity of his premiership (2 March– 20 October 1875), was visibly dismayed as he spoke. Not even compliance with parliamentary form and courtesy could conceal the sharp ring of his irate words. In the course of his opening remarks he took exception to Istóczy's seemingly interminable speech and concluded his statement by noting wryly that his answer satisfied none of the points which the interpellation had raised. "The government does not and may not pursue a policy with respect to the Jews or any other group other than the one I have outlined," Wenckheim declared, and he continued:

> By acting to the contrary, the government would sin against humanity, civilization, and truth, but above all those laws of the land which assure all citizens, without regard to religion, language, and race, equal civil rights.[25]

Istóczy made sure that the Prime Minister's reply would not be the last word on the subject. He rose quickly to present his observations. He declared that he viewed the Jewish Question not as a religious question, but a socioeconomic one. Hungary had become the principal staging area of "Jew-politics," dependent on Jewish haute finance. Although he had anticipated the government's response, not for a moment expecting it to be satisfactory, his responsibility as a representative compelled him to go through with the interpellation. "The time will come when my views are not thought of as mere chimeras—may Providence not allow it to come to pass. Let me then be, in this respect, Hungary's Cassandra."[26]

The die had been cast. Although Istóczy acknowledged the Prime

Minister's reply, it did not alter his views. Nor did it dissuade him from pursuing the dream of becoming Hungary's self–appointed savior. However eloquently and firmly Baron Wenckheim dispelled any hope of Istóczy's interpellation earning merit, "Hungary's Cassandra" was clearly convinced that he had acquired a distinct oratorical style and found a niche of his own in the Mecca of his nation's politicians. "I woke up the next morning to find that I had become famous not only in Hungary but all over Europe as well," he noted proudly.[27]

The consequences of Istóczy's first major anti–Semitic speech in the Diet were for him less than gratifying. There was no fanfare, no limelight in which to bask. Aside from the Prime Minister's obligatory reply, the speech elicited neither criticism in general nor rebuttal from any of the Jewish representatives. The latter attributed little or no significance to Istóczy's rabid Judeophobia and let the Prime Minister be their spokesman. That may indeed have been the best solution for the time being. In the long run, however, the failure of the Jewish representatives to respond to the challenge and the unwillingness of the leaders of Pest's Jewry to organize against the newest manifestation, however isolated, of that timeless anti–Semitic phenomenon proved to be communal negligence for which they paid a high price within a decade. Their public indifference to anti–Semitism and excessive faith in the ability and willingness of the government to protect the country's Jewish citizens was a tragic institutionalized miscalculation.

Despite his growing newsworthiness, Istóczy remained one of the least visible members of the Diet, speaking infrequently. More than six months passed before the parliamentary minutes again showed extended activity on his part. During that time he won reelection, confirming the suspicion that voters in certain election districts did not consider the pursuit of anti–Semitic ideals and goals as a liability impeding one's political career or adversely affecting one's personal integrity. Yet, on 12 November 1875, when the representatives leaned back in their seats in anticipation of another lengthy anti–Semitic tirade from the designated speaker, their wait for the words of anger and accusation went unrewarded.

Istóczy's tightly structured speech—in marked contrast to the interminably rambling interpellation concentrated on two improperly managed and inefficiently utilized sources of national revenue: the Stock Exchange and the railway system. Political leaders and financial experts struggled desperately to extricate the country from the shadow of the disastrous crash of the Vienna Stock Market in 1873. In 1874 the national deficit exceeded 40 million. The immediate prospects looked inauspicious. In 1878 the government floated a public loan of 153 million forints at excessively high interest rates. Finance Minister Károly Kerkápoly (1824–1891), a man of impressive economic and political credentials, fell victim to the controversy that erupted in connection with the "usury bond," the sobriquet given to the aforementioned public loan. His successor, Kálmán Ghyczy, endured less than a year. Hungary's deficit–ridden economy languished helplessly until almost the end of the century. The state fared no better sharing in the increasingly profitable railway system. Nearly all lines before 1867 were constructed by Rothchild–owned or influenced companies which also received state support. Railway construction suffered a predictable setback in the aftermath of the panic of 1873 but managed to recover by the early 1880s.[28]

If Istóczy's ill–tempered anti–Semitic outburst chagrined Ghyczy and other members of the Diet, his anguish over the country's tattered economy and finance had a correspondingly opposite effect on the former finance minister who was occupying the chair of the president of the Diet. The speech, uninterrupted by impatient reminders of impropriety and frequently prodded along by expressions of approval, gave a sobering revelation of the kind of politician Istóczy might have become had his mind and career not been so exclusively pressed into the service of anti–Semitism. He reviewed the oppressive state of the economy and voiced hope in the government's ability to regain control and institute reform. He called for the impositon of a stock exchange tax, citing a similar effort in Germany, and the issuance of documentary stamps. These measures were justified, he argued, in view of the fact that "the Stock Exchange caused commerce to suffer the deepest wounds." Turning to the railway system, the construction of which was viewed as symbolic of the modernization of the Hungarian economy, Istóczy called for state ownership, a dramatic turnabout that was to be realized before the end of the decade. His plan, bolstered by a mass of data and suitably relevant arguments, sounded impressive. "In those days I alone spoke in the Diet in favor of a system of state railways," Istóczy recalled with justifiable pride.[29]

The most remarkable feature of Istóczy's speech was not what it contained but what it omitted. For reasons that defy explanation he chose not to bolster his arguments by reverting to scapegoatism, a technique he had undoubtedly mastered. Not once did he mention Jews, though both themes were inviting. Jewish financiers and investors were the indispensable concomitants of not only the banking system but the infrastructure of Hungary's economy as well. Yet Istóczy's reference to the "cosmopolitan visitors to the Stock Exchange" was casual, brief and devoid of malice. Nor did he venture to mention the virtual Jewish monopoly of the Hungarian railway. Two easy preys lay within close range of the persistent hunter. Yet no shots were fired. Was Istóczy trying to establish credibility as a versatile politician and avoid being stigmatized as a one–issue huckster? Was he trying to impress his fellow representatives with his ability to grasp complicated issues of national importance, master and utilize a multiplicity of technical data, advance cogent arguments, and offer pragmatic solutions? Or was he in fact a political neophite, inconsistent and unpredictable, whose public utterances lacked structure, depth, and purpose? The validity of none, some or all of these hypotheses can be proven. Inexplicably and mysteriously, the speech went unnoted.[30]

Anyone who was puzzled as to why Istóczy neglected his Judephobia and forayed into the realm of conventional politics soon had plausible explanations. The mirage lasted less than five weeks. On 17 December 1875, the debate over the passage of a bill that sought parliamentary approval for a commercial treaty with Romania provided Istóczy with a vehicle by which to return to his true form. The discussion was bound to create tension and acrimony. Even though Representatives Chorin and Wahrmann, prominent leaders of Hungarian Jewry, spoke for ratification, an undercurrent of uneasiness attributed to causes unrelated to the economic implications of the treaty were clearly discernible. Chorin and Wahrmann voiced concern over Romania's anti–Jewish laws. Indeed, for nearly ten years Romania had been the scene of violent demonstrations, often pogroms, against Jews. Outraged mobs in Bucharest prevented the legislative assembly from discussing the question of Jewish emancipation. Jews accused of causing a cholera epidemic were expelled from villages; synagogues and cemeteries were desecrated. Considering the Jews aliens, the government provided only a modicum of protection but only in deference to the mounting international pressure.

To Istóczy, Romania was a familiar stamping ground. A portion of the chapters that he had translated from Du Mesnil–Marigny's works contained the copy of a document signed by thirty–one members of Romania's national assembly. It painted a terrifying picture of devastation and exploitation among the people of Romania. The perpetrators, the document alleged, were among the steadily increasing population of Jews whose monopolistic machinations had ruined Romania's trade and commerce and whose rejection of solidarity with the Romanian people had caused a grievous social imbalance. The passage of protectionist laws was supported by the undersigned representatives "to protect Romanians from Jewish exploitation."[31]

Istóczy wasted no time in grasping this opportunity to speak at the debate. Nor did the representatives seem eager to call for adjournment even though Istóczy requested to speak at the end of the daily session. The promise of another round of verbal histrionics was obviously too good to postpone, and Istóczy would prove them right. Two obstacles, Chorin and Wahrmann, blocked the path to his target. They were, however, more illusory than real. Istóczy was convinced that the two Jewish representatives supported approval of the treaty for well–concealed, ulterior reasons: to create a deceptive climate for their deceitful propaganda "against the constitution and laws of a neighboring friendly nation, and to persuade the Diet to initiate a moral intervention in its internal affairs." The people of Romania, Istóczy noted, had fallen prey to the Jews' usurious and exploitive business practices. For dramatic effect he produced the text of the declaration of the thirty–one Romanian representatives and read it from start to finish.

Although the basic components—the venomous description of Jews, the power of the Jewish–controlled press, and the right of the people to self–defense against Jewish exploitation—remained the all too obvious hallmarks of Istóczy's third major speech in the Diet, there was a new, previously undetected, element that should not be underestimated: flashes of a biting wit. Twice he caused his audience to burst into approving laughter: first, when he warned the Diet against "lending a helping hand to a moral crusade in the Jewish interest"; and second, when his reading of the Romanian representatives' declaration, Istóczy added emphasis to the words that attributed the Jews' proclivity for usury to "their instinct for beastlike rapacity."

Two unexpected snags, however, spoiled Istóczy's hopes of completing his speech unchallenged. Lajos Csernátony[32] interrupted, accusing Istóczy of voicing views tantamount to religious persecution, a charge the latter indignantly denied. Istóczy, however, blundered in qualifying his previous disparaging statement concerning the press, restricting it to the Jewish–controlled newspapers from which he exempted Csernátony's, in a snide allusion to the series of articles Csernátony had written about the Jews. It was then that an impatient Kálmán Ghyczy cut Istóczy short by ruling his comments about the press irrelevant to the discussion in progress.[33]

Few topics of parliamentary discussion were more conducive to Istóczy's purposes than the bill calling for the modification of the laws of usury. What other occasion would be more appropriate for a prolonged chastisement of his favorite whipping boys, the "usurious Jews"? His speech in the Diet on 23 January 1877, after more than a year of keeping a low political profile, revealed evidence of his inexplicable fluctuations between his accustomed reserve and a surprising versatility. It was a strangely brief but eloquently worded speech, filled with almost pedantic objections to the indiscriminate practice of Manchesterism. It precipitated the spread of unregulated usury that resulted in the expropriation of the possessions of small landholders and the near economic ruin of the gentry, once the healthiest segment of the population. Astonishingly, Istóczy made not one direct reference to the Jews,[34] although his veiled allusion to "the everspreading indebtedness of our people to the usurious speculating innkeepers" had an all too obvious intent.[35]

Chapter V
The Palestine Speech

The egomaniac sees the path of illusions as filled with the promises and rewards of his permanent metamorphosis. It transforms the amateur into a professional, the bungler into a perfectionist, and the practitioner of mediocrity into a seeker of excellence. In politics it allows the provincial mind to exchange its limited horizon for the panorama of statesmanship. Amid the applause of newly acquired admirers, the egomaniac hears the muffled sounds of self–delusions with the sharp ring of reality.

Within three years of his election to the Diet, the inexperienced representative from Vas County had found a style, a voice and a vehicle. They enabled him to speak on both matters of national importance and issues of foreign politics with enthusiasm and assurance. He had clearly become the darling of the anti–Semites all over Europe.

Since 8 April 1875, through the years, thanks to my subsequent anti–Semitic speeches in which I took due care to concern myself not only with conditions in Hungary but those prevailing all over Europe as well, a constant stream of letters, sending congratulations and encouragement and seeking guidance, have reached me not only from my own country but also from Austria, Germany, and France. Following in my footsteps, anti–Semitic writers, among them Edouard Drumont[1] in Paris, have sent me copies of their works inscribed with flattering dedications. Interviewers from Paris and Berlin sought me out . . . I became the leader of a political movement that was called by then anti–Semitic not only in Hungary but other European countries as well.[2]

Istóczy had already shown a fledgling interest in foreign affairs during his intemperate outburst during the debate on the ratification of the commercial treaty with Romania. Yet it was not until the summer of 1875 that he unveiled his grandiose plan for the systematic de–Judaization of Europe. On 24 June 1878 Istóczy delivered the most memorable and controversial foreign policy speech of his political career. Entitled "The Restoration of the Jewish State in Palestine," it was subsequently better known as the "Palestine Speech." With it "I

gave [the development of the] Zionist organization a decisive push,"
he concluded.[3]

Istóczy's bombastic, self–aggrandizing statement was invested
with a ring of truth and surrounded with an aura of political sanctity
by subsequent generations of anti–Semites for whom he had become
a seminal, though not always easily discernible, force. An objective
examination of the antecedents and circumstances, however, yields a
considerably less flattering view of the contents and significance of
the "Palestine Speech," and casts a less than luminous glow on its
maker. Taking credit and deserving it, in Istóczy's case, were mutually exclusive undertakings.

Except for the possibility of simple ignorance, it is difficult to
identify the rationale or stimuli that prompted Istóczy to stake his
claim. By 1878 the works of proto–Zionists, such as Moses Hess and
the rabbis Yehuda Hai Alkalai, Zvi Hirsch Kalischer and József Natonek, had formulated the ideology, charted the direction and defined
the goals of Jewish nationalism.[4] Istóczy, a knowledgeable Jew–baiter,
pretended to be or actually was unaware of the early stirrings of the
Zionist idea. Despite the geographic proximity of at least two sources
of proto–Zionism, his state of mind yields no more puzzling challenge
than Herzl's statements about his not having been exposed either to
the manifestations of anti–Semitism prior to his taking up permanent
residence in Vienna in 1878 or the works of Zionist thinkers that preceded the publication of his *Der Judenstaat* in 1896. Alkalai, rabbi
of the Jewish community of the Serbian city of Zemun (Semlin), then
called Zimony and located in the southernmost portion of Hungary's
Szerém County, had been a supporter of the ideals of the 1848 Revolution and Natonek, who by the early 1870s had settled in Budapest
and, to the chagrin of the capital's assimilationist Jewry, become the
editor of the short–lived *Das Einige Israel*, the first Zionist weekly.[5]
Istóczy was equally oblivious of the incipient Arab nationalist movement, inspired by Lebanese intellectuals, the Christian Nasif Yazeji
and the Muslim Butrus Bustani, which made the ever–suspicious Ottoman government even less receptive to Zionist aspirations than it
might have been otherwise.

Istóczy's self–assembled statesmanship reflected the prevailing
mood of public opinion on the Balkan Question. His perception
of it was molded by the conflicting Austrian and Russian interests
in the turbulent Christian–dominated Ottoman provinces, the ensuing Russo–Turkish War of 1877 and his own personal interpretation
of the implications of big–power politics at the Congress of Berlin
(1878). The Hungarians' dislike and fear of Russia, institutionalized by Nicholas I's assistance in the suppression of the 1848 Rev-

olution, and concerned with the nationalist disturbances in Croatia and among Hungary's South–Slav minorities, created a nationwide support of the Turks. The Hungarians' pro–Turkish sympathies help explain Istóczy's interest in the Ottoman empire but shed no light on his reasons for believing himself an expert on its internal structure and political and economic priorities. No less puzzling is Istóczy's almost phantasmagoric vision derived from the irreversible territorial shrinking of the Ottoman empire and the detailed explanation with which he bolstered his multidimensional argument. His views, to be sure, were based on facts: the Russo–Turkish Treaty of San Stefano (3 March 1878) guaranteed full independence to Serbia, Romania, and Montenegro and created a "Greater Bulgaria" which incorporated much of the Ottomans' remaining European holdings; and the subsequent Congress of Berlin (June–July 1878) restored to Turkey a portion of the area that had been ceded to Bulgaria but gave occupational rights to Austria in Bosnia and Herzegovina. (The Hungarians found themselves in a difficult position. They were heartened by the high visibility of Count Gyula Andrássy, who since his appointment on 14 November 1871 had served as the monarchy's foreign minister. However, the occupation of Bosnia and Herzegovina caused considerable anguish, prompting a gloomy Ghyczy to dispute its benefits to Hungary and voice concern over grave financial and political implications.)[6]

The "Palestine Speech" was preceded by a brief motion which gave an ominous warning of both the scheme of twisted and cunning logic and the bizarre state of the mind from which it hatched.

> May the House declare that not only the Eastern peoples' aspirations for freedom be realized but also justice be rendered to the Jewish people forced to abandon its ravaged homeland eighteen centuries ago; that its native country, Palestine, be enlarged under the Sublime Porte as an autonomous province or restored as an independent Jewish State, thereby creating a Jewish people, which at its present rate of growth hinders the development of European nations and threatens the Christian civilization. Their national government and institutions, amid kindred Semitic tribes in the enfeebled and backward East, may make it a vigorous, powerful and new element and an influential ingredient of civilization.[7]

As if wanting to harness the momentum generated by the ongoing deliberations at the Congress of Vienna to gain credibility for the theme of his motion, Istóczy in the "Palestine Speech" used the systematic reduction of the Turks' European possessions as a virtual rider to his master plan. Its structure was deceptively cultured and pragmatic, belying the incivil language, the flawed logic, and the insupportable characterization of the Jews. Istóczy declared:

> During the over a millennium-long titanic struggle between the Christian West and the Mohammedan East the Hungarian nation, bleeding from thousands of wounds, obliged the European family of peoples to eternal gratitude with standing fast for centuries as the bastion of its civilization.

The threat of Arab Mohammedanism was brought to the heart of Europe by the Ottomans who were subsequently forced to change the old policy of aggression into one of self-defense within ever-narrowing borders. The Christian peoples of the Balkan peninsula were gaining independence, either by reaching peaceful resolution to differences at the Congress of Vienna, or by the force of arms. "Europe must, by whatever means, prevent the newly liberated Christian peoples from coming under Muscovite despotism," he warned.

Istóczy planned to create an uplifting mood in his audience by presenting the dramatic spectacle of Christian triumph over Muslim aggression. He then changed the mood by faltering on a long-entrenched obstacle. He declared dramatically:

> After the gradual disappearance of the Mohammedan element from Europe, only one single alien, a completely isolated element has remained. That alien element is the Jewry. With feverish excitement and indefatigable activity the Jewish people strive to realize their bold plan of acquiring control over the peoples of Europe and enslaving them.

Amid choruses of "Hear! Hear!" Istóczy went on to recap briefly the message of his previous speeches. The ignorance of people and the ingenious machinations of the Jewish-controlled press, Istóczy charged, succeeded in putting a veil of secrecy over the real objectives of Jews. As time went on, his accusations began to sound monotonous and his reasoning belabored. Suddenly he shifted gears. The lesson in demography which the translation of the Du Mesnil-Marigny chapters had taught him came in good stead now. Facts, he felt, would make a more dramatic impression than theory. The hunch, leading to an effective, albeit alarmist, argument proved him right. According to census figures published at irregular intervals between 1785 and 1870 the number of Jews residing in Hungary showed an eightfold increase, from 75,089 to 552, 133. Statistical analysis, Istóczy inferred, would support the theory that "the Jewish element in our country doubles itself every thirty years."[8] His prediction of the presence in Hungary of 1,100,000 Jews in 1900, 2,200,000 in 1930, 4,400,000 in 1960, 8,800,000

in 1990, and 17,600,000 in 2020 caused ripples of laughter among
the representatives. He predicted that within 150 years, taking into
account the less than two-fold increase of the number of non-Jews
between 1785 and 1870 and the irrefutable biological, historical, and
statistical evidence that Jews were spared the ravages of epidemics,
"Jews would outnumber the non-Jewish population of St. Stephen's
domains by two million." Istóczy even cited a number of telltale signs
of the Jews' plotting to achieve dominant positions:

> Many live to a ripe old age. . . . They avoid all work that
> requires physical exertion . . . they are represented min-
> imally in the army, and army doctors and often well-paid
> noncombatants make up half of even that small number . .
> . they derive great profits from destructive wars . . . they
> lead the legions of Social Democrats in economically ruined
> countries . . . they poison the relations among Christian
> peoples . . .

The choice, as Istóczy saw it, was clear:

> Living as we are, side by side, inevitably, one of the two will
> have to perish unless an alternative is found . . . Fortu-
> nately the necessity to resort to the *ultima ratio* exists no
> more, provided the Jewish people itself would lend a hand
> to the solution of the Jewish Question in accordance with
> the prevailing spirit of our time. The solution is none other
> than the reestablishment of the onetime Jewish state.

With his brief history lesson and overview of socioeconomic and
political complexities, Istóczy demonstrated the desirability and in-
evitability of the restoration of the Jews to their renascent national
state, an idea to which Roman and Christian emperors, Muslim Arabs
and Ottomans had introduced insurmountable obstacles. "From time
to time the burning problem that the Jewish Question created was
resolved by the mass execution of Jews," Istóczy noted, his words
causing "much amusement." For the "injustices and cruelties that
had been perpetrated against their ancestors, the Jews have taken
revenge by subjecting the European peoples and their governments
to torture."

Midway through the speech he stunned his audience with making
a rare display of modesty, although nearly half a century later, clinging to the last fragile straws of a discredited and forgotten career, a
disillusioned and dispirited Istóczy would claim that he had virtually
given birth to the Zionist movement. He denied having originated his
plan. He noted that men before him had raised the idea of the return
of the Jews, citing Luther and Fichte and one Goldwin Smith, who

in the May 1878 edition of the British monthly, *Nineteenth Century*, had suggested, in view of the financial woes of the Ottomans, the feasibility of the restoration of the Jewish state. However, Istóczy made no mention of a Jewish contributor to the idea.

Precedent, Istóczy reasoned, confirmed the desirability of the plan. In 1867, Hungary had regained its national sovereignty, lost at Mohács.[9] The Greeks and other Christian peoples of the Balkan peninsula had already been restored to the state of nationhood that existed prior to the Ottoman conquest, or were in the process of achieving it; Barbarossa's (Frederick II) empire came to life again [in Germany] six hundred years after it was conquered; and Italy reestablished its unified national structure nearly a millennium and a half after the fall of the Roman Empire. Why could a Jewish state, destroyed 400 years earlier, not experience a similar national renascence?

His argument of historical precedents, however, quickly bogged down in the quagmire of anti–Semitic fallacies. Somehow, when applied to the Jewish Question, the universal experience of rebuilding nations, that harmonious blending of exalted communal and individual aspirations—often to dazzling and deceptive heights—was instinctively demoted to the level of base machinations and invested with odious characteristics. The Jews had already formed a state within the state, Istóczy declared. The institutions and leaders of no state could bear favorable comparison with the universal republic of the Jews [i.e., the Alliance Israélite Universelle] and its president. The Jews preserved their ancient ties to their homeland, their traditions and festivals, and their customs of making pilgrimages to Jerusalem and scattering the dust of Palestine over their graves. Nor could Istóczy bring himself to explain in a respectful manner the manifold efforts to rekindle the fire on the altar of Jewish nationalism, a gesture he so readily accorded others. The opportunity to engage in profanities was all too tempting and free of risk. His tolerant audience apparently listened good naturedly, taking no offense as he oscillated between solemnity and irreverence. "The majority of the even now nomadic Jewish people, the most mobil element in the world," Istóczy sneered, stirring laughter,

> could convert most of its possessions into movable property and change residences within forty–eight hours. It is an anthropologically demonstratable fact that no people can establish itself as easily as the Jews. Returning from all corners of the earth they will acclimatize to their ancestral land without difficulty.[10]

Drawing no warning from the president of the Diet for straying from the topic of his motion almost at will, an emboldened Istóczy proceeded to introduce the details of his multidimensional master plan. Jewish immigrants from Europe and the Arab provinces of the Middle East would gradually increase Palestine's small Jewry. The establishment of a Jewish state was a political necessity and would benefit the entire region; the Arabs had already played out their historic role; the vitality of the Egyptian state was uncertain; and the Ottoman empire lacked the material and moral resources that were the guarantees of a healthy and durable state system. The East had spent its rage and its once iron-fisted rule had become enervated. A vibrant, intelligent, progressive, and diligent element, like the Jews, was needed to assume positions of leadership and demonstrate compatibility among racially and spiritually kindred peoples. Istóczy argued that:

> Possessing intellectual talents of high quality, conspicuous political, legal, commercial, and financial expertise, but above all the enormous power of wealth, the Jews might effect the regeneration of the Ottoman empire, long suffering from a chronic shortage of funds in Asia.

This reasoning triggered another outburst of appreciative laughter.

Istóczy's next target was the *Weltanschauung* of Central and West European Jewry, an integrated community known for its multifaceted patriotism. Attacking it, however, necessitated the deployment of new weapons. The impact of rationalization and sarcasm would be minimal, their effects short-lived at best. Supporting nationalistic impulses in the Jewish mind, character and lifestyle had to be detected, unearthed and revealed. He named identical reports that appeared two years earlier in the *Pester Lloyd* and *Nemzeti Hírlap*, two popular Budapest dailies, quoting a letter in *Ha-Maggid*, the first Hebrew-language newspaper based in East Prussia. According to that source of information, the Ottoman government had offered its Jewish creditors in England a portion of Palestine and agreed, as rumors circulating in Istanbul had it, to the formation of a consortium of wealthy English, French and Austrian Jews which would eventually acquire the entire Holy Land. The reason these plans had not been realized, Istóczy argued, was a contrary, connivingly concealed aspiration. Influential Jewish statesmen and politicians tightened their control of European capitals and promoted the parasitic existence of Jews, hoping to slowly strangle the non-Jewish society, and replaced it with an exclusively Jewish one. He challenged those Jews who viewed themselves as strangers in Europe, unwilling to make peace with the European state system and unquestioningly accept the Christian civilization, to leave. "Our most heartfelt wishes for happiness, well-being and good fortune will accompany their return to their homeland from which they had been exiled for 1,800 years."

Suddenly—and inexplicably—the combative elan that had sustained much of the speech dissipated. Almost as an afterthought, Istóczy stopped short of embracing the radical views of racial anti-Semites who on the basis of irreconcilable racial differences advocated the complete removal of Jews. He made an unexpected and surprising call for an orderly and mutually beneficial, albeit conditional, rapprochement.

> May those who wish to stay among us in Europe for whatever reason cease forming a state within the state and abandon forever all the politics of extermination. May they, without any *arrière-pensée*, embrace our customs, reconcile sincerely with the Christian civilization, and assimilate into us, becoming one with us in body and soul. Then we shall welcome them in our midst with the most heartfelt joy.

Although the words were clear, their meaning—perhaps intentionally—was ambiguous. Did they call for only assimilation or imply conversion? Were they, due to Istóczy's inexperience, uttered in an inconsistent moment, or were they a well-timed, cathartic homage to pragmatism? Even though he was the first practicing—and largely self-taught, often impulsive—anti-Semitic politician, Istóczy had after all been honing his powers of persuasion through two parliamentary terms. By all counts, six years in a political career constitute an adequate period to gain the required grasp of issues, procedures and rules; develop a style in parliamentary rhetoric; learn to gauge the attention and interest span of the audience, and, if sufficiently motivated, establish a persona and develop a commitment to a cause. Istóczy had already demonstrated an ability to control his obsessive Judeophobia through an entire speech and manage to sound well prepared, persuasive and intelligent, even sagacious at times. The brief foray into the realm of socioeconomic pragmatism was clearly a well-prepared attention getter.

In the concluding portion of the speech Istóczy reverted to the accustomed claptrap presentation of his political vision, a melange of biting anathemas and flashes of genuine deductive reasoning, the style and content everyone readily associated with him. Indeed, the restoration of the Jewish state, Istóczy observed, no longer belonged to the "realm of chimaeras." Yet, only wishful thinking could breathe life into a presumed configuration of personal preferences and *raison d'état* at work at the Congress of Vienna. (Ironically the Zionists would subsequently prove that wishful thinking transformed into the power of will could make a dream a reality.) Istóczy envisioned the Congress as a sort of exclusive club of Europe's leading Jewish statesmen where only one word from them could change fiction to fact: Britain's Disraeli; the French Leon Gambetta; Eduard Lasker, then still a political ally of Bismarck; and the Austrian Minister of Justice, Julius Anton Glaser; and Joseph Unger, a minister without portfolio. The latter two were in the government of Prince Adolf Auersperg.[11]

National interests were no less accommodating, Istózy reasoned. The Ottomans, in dire financial straits and in deference to European Jewry that had demonstrated sympathies for them during the Russo–Turkish War, would agree to the creation of either an autonomous Jewish province under Turkish sovereignty or even an independent Jewish state; the Dual Monarchy, beset by a variety of pressing woes, would favor "the radical solution of the Jewish Question." Hungarian public opinion and national interest in particular would be ill-served if the Foreign Ministry did not support the plan of restoration, should the government of a European country or the leaders of European Jewry initiate an effort to implement it.

Imagination can play tricks on the retrospective observer. He would expect the concluding words of the first anti-Semitic—and proto-Zionist—speech in a parliament to be followed by a round of applause, audible expressions of approval or indignation or the silence of astonishment or indifference. However, the remarks of Kálmán Ghyczy, the president of the Diet, must have caused the exhausted speaker considerable consternation, but not for the reason he had come to expect. Indeed Istóczy must have wondered why the accustomed words of warning had been withheld so conspicuously. When at long last Ghyczy spoke, his words created an almost comic relief, leaving Istóczy incredulous and stupefied. An old ghost had returned to haunt the solemn chamber. "The acoustics of the building are so bad," Ghyczy said, "that even the sounds of the distinguished representative's speech were only sporadically audible here." After he was reassured—incorrectly—that he had been misinformed about Istóczy having made the statement about the solution of the Jewish Question by mass execution in the Middle Ages, Ghyczy even withdrew a belated warning and called for questions.

Although the actual number of representatives who heard the "Palestine Speech" from start to finish may never be verified, a member of Prime Minister Kálmán Tisza's government was one who did and offered an unhesitating rebuttal. The response by Minister of Cults and Public Instruction Ágoston Trefort was condemnatory in both brevity and content. He voiced regret that doctrines in such marked contrast to the "humanitarian ideals of the age and the noble spirit of this House could have been expounded, spurring inaccurate and harmful interpretations." He questioned the very propriety of Istóczy's speech and expressed the hope that "the sounds of this literary essay have already faded without leaving a trace or an echo in the Diet." A few audible expressions of support in the course of the speech notwithstanding, the mood of the representatives was of virtually uniform disapproval. Seeing his hopes dashed and sensing defeat, Istóczy retreated quickly. Trefort's strongly worded statement had already blocked a full debate on the floor. "I hereby withdraw my motion," Istóczy announced. "I call on future generations to testify to the propriety of my words." [12]

Although Istóczy offered surprisingly weak resistance and eventually made an almost meek submission to the mounting forces of opposition—Trefort's forceful intervention and the ubiquitous Ghyczy's zealous and unyielding guardianship of parliamentary propriety had within minutes diffused the threat of a potentially controversial, and for the government embarrassing, debate—he was not disheartened by the ignominious aftermath of the "Palestine Speech." It was anticlimactic, giving him no cause for grievous concern. The events of the first six months of 1878 had been amply suspicious. He succeeded in transferring political anti–Semitism from the stultifying milieu of the Diet, where his request to organize a non–Jewish caucus had been rejected, into the spectrum of public opinion. Convinced of his ability to evade "the oppressive Jewish monopoly of the press," Istóczy started a weekly journal, *Jövőnk* [Our Future], the first exclusively anti–Semitic publication in Hungary. An admittedly risky undertaking even under less controversial circumstances, the *Jövőnk* was doomed to an early failure. During a faltering five–month operation it succeeded neither in reaching a sizeable readership nor in attracting the number of subscribers needed to cover the costs of publication. [13] Still, Istóczy's stature and political career had become visible, firmly etched in the minds of his contemporaries. He had emerged from the anonymity of political apprenticeship and outgrown the limitations of his provincial base. As long as the voters in the district of Rum were willing to return him to the Diet and have themselves represented by a man whose most recognizable trait was anti–Semitism, Istóczy had a secure niche in national politics. Within six years the pesky nuisance had become a political persona.

Chapter VI

The Alliance of Hungarian Non-Jews

Whereas the speakers in the parliamentary proceedings were hampered in varying degrees by the bad acoustics of the chamber of the Diet, the public opinion was not handicapped by similar impediments. Istóczy's message, often unheard or ridiculed in the Diet, found a surprisingly unobstructed exit into the streets of Budapest and the towns and villages of the countryside. The echo that Trefort had hoped would not be generated gathered momentum and reverberated with growing intensity. The tools that manufacture popularity sometimes are found in the storehouse of setbacks. The apparent lack of support in the Diet and the short life of *Jövőnk*—its faltering course uncorrected, it ceased publication in the autumn of 1878— did not turn Istóczy into a disillusioned man or deter his quest for nationwide attention and support.

Impatient yet calculating by nature, Istóczy decided to not wait and see if his investment of speeches to his fellow representatives would pay dividends. Wherever he detected even faint echoes of his speeches he moved with resolve. The early results of his decision convinced him that he had found receptive segments in the population. The Catholic lower clergy, the gentry, and university students, groups Istóczy had known all too well, easily absorbed the anti-Semitic agitation and quickly gave credence to the poisonous words of Jew baiters. By the late 1870s Istóczy also gained footsoldiers among the factory workers for his "crusade against the parasitic Jews." Victimized by primitive conditions in factories and the callous indifference of factory owners and managers, workers were easily persuaded to vent their anger and frustration at the perpetrators of their misfortune. For many foreign workers from "Vienna, Bohemia–Moravia, and even Germany, and Hungarian journeymen traveling abroad in compliance with long standing custom,"[1] anti-Semitism was a familiar opiate.

To Istóczy, the principal theoreticians of the international labor movement were Jewish enough to be distrusted and feared: Ferdinand Lasalle, Karl Marx, and Leó Frankel,[2] their most dedicated Hungarian disciple and one of the leaders of the Paris Commune of 1870–1871 who was allowed to return to Budapest in 1876. The ominous implications of the "Jewish monopoly" of the leadership of the Hungarian labor organization, however, were neutralized by the increasingly politicized labor leaders. In response to the government's decision to disallow the formation of the Party of the Disenfranchised, which called for universal suffrage, the labor leaders urged workers to support the Independence Party and vote for its candidates in the national elections of 1878. In return, the Independence Party supported some of the workers' demands.[3] However, the party also happened to be the political base of some of Istóczy's earliest and most fervent disciples.

The time-consuming efforts required to lay the foundations of extra-parliamentary support did not render Istóczy inactive in the Diet. In a carefully orchestrated sequence of speeches he addressed problems that concerned three of the four bases of his expanding constituency. In 1879 he spoke in support of the establishment of a government-sponsored national monetary fund that would extend mortgage credit to small landholders and thus protect them against "the devastation of usury and the invading foreign element that threatens the very existence of our nationality and society."[4] He also spoke in defense of Hungarian agriculture—Hungary was particularly hard hit by the United States' massive grain shipments to the European market in the late 1870s. The United States, Istóczy charged, had nearly been ruined by laissez-faire capitalism "unrestrained by material and moral fetters, and could only recover by means of self-help rather than parliamentary legislation or government intervention."[5]

Commencing auspiciously, the year 1880 would rank as a watershed in the early phase of his political career. Istóczy stepped out of his role of self-annointed savior of rural society and took an unprecedented, albeit brief, excursion into Budapest's turbulent municipal politics. His speech, delivered on January 28, was one of the most abusive Jew-baiting outbursts on record. Istóczy attempted to divert the political orientation of the workers from the Independence Party to himself. The violent street demonstrations that had created havoc in Budapest earlier in the month served as the backdrop of Istóczy's newest attack on "the Jewish malady of our society." The Jews, Istóczy charged, without citing a single corroborating example, were responsible for corruption of all sorts. "Beyond every affair, like a Mephisto, stands a Jew," he exclaimed, drawing as he often did a mixture of incredulous laughter and knowing smirks. "History marches unstoppably in its path," he warned ominously. "The radical solution of the Jewish Question is not far off." Much of Istóczy's rancor, however, was lost on his audience, unusually jovial but not now in the mood to take him seriously. Even the new president of the

Diet, József Szlávy,[6] a distinguished, much–respected political stalwart, indulged himself in issuing a truculently sarcastic reprimand. "I enjoin the honorable representative to adhere to the subject or at least draw near it," Szlávy grumbled. The chamber exploded in deafening laughter.

Istóczy had been forced to become impervious to being the inevitable butt of frequent manifestations of parliamentary levity. However, although resigned, he skillfully avoided becoming passive. When one avenue seemed blocked, he sought out another with renewed vigor. Instead of heeding Szlávy's warning, Istóczy turned in another direction which appeared to be even less relevant than the one he had been requested to abandon. He proposed to read a seventeen–article long document, entitled "The Charter of the Central Association of the Federation of Hungarian Non–Jews,"[7] hoping to stir up interest in and support for the creation of a parliamentary group modeled on the Berlin *Antisemiten–Liga,* "against the aggressive and demoralizing Jewish power." Again his attempt failed. The occasional voices of encouragement were drowned by a chorus of mock–heroic heckling, causing Istóczy to briefly lose his usually unfailing repose. The coup de grace was delivered by Szlávy, when he said sternly:

> As my request to that end has gone unheeded, I must now demand that the Honorable Representative return to the topic on the floor, for the charter of such an association has no connection with the item on the agenda.

Istóczy complied, but not without uttering a parting slanderous remark: "Let the world know that in our midst, too, in most cases the corruptors are the Jews."[8]

The overwhelming expression of disapproval of Istóczy's proposed reading of the charter proved to be only a short–lived setback. Within twenty–four hours after Istóczy failed in his laborious attempts to gain limited exposure for the charter, it was thrust into the limelight of public opinion by a means that did not even require his machinations. The January 29th edition of the *Egyetértés,* a left–wing daily, whose oversized pages devoted to sensationalism assured both its popularity and dubious reputation, published a three-part, abridged version of the charter. It characterized the proposed organization as an apolitical gathering place of non–Jewish representatives in the Diet and other like–minded individuals for the purpose of "protecting our nation from further moral and economic deterioration caused by the Jews." To accomplish that objective the organization would resort to only legal and permissible tactics, avoiding incitement of all sorts. The charter also gave a detailed blueprint of the subsequent establishment of organizational branches in various counties and the development of ties with fraternal associations in foreign countries. A unique feature of the charter, attesting to Istóczy's somewhat cavalier attitude toward the dictates of racial anti-Semitism, envisioned the admission of converted Jews with limited membership rights.

A far more immediately useful event with more portentous long-range consequences than the publication of the charter ended Istóczy's lonely isolation in the Diet. Despite the occasional sparse signs of audible support, usually overwhelmed by the vociferous opposition, Istóczy was the only professing anti-Semitic representative in Hungary's post-*Ausgleich* political structure during the first six years of his parliamentary career. His zeal, unswerving tenacity and anti-establishment program attracted at long last a following of two men of considerable achievement and prestige: Gyula Verhovay and Iván Simonyi.

More suitable disciples for embracing political anti-Semitism, nor more auspicious circumstances and timing could hardly be found. Both men were parliamentary representatives and Istóczy was provided with a numerical, albeit minuscule, base of identifiable support in the Diet. Both were experienced journalists and skilled writers, thus Istóczy and his hate-filled message were assured a consistent, nationwide exposure, which could transform his one-man crusade into a movement of predictable growth in size and influence.

Gyula Verhovay (1849–1906), like Istóczy, was a country-born lawyer turned politician. For nearly ten years he was affiliated with two popular Budapest dailies, the *Ellenőr* and the *Egyetértés*, the official organ of the Independence Party. In 1878 he ran on the Independence Party slate and was elected into the Diet by voters in Cegléd, an historic 700-year-old town to the southeast of Budapest. An emotion-stirring political commentator who combined a writer's fluid style, a revolutionary's passionate fervor, and a demagogue's boisterous lack of discipline, Verhovay was a consistent and biting critic of the policies of Prime Minister Kálmán Tisza. His journalistic talents and indefatigable labors for Hungary's independence of Austria won him a national reputation. He was frequently called "little Kossuth," a sobriquet he cherished for its flattering comparison to the exiled leader of the 1848 Revolution. He was proud to be the representative of the town whose residents had made Lajos Kossuth an honorary citizen. In December 1879, following an acrimonious clash with Károly Eötvös, a fellow employee, who was one of the leaders of the parliamentary opposition, Verhovay left the *Egyetértés* and founded a newspaper of his own, the *Függetlenség*, which he put in the service of Istóczy's relentless anti-Semitism.[9] Like the constituents of the district of Rum, Istóczy's electoral base, the voters of Cegléd, where members of a small but active Jewish community had been permitted to settle since 1855, saw nothing wrong with having their parliamentary representative linked with the propagandizing of the emergent anti–Semitic movement.

A no less formidable and reliable pillar of support was Iván Simonyi (1836–1904). His conversion to political anti–Semitism was virtually preordained by an unsavory trait of the city which served as his political base. An acid–penned critic of the government's economic policy, Simonyi sought to ameliorate the seemingly irreversible deterioration of the conditions of small landowners. One of the most surprising features of his program was the inclusion of moneyed Jews as agents of agrarian reform. His efforts, however, came to naught. Blaming the Jews for his failure, he decided to run for public office. Pozsony (Bratislava) was the first recipient of the vituperative anti–Semitic propaganda which Simonyi disseminated through his newspaper, the *Westungarisher Grenzbote*. Unlike Istóczy's Rum and Verhovay's Cegléd, Pozsony had been a stronghold of anti–Semitism since the fourteenth century.[10] After electing Simonyi to the Diet, its citizens fell easily in line with their irascible envoy.

Despite Istóczy's disappointment over the demise of *Jövőnk* and his sudden and unexpected gain of publicity through two experienced and well–known journalist–politicians no compelling reason for Istóczy's decision to start a new anti–Semitic publication emerges. Obviously, he was motivated by his self–aggrandizing ego rather than practical necessity. Both the leader and following of a self–contained political cell, he was clearly no prophet in his own country. In moments of unyielding loneliness and bitter frustration, Istóczy drew encouragement from the many expressions of ideological camaraderie he received from anti–Semitic organizations in Austria and Germany. He was heartened and felt vindicated by the declaration of support from Verhovay and Simonyi. Yet the prospect of sharing the unaccustomed light of publicity, an implied threat to his leadership, with two well–known public figures who were his intellectual superiors, virtually coerced Istóczy to keep abreast of them.

It was to that end that on 15 October 1880 the monthly *12 Röpirat* commenced publication. Istóczy viewed it as the mouthpiece of the movement, outranking Verhovay's *Függetlenség* and Simonyi's *Westungarischer Grenzbote*. It served as a repository of his anti–Semitic theories and accusations, many derived from his speeches in the Diet, and a blueprint for action for his sympathizers and would–be supporters.[11] It also reflected Istóczy's preoccupation with transforming his personal philosophy, generally considered as a *corpus vile*, into a scientifically and historically justifiable *Weltanschauung*. Lastly, it reinforced his conviction that he was the founder and principal theoretician of a delusion that became a reality for him. He assiduously collected all references made to him in the foreign press and was particularly proud of a gift—a beer service consisting of a pitcher on whose lid the words *Vier dankbare Deutsche* (four grateful Germans) had been inscribed and three steins—he received from Bernhard Förster in 1880. Förster was the organizer of an anti–Semitic petition campaign in Berlin, an event that, Istóczy believed, started the German anti–Semitic movement.[12]

Istóczy's next target, the university students, a particularly promising, and useful segment of his growing constituency, waited to be addressed officially. Istóczy had already expressed concern over Jewish education, much of which he found odiously anachronistic, conspiratorial and separationist.[13] He was resolved to keep his views and arguments on the subject well–honed. However, his speech, delivered on 11 March 1880 in the Diet was a meaningless déjà–vu. He berated the Jews for being a separate caste and race, disputed their intention to assimilate through intermarriage, resurrected his distorted vision of Jews exploiting and ultimately absorbing their non–Jewish countrymen, and rejected linguistic assimilation as a criterion of social integration. Ignoring Diet President Szlávy's sharply worded admonition for repeatedly treading on irrelevant grounds, Istóczy questioned the loyalty of Hungarian Jews by making an offhanded reference to the Jewish School Fund, the real topic of his speech, which he described as a reward for the machinations of the Austrian–turned Jews, the greatest and deadliest enemies of the Hungarian people. His closing remarks, as usual, called for the radical solution of the Jewish Question.[14]

In an earlier phase of Istóczy's career such a rambling diatribe would have been attributed to his inexperience as a public speaker and the structural and ideological infirmities of his political philosophy. To listeners of the same speech in 1880, the year of his ideological maturity and consecutive political triumphs, an unmistakable purpose and direction became discernible. As an all–purpose anti–Semite, Istóczy could cater to the manifold interests of a varied constituency. After endearing himself to the industrial workers and the "proletarians of the agrarian economy," i.e., the gentry and the peasants, with incendiary speeches, Istóczy was ready to address the concerns of university students. What better credentials could he present than the revelation of the "deadliest enemies of the Hungarian people" whose offspring were already besieging Hungary's institutions of higher learning in alarmingly great numbers, and who would, by bitter competition, entrench themselves in positions forever lost to non–Jewish graduates? The specter of a self–perpetuating Jewish supremacy loomed menacingly over university students anxiously weighing their future prospects.

The long–range objective of Istóczy's second speech on the Jewish School Fund remained obscured for months. Although he had been striving to create an atmosphere of spiraling, fear–inducing hatred of Jews among university students for some time, his latest outburst served as a means of reactivating his concern over what he believed were the ominous social ramifications of Hungary's Jewish-dominated system of education. On 10 February 1881, a 25–member delegation of university students visited Istóczy in his office, located in the Diet building. He was handed a document of virtual ideological fealty which expressed the students' admiration and support for him and their intention to obstruct Jewish students in the performance of their academic duties.[15] Subsequently, the university was the scene of noisy anti–Jewish demonstrations which included incidents of physical assault against Jewish students. When ordered to appear before the rector, a certain Dr. Berger, the ringleaders of the protests presented their grievances concerning the Jewish students and demanded that their number be reduced and made commensurate with the percentage of Jews in the country. In defiance of the rector's strongly worded admonition, the students called a general meeting for the 17th of February. However, the police of Budapest, commanded by Elek Thaisz, the heavy–handed, autocratic guardian of law and order, banned the meeting, citing incitement to race hatred as a threat to public safety.[16]

However, Istóczy left unmentioned another manifestation of anti-Semitism. In the spring of 1881, two towns in Nógrád County in eastern Hungary were rocked by violence. In Losonc and Pásztó, Jews were beaten and their homes and shops looted.[17] The culprits were pan–Slav agitators who used the attacks on the Jews as a means of diverting attention from their struggle for independence, the real cause of their misconduct. Although Russian patrons undoubtedly induced the anti–Semitic atrocities, Istóczy was forced to acknowledge the underlying motive for what were for him otherwise auspicious events. Paying lip service to traditional accusations the pan–Slav nationalist exploited the popular perception of the Jews as economic rivals and the objects of traditional religious hatred. However, the brutal attacks were principally motivated by a deep resentment of the Jews for being patriotic Hungarians, virtual fifth columnists whose very presence was viewed as a retardant in their political struggle.

No such compunction troubled Istóczy's conscience when he took the university students' cause to the floor of the Diet. The purpose of his request, approved by Tamás Péchy,[18] the new president of the Diet, was to interpellate the views of Prime Minister Kálmán Tisza in his capacity as minister of interior, that had prompted him to approve the police authorities' decision to ban the anti-Semitic students' proposed meeting.

The text of the interpellation, consisting of a single sentence, is but a brief preamble to a lengthy, uncharacteristically disorganized and predictably circuitous discourse. Yet some of its components are significant enough to bear mention, even though unrelated to one another or the subject of the interpellation. Istóczy's opening remarks, indignant and admonitory, revealed his growing recognition of the true nature of the outbursts of laughter his views elicited from time to time. Some of his statements, however offensive, testified to the workings of his cutting wit. He had come to realize that many of his fellow representatives were not laughing with him but at him. "The Jewish Question has not been mocked or beaten to death," he scoffed. "On the contrary, it has become a fixture of parliamentary discussion." The bulk of Istóczy's comments centered on the Talmud, that repository of legalistic opinions and teachings which had long been viewed by Jew-baiters as the source of the Jews' evil ways, duplicitous business practices, and hatred of Christians. The source of Istóczy's newly acquired knowledge of the Talmud was *Der Talmudjude*, a work by August Rohling (1839-1931), professor of Semitic languages at the University of Prague. Rohling cited out-of-context references, inaccurate translations and distorted interpretations in an effort to demonstrate the timeless validity of the Jewish insults of Jesus that had so angered the early Church Fathers; and the sanguine description of non-Jews, especially Christians, as *goyim*, a term which institutionalized Jewish separatism in Christian society and inspired subsequent generations of Jews to conspire against, and even murder, Christians.

With Péchy's approval and his colleagues' exclamatory vote of assent, Istóczy proceeded to enlighten his audience about "that dubious-natured, mysterious book that serves as the murky, unexplored background to the well-known machinations of the Jews." He had carefully selected excerpts from *Der Talmudjude*, tracing the leitmotiv of Jewish hatred of Christians through examples of permissible socioeconomic misdeeds. Ignoring shouts of objection, Istóczy cited Talmud-sanctioned transgressions—the inhumanity of Christians, the indiscriminate legal and financial shortchanging, merciless exploitation, callous domination of defenseless Christians, and the exclusion of Christians from the biblical prohibition against killing—as convincing evidence of the

> unrestrained impatience and race hatred with which the
> Jews have declared a social war of extermination on us,
> perpetrating, with impunity, the most heinous crimes and
> rankest injustices, and believing themselves superior beings
> while regarding us a horde of rightless beasts.

Only after he carefully erected this forbidding backdrop
did Istóczy touch briefly on the real subject of his interpellation.
Hungary's Jewry, he noted, constituted only 5 to 7 percent of the
population. Yet the number of Jewish students in law and medical
schools corresponded to 26 and 36 percents, respectively, and was
rising steadily. "What could the future hold for our youth if Jewish
graduates, proliferating like mushrooms and aided, as is customary,
by other Jews, crowd the professions?" Neither the government, dependent on Jewish money to finance the national deficit, nor the
press, controlled largely by Jews, could be expected to show sympathy, Istóczy reasoned. The opposition, which shirked its responsibility to start political movements, should be the principal advocate of the solution of the Jewish Question. His long–winded tirade
notwithstanding, Istóczy's attempt to expand his minuscule group of
followers by implication backfired. His remarks about the many undeclared comrades–in–arms who would support him in a secret ballot
were interrupted by choruses of incredulous and derisive laughter.
The fractured logic of Istóczy's concluding statements elicited a less
than heartening response. If Jews did not exercise power and influence, disproportionately greater than their number in Hungary, there
would be no political anti–Semitism, he reasoned. The discussion
of the Jewish Question had been precipitated by self–defense rather
than race hatred. His caustic legal argument proved even less convincing. Noting that the penal code contained no reference to the
incitement of race hatred, Istóczy declared that he viewed the Jews
neither as a religious nor a social group, for "by Semites one under-
stands both Jews and converted Jews as they are hand and glove with
one another, nor a nationality, for they keep arguing that they are
Frenchmen, Germans, Hungarians, etc." He also questioned the le-
gality of government and police interference in "an internal university
matter."

Responding amid expressions of support voiced by the majority
of the representatives for him, Prime Minister Tisza firmly defended
the government's decision and reaffirmed his responsibility to prevent
incitement aimed at creating friction among social classes, nationalities, and religious groups. He cited the proposed meeting of univer-

sity students as an event whose "sole purpose is to create excitement against a religious and racial group . . . and the Jews, after all, are both."[19]

Istóczy acknowledged the prime minister's reply, noting he had anticipated its substance. His combative mood, however, remained undiminished. He expressed hope that the results of the next parliamentary elections would vindicate him. "Let's not lose heart! To work! We shall triumph! The future is ours!" he shouted defiantly.[20]

The meeting of the university students came to naught, rendering Istóczy's interpellation yet another exercise in futility. However, the echoes of his defiant battle cry did not fade.[21] Neither was the interpellation buried in the thick folios of parliamentary records. One statement, the reference to the permissible killing of Christians, would soon become Istóczy's inadvertent contribution to an unplanned medieval house of horrors, modern Hungary's badge of shame.

Chapter VII

The Blood Libel of Tiszaeszlár

As a prognosticator, Istóczy again proved himself to be a creature of habit, equaling his record of accuracy he set as a politician, public speaker, newspaper editor, lawyer, sociologist, economist, and Talmudic authority. The 1881 elections returned him[1] and his small group of followers to the Diet, yet without an outpouring of public support for the launching of an anti–Semitic movement. It was an unexpected and disappointing setback for Istóczy in the wake of a sequence of promising gains. In the Diet he had consistently addressed the grievances of his principal bases of support and managed to end his seemingly unyielding isolation as the sole proponent of political anti–Semitism. He had developed the *12 Röpirat* into a recognizable ideological mouthpiece, printing the recurring topics of his speeches in the Diet and featuring journalistic variations on the permanent themes of Jewish misdeeds and inadequacies—usury, parasitism, disloyalty, monopolistic exploitation, separatism, and hatred of Christians—and on the anti–Semitic solutions of the Jewish Question—legitimization of pogroms, revocation of the emancipation, social boycott, restriction of intermarriage, and forced emigration. Because of the diverse social and intellectual backgrounds of the contributors as well as Istóczy's often repeated editorial policy to establish and sustain the claim that it was the "first scientific journal dedicated to the Jewish Question," the *12 Röpirat* was an easy target for literary critics who found little, if anything, of redeeming value in its purpose, content and style. "In his pamphlets, as it's generally known, Mr. Istóczy struggles with Jews, syntax, and grammar," observed Kálmán Mikszáth (1847–1910), one of Hungary's most popular writers. The parliamentary correspondent of the *Pesti Hírlap* in the 1880s, Mikszáth wrote numerous scathingly witty, albeit at times felicitous, sketches of the proceedings and personalities of the Diet.[2]

Despite the notable inroads they made among the industrial workers and university students in Budapest, neither Istóczy nor the *12 Röpirat* could breach the ever–thickening wall of resistance which the hostile government, the majority of the Diet, the country's progressive and culturally elite, and Pest's influential Jewry had built around all manifestations of anti–Semitism. Istóczy's vision of a de–Judaized Hungary reached an impasse. There were telltale signs of stagnation, even attrition, as the echoes of Istóczy's defiant victory-promising cry began to fade. It became increasingly apparent that political anti–Semitism was destined to expire by political strangulation in pragmatic, progressive Budapest. Only an expansive breathing space, more traditional and backward–looking supporters and, above all, a new momentum could extricate Istóczy's pubescent movement from its demographic constraints.

Istóczy needed little expertise and time to identify susceptible targets for his ideology. Even a superficial survey of the subscribers of the *12 Röpirat* reveals that the great majority of Istóczy's supporters were of the people of the towns and villages of the Hungarian countryside.[3] It was among them that the Catholic lower clergy, a reliable base of Istóczy's support, still exercised enormous influence as the annointed guardians of individual souls and the self–appointed molders of public opinion. A no less influential role was played by many a village schoolteacher who regarded the spreading of Istóczy's message as the natural extension of an institutionalized rural tradition. Small wonder that the *12 Röpirat* frequently praised these inculcators of youthful minds as "our most trustworthy allies and enthusiastic standard–bearers."[4] However, such views were held by only the most conservative stalwarts of rural society dedicated to preserving a romanticized, anachronistic, and insulated way of life.[5] Economic considerations—the business acumen and financial expertise of Jews were frequently utilized to increase the wealth and influence of the Hungarian Catholic Church[6]—and corresponding moral obligations prompted Cardinal Primate János Simor (1813–1891), whose pragmatism and flair for diplomacy were instrumental in the orderly conduct of Church–State relations, and the episcopate to reject Istóczy's program and issue periodic statements decrying the spread and manifestations of anti–Semitism. Equally, if not more, condemnatory was the position of Minister of Cults and Public Instruction Ágoston Trefort, a conscientious and efficient administrator and loyal, outspoken defender of the policies of the Tisza government. However, in the ranks the copies of *12 Röpirat* generated greater enthusiasm than the rescripts of the governing authorities.

The sagging spirits of Istóczy and his coterie were more than mildly shaken by the results of two elections. In neither instance should the winner have won, least of all where he in fact had. In January 1882, the Jewish Zsigmond Frankl and József Mayer were elected village judges.[7] Not only were their respective villages located in Vas County, Istóczy's birthplace and stamping ground, but also in Rum, the very district whose voters had twice elected him as their representative in the Diet. Moreover it looked as if fate wanted to rub the proverbial salt into his political wound. Mayer's village was Baltaháza—Frankl's was Kisbér—where the ill-fated auction that launched Istóczy's vengeful political career had been held.

On 18 February 1882 Gábor Baross,[8] the Secretary of the Diet, read aloud the text of a brief petition that the Catholic clergy of the district of Vasvár had submitted. The priests, who had been organizing politically since the autumn of 1881, called for "the withdrawal of the motion to sanction marriages between Christians and Jews and the abrogation of Law 1867:XVII that proclaimed the civil equality of the Jews." Following Baross's presentation of the Vasvár petition, Albert Berzeviczy,[9] a referee of the Petitions Committee of the Diet, acknowledged the receipt of the petition. The committee, Berzeviczy noted, would study the part relating to intermarriage, but he characterized the demand for the abrogation of Law 1867:XVII as not meriting parliamentary response.

When Péchy, President of the Diet, granted Istóczy's request to have the petition placed on the floor, few of the elected representatives of the Hungarian people had even the slightest inkling that they were to witness the birth of anti-Semitism as a political movement. Istóczy opened his speech with the customary raving and ranting about the "alien" Jews and the machinations of the Jewish-controlled press. Proudly he reaffirmed his claim to having been the one to "raise for the first time the Jewish Question in a European parliament" and to having done the right thing despite his being frequently ridiculed. With an almost visible bow to rhetorical sophistry, he characterized the nineteenth century as the century of enlightenment in which "a virtual Egyptian darkness engulfs the Jewish designs against us," of humanism, "the benefits of which only the Jews enjoy," and of patience although "just try and let anyone dare make the Jews the subject of even the mildest criticism."

Suddenly the thin veneer of civility and parliamentary discipline crumbled. It was as if the tip of an ageless iceberg, long restrained by the lack of visible support and the disheartening sounds of derisive laughter, had broken through the fetters of modernity. It was the prophet of retribution, not merely a harbinger of bad tidings, that thundered a message of punishment and doom. Clearly, Istóczy was a changed man. Encouraged by the unmistakable signals from the steadily broadening base of provincial support, emboldened by the presence of sixteen fellow representatives who had openly declared themselves to be his ideological comrades-in-arms, Istóczy either lost control, or perhaps, unaccustomed to the protective ring of supporters, purposefully broke with his self–imposed pragmatism that had always enabled him to retreat without losing faith before the opposition's predictable show of force. No such torrent of profanities had ever been heard in the solemn chamber of the Diet. Not even the often mercifully bad acoustics muted its ferocious intensity. "This parasitic and shochetizing[10] semi–nomadic horde . . ." Istóczy shrieked. Although a stern warning by Péchy, the president of the Diet, prevented Istóczy from completing his sentence, the tone of the new anti–Semitic movement had clearly been set.

Istóczy looked beyond his prediction that the Diet would not pass the motion sanctioning civil marriages of Jews and Christians.

> What should then happen to that alien organism feeding on the nation's body? The rejection of the motion must serve as a point of departure from the old policy on the Jews to a new one, the first objective of which must be the abrogation of the emancipation of the Jews.

He repeated his favorite litany of statistical inequities favoring Jews at the expense of Christians; their very mention rarely failed to bring smiles to the faces of his listeners. Then Istóczy plunged into a shocking, unparliamentary tirade. He bored through the many layers of unsubstantiated accusations which generations of like–minded predecessors had so patiently gathered.

> The Jews are engaged in usury and easy tavern–lending, sell tainted wine and flour mixed with sand, weigh the scales, encourage drunkenness, sell the meat of dead cattle, engage in white slavery, bear false witness, avoid heavy work and army service, do not return paid–up notes of debt, mock Christians, practice shotgun journalism, and avoid punishment by escaping to America.[11]

Such reasons, Istóczy claimed, amply justified a motion in support of the Vasvár petition. When Secretary Baross finished reading the text of Istóczy's motion a big sensation was created by the inclusion of the names of sixteen representatives who acted as cosponsors. Hungary's once lonely Cassandra was alone no more.

Istóczy would have preferred to have the motion put to a vote directly. However, the government could hardly let such a slanderous outburst go unchallenged. The intent of the petition and the motion was to introduce the ancient conundrum of the Jewish Question, yet by implication, also indicted the government for its commitment to the preservation of the spirit of Law 1867:XVII and its protectionist attitude toward Jews. Prime Minister Tisza wasted no time in taking the lead to assure the defeat of Istóczy's motion. He spoke briefly. His

words, laced with a generous dose of sarcasm, hit their target hard.
"I cannot be expected to follow every detail of the Honorable Representative's motion," Tisza declared, impugning the sensationalism
of Istóczy's speech. He expressed little admiration for the attitude of
the Russian government toward the Jews and voiced respect for the
German nation even though "in its bosom sickly movements come to
life from time to time." Jews, he noted, practiced usury to no greater
extent than Christians. He took pride in Hungary's parliamentary
politics and its success in eliminating the vestiges of age–old injustices. He called on the Diet to accept the recommendation of the
Petitions Committee, an act which would automatically mean defeat
for Istóczy's motion in support of the Vasvár petition.

The subsequent vote put the stamp of overwhelming approval on
the prime minister's statement.[12] On all counts, the year 1882 showed
auspicious signs of a respite from strife and misfortune, promising
the people of Hungary social well–being and economic stability. The
waves of emotion that the elections had stirred up were subsiding.
The economy, largely through a fourfold increase in foreign capital
investments, the rapid growth in industrial production, and a policy of
protective tariffs nurturing the products of agriculture against foreign
competition, was well on its way to recovery from the devastating
effects of the crash of 1873. The new boom in railway–building created
thousands of jobs and impressive visual evidence of progress. There
was an illusion of tranquility in European politics which the Dual
Monarchy had promoted in its efforts to retain its position in the
balance of power. The renewal of the Three Emperors' League in
1881 and the expansion of the Dual Alliance of Austria–Hungary and
Germany to facilitate the entry of Italy in 1882 were viewed as strong
guarantees of national security.

On Saturday, 1 April 1882, Eszter Solymosi, a fifteen–year–old
servant girl disappeared from Tiszaeszlár, a town in the northeastern
county of Szabolcs. Her mother, a hard–working sickly widow of a
poverty–stricken Calvinist peasants was left with the difficult task of
caring for three children. She started a desperate search, questioning
neighbors and passersby. No one had seen Eszter or could offer clues
concerning her whereabouts. One of Mrs. Solymosi's neighbors was
József Scharf, a pious but simple–minded Jew and himself the father
of two young sons. He offered her words of consolation, citing a similar
case of disappearance in a nearby town. "People there already started
saying that the Jews had gotten hold of her," Scharf said. "But then
she came home." Within two days the words of consolation created
horrifying images of a bloody sacrificial murder in the mind of the
increasingly irrational, grieving mother. The pieces quickly fell into

place: Scharf lived in a house adjacent to the synagogue; someone, the last person to see her alive, had observed Eszter pass by the synagogue; and two women reported they had overheard Scharf's younger son telling some children of a Hungarian girl who was "cut" by a religious slaughterer in the synagogue. The day she disappeared also happened to be the Sabbath preceding the start of the Jewish Passover. The hysterical mother confronted the authorities with her suspicions.

The county court at Nyíregyháza, the administrative seat of Szabolcs County, ordered a full–scale investigation of the allegations. József Bary, an ambitious, aggressive man of twenty–four and a graduate of the law school of the College of Sárospatak, the famed intellectual bastion of Calvinism in Hungary, was put in charge of the investigation. To Ferenc Korniss, the president of the Nyíregyháza court who was known for his dislike of Jews, Bary looked like an excellent choice. Bary's enthusiasm and legal training would guarantee an expeditious and properly conducted investigation. Above all, however, Bary had already acquired the reputation of a man possessed by hatred of Jews. Of the Jews in Tiszaeszlár he observed, "They are without exception uncultured, unwashed persons, living in moral and bodily filth, Yiddish–speaking and evil–looking religious fanatics who harbor a burning hatred of Christians."[13] To the twenty–five families of the Jewish community of Tiszaeszlár, the tone of the official proceedings and the rumors that seemed to be on everybody's lips had an ominous, familiar ring. Deeply engrained in the consciousness of the people of the countryside was the explanation for misfortune of all kinds: the age–old accusation that the hate–filled Jews possessed murderous instincts which prompted them to obtain the blood of Christians for the Passover and other rituals.[14] Since the end of the fifteenth century, five cases of ritual murder had given ample weight to the vivid earthiness of folksongs and folktales and to the frightening imagery of brimstone sermons, thus molding popular views of the "miserable Jewish people" and perpetuating the menacing figure of the mysterious wandering Jew.[15]

To the forces of anti–Semitism, the events of Tiszaeszlár were rapidly becoming an opportunity of unique, even historical, significance. Despite the growing popularity of the *12 Röpirat*, Istóczy's political program, however pedestrian in tone and presentation, remained a parliamentary sideshow beyond the conceptual framework of the majority of the people for whom anti–Semitism was a simple self–defense mechanism against the Jews' ever–tightening grip on the national economy and culture. Despite the intensification of anti–Jewish activities abroad—the proliferation of pogroms in Russia in the aftermath of the assassination of Czar Alexander II on 13 March 1881, the heightened political visibility of Adolf Stöcker in Germany and the rise of the *Verein Deutscher Studenten* (1881), an anti–Semitic students' movement, and the early anti–Semitic speeches of the Austrian Georg Ritter von Schönerer—only a carefully detonated explosion that unleashed an avalanche of anti–Semitic histrionics and a skillful manipulation of popular support could extricate Istóczy's movement from the parliamentary and journalistic quagmire. Tiszeszlár provided the trigger, and Istóczy pulled it without hesitation.

Whether or not the waves created by the blood libel of Tisza-eszlár, allowed to run its course without interference by outsiders, would have broken on pragmatic national priorities is a matter of conjecture. Istóczy and his followers made sure that the Tiszaeszlár case not only did not remain a mere local irritant but that the very mention of the name would stir a ring of evil and infamy long, if not forever, after the particulars had sunk into oblivion. A combination of carefully planned maneuvers and unforeseen but welcome developments created an almost predictable victory for the anti–Semites. Bary, the investigating magistrate, was not only inclined to believe in the Tiszaeszlár Jews' guilt, but he conducted the investigation with uncommon zeal and thoroughness. He also became, contrary to prescribed criminal procedure, a virtually inexhaustible source of detailed, albeit tainted, information to sensation–seeking journalists who descended in droves on the small town. The grapevine of the Catholic lower clergy was an equally efficient conduit linking the events at Tiszaeszlár with the *Magyar Állam*, the Catholic newspaper that was the first Budapest daily to break the story in its May 10th edition.[16] The report described the mysterious disappearance of the young girl and the suspicious circumstances surrounding the presence of two ritual slaughterers in the Tiszaeszlár synagogue. The charge of ritual murder had not been made even though the implications of the case were sufficiently condemnatory.

The third, and possibly most important, link in the anti–Semitic chain reaction to the Tiszaeszlár affair was Géza Ónody, who could easily be nicknamed "little Istóczy." He was born in 1848 to a family of impoverished nobles, one of whose estates, a large piece of land in the vicinity of Tiszaeszlár, had been sold to the Jewish Simon and György Pöhm. Ónody leased a portion of that property, eking out a considerably more humble existence than his predecessors and lamenting his misfortune. The Jewish ownership of his ancestral inheritance made his situation all the more humiliating. Eventually, he entered local politics. In the 1881 elections he won a seat in the Diet as the representative of the district of Hajdúnánás, in whose electoral jurisdiction Tiszaeszlár belonged.[17] Unlike Istóczy, who was a member of Prime Minister Tisza's ruling Liberal Party, Ónody ran as an Independence Party candidate. The years of financial uncertainty and social misfortune, which left him embittered and caused him to find solace in the practice of scapegoatism, made Ónody easy prey to Istóczy's vulgar and irrational philosophy. He embraced anti-Semitism, becoming, like Verhovay and Simonyi, a source of considerable embarrassment to Dániel Irányi, chairman of the Independence Party.[18] Irányi found himself in a no more enviable situation than Prime Minister Tisza, his counterpart in the Liberal Party. Both leaders attempted to disassociate the political philosophy and program of their respective parties from the views which the increasingly undisciplined anti-Semitic members espoused.

As the anti-Semites' expert on Tiszaeszlár, Ónody managed to raise his otherwise imperceptible parliamentary presence and undistinguished political career—like Istóczy he showed little, if any, promise during his first year in the Diet—to the level of notoriety. Of the seventeen anti-Semitic representatives, Ónody was the first to make a public speech in the Diet about the unfolding drama in Tiszaeszlár. It was, however, not a spontaneous outburst of a deeply felt indignation but the initial salvo of a carefully orchestrated barrage of anti-Semitic accusations—making a mountain of the proverbial anthill. Delivered on May 23, his speech opened a floodgate of concealed emotions and bitter accusations.

Ónody was Istóczy's clone, undisciplined, abusive and hateful. It was during a debate on Hungary's share in contributions to the imperial Austrian military expenditures that he requested permission to speak. Following a circuitous line of befuddled reasoning which no one, save Istóczy, was able or cared to follow, Ónody noted that Germany and Russia had encouraged the Dual Monarchy to occupy Bosnia in hope that the occupation would eventually exhaust the peoples of the empire; and the pan-Slav agitators in Russia were behind the sweeping attack on the Jews who subsequently took flight and settled in the neighboring regions of the Dual Monarchy. Eventually the "dangerous current" reached Hungary. On 1 April 1882, a young girl disappeared as she passed by the synagogue of Tiszaeszlár. Later it was discovered that a ritual slaughterer had invited her in, tied her arms behind her back and gagged her. No one knew what happened to her after that.[19]

No one knew, and apparently no one cared. Aside from the predictable warning that Diet President Tamás Péchy issued to Ónody for straying from the debate topic, the speech elicited only the laughter of incredulous representatives and then suffered the familiar fate which Istóczy anticipated.

Few masters cherish the prospect of being outshone by their disciples. Istóczy was neither charitably deferential nor accustomed to
standing in anyone's shadow. Ónody had stopped short of calling the
Tiszaeszlár case a ritual murder and the echoes of the speech were fading quickly. A momentum of historic import was gathering; it must
not be allowed to slip away. The following day—May 24—witnessed
the birth of the blood libel of Tiszaeszlár. Istóczy asked to be allowed
to interpellate Prime Minister Tisza and Minister of Justice Tivadar
Pauler, his erstwhile law professor, on the government's perception of
and attitude toward the Tiszaeszlár affair. A creature of rhetorical
habit, Istóczy's hunger for controversy could not be satiated by simply posing the three short questions of the interpellation. It served as
a mere perfunctory concession to required parliamentary procedure,
legitimizing the lengthy presentation of a prefabricated scheme that
often consisted of irrelevant ingredients. Apparently misinformed of
Bary's unscrupulous—and at times illegal—investigation and intimidating interrogation of most of Tiszaeszlár's 200 Jewish residents, a
fact that spoke well neither of the journalistic ethics of the four principal anti–Semitic publications nor of Ónody's reputation as the expert
analyst of the events in Tiszaeszlár, Istóczy decried the tardiness of
the Tiszaeszlár authorities and the county court in Nyíregyháza in
pursuing the investigation of the case. Yet despite his legal and juridical experience, Istóczy did not hesitate to lace his own prejudices
and misconceptions with unfounded rumors, spinning from them circumstantial evidence which he deemed sufficiently valid to sustain a
conclusion of guilt. The possibility of logical alternatives to murder,
such as accidental death or suicide, did not enter his hate–filled mind.
Nor did he doubt the identity of the perpetrators of the crime.

If a Christian was murdered, the murderers could only have been
Jews. Istóczy declared:

> The suspicion of ritual murder is strengthened by the cir-
> cumstance that the murder took place in the synagogue be-
> fore the Jewish Easter and by a ritual slaughterer trained
> to perform ritual murder. Since the advent of Christian-
> ity, the suspicion has never dimmed in the consciousness
> of Christians about the Jews' need—only the Orthodox, of
> course—for Christian blood for their Easter rituals.

As convincing proof of the veracity of his statement, Istóczy quoted
a lengthy portion of Rohling's *Der Talmudjude,* his favorite source
of "scientific information," which consisted of a detailed, concocted
anti–Semitic version of the Damascus Affair of 1840, involving the

disappearance of a Capuchin monk, and a reference to an 1831 trial in St. Petersburg of Jews accused of murdering a young Russian soldier. Like the skewed logic of Ónody's spech, Istóczy's irresponsible ramblings elicited harsh words of warning from an angered Diet President Péchy. He admonished Istóczy for quoting excessively from *Der Talmudjude* and for stirring up emotions. Istóczy's lame attempt at self-defense—"I do not a priori wish to state that the case in question involves a murder spawned of religious fanaticism"—only added to Péchy's exasperation. The Diet President fumed:

> I ask the Honorable Representative to consider what terrible consequences such an accusation may have in certain places. And to make an accusation like that with such certainty is, in view of the absence of verification, a little too much. Please consider that the accusation affects a sizeable, diligently working segment of the Hungarian people.

Somewhat taken aback by Péchy's uncommonly vigorous guardianship of parliamentary propriety, Istóczy quickly disclaimed any intent to engage the incensed Diet President in polemics. His reply, however, sounded ominously prophetic.

> It is not impossible that there is in fact a case of a mysterious religious murder or human sacrifice, the uncovery of which will have a decisive effect on the fate of the whole of Jewry in the centuries to come. This criminal case will become a worldwide *cause célèbre*.

Istòczy's brief, three-part interpellation also called the attention of the Prime Minister and the Minister of Justice to the local and county authorities' negligence in starting the investigation thus causing it to be delayed for weeks. Istóczy wanted to know what action the government planned to take in an effort to hold the aforementioned authorities accountable for their negligence to assure, despite the anticipated upsurge in countermeasures taken by wealthy Jews, the just punishment of the guilty Jew or Jews.

The Prime Minister had repeatedly proved that he was more than willing to respond to Istóczy's theatrics in kind, albeit in an abridged version and in a more controlled tone. "My initial observation," Tisza said, "is that it is incorrect to state about any race or religious group living in our nation that it is deserving of dastardly, unqualified contempt." He claimed no knowledge of the events in Tiszaeszlár and promised a thorough investigation. As minister of interior, Tisza felt obliged to issue a warning that anyone who caused danger in the streets by incendiary words spoken in the Diet would be prosecuted with the full force of the law. Minister of Justice Tivadar

Pauler spoke briefly in the same vein.[20]

Following the ministerial replies, Istóczy and Ónody suffered a humiliating, albeit temporary, setback. Dániel Irányi, the influential leader of the Independence Party, of which Ónody was a member, condemned the persecution of the Jews in Russia, comparing it favorably with the barbarism of the Middle Ages and characterizing the Russian government's inaction as "horribly negligent." He denounced the charge of ritual murder and reminded the government that it was responsible for the protection of the lives and property of the Jews.[21]

Istóczy's optimism about the potential of the Tiszaeszlár case to become the *cause célèbre* of political anti–Semitism turned to anguish as he pondered the slow pace of provincial investigation which he attributed to a government–inspired coverup. Little did he suspect that his perceptions had evolved due to not the investigation, but to the slow release of the information by the Nyíregyháza authorities, Bary in particular. No friend of the Jews, Bary was resentful of both Istóczy and Ónody—however, he admired Verhohay's journalistic talents and the "impartiality" of the *Függetlenség*—for making speeches in the Diet about the Tiszaeszlár case. "From Istóczy's perspective," Bary recalled, "it was not important whether acts of negligence had taken place or the facts that served as the basis of his interpellations were accurate. The Tiszaeszlár affair was merely a weapon in his bitter, theretofore unsuccessful and futile struggle against the Jews."[22] The case did become a *cause célèbre*, exploited in full by Istóczy and his collaborators. Only the prophets of doom would have appreciated what it might have turned into had Bary and the Nyíregyháza authorities joined forces with the political anti–Semites.[23]

The Tiszaeszlár case generated enormous interest nationwide. More and more newspapers sent correspondents to the small town in northeastern Hungary. In daily dispatches, they analyzed and interpreted every detail of the strange case, every unexpected turn of events. There were interviews with local and county officials and character sketches of the accused Jews. Adding generous doses of hatred to the gradually mounting tension were the steadily proliferating pamphlets. They contained explanations of ritual murder, crude, inflammatory anti–Jewish slogans and offensively exaggerated and distorted drawings. Not much incitement, to be sure, was needed to inflame the countryside. Surprisingly, despite the nationwide agitation, anti–Jewish demonstrations were confined to the northwestern counties of Hungary. In July 1882 Prime Minister Tisza, acting on the recommendations of Chief Prosecutor Sándor Kozma whose detailed report identified a number of anti–Jewish publications and described their effect on the people, ordered law–enforcement authorities nationwide to prevent the spread and sale of such pamphlets. Taking refuge in the government's guardianship over the constitutionally guaranteed freedom of the press, Istóczy's *12 Röpirat* was clearly a pacesetter. The Tiszaeszlár case, the difficulties in communication with the investigating authorities notwithstanding, became the all-purpose clay from which the anti-Semitic publicists molded their images. Its resolution by trial—the guilt and punishment of the accused Tiszaeszlár Jews were taken for granted—would inevitably lead to the removal of all Jews from Hungary; catapult Hungarian anti-Semitism into a position of worldwide respect and leadership; demonstrate the culpability of the whole of Hungarian Jewry and contribute directly to the solution of the Jewish Question.

The anti-Semites' hope notwithstanding, the Tiszaeszlár case proved to be the illusory foundation of their house of cards. Ónody, Istóczy's ritual murder expert, worked feverishly on a "definitive study" of the Tiszaeszlár affair. However, the product of his labors, published in 1883, did a great injustice to Istóczy and the whole movement. Of all the books written about Tiszaeszlár, Ónody's acquired the dubious distinction of being the most vulgar, inaccurate and irrational. Excepting those who believed in his observations and conclusions, Ónody's *Tisza-Eszlár* leaves its reader with a pounding head, clenched fists, outraged and frustrated with the unfathomable intricacy of Ónody's warped mind. Even Istóczy found Ónody's expertise unsatisfactory. A number of issues of the *12 Röpirat* contained an announcement soliciting from the readers written accounts of cases similar to Tiszaeszlár's. The replies ranged from witches' tales to tales of horror, each more incredible than the other.[24]

For Istóczy the most exasperating aspect of the Tiszaeszlár case was the slowly turning wheels of provincial justice. Bary's thorough, at times contrived and often illegal, methods of investigation forced the anti-Semites to reconcile themselves to the sequence of events which the Nyíregyháza court had determined. Despite the machinations of Istóczy and Ónody in the Diet and the howling charges of anti-Semitic propaganda that the Tiszaeszlár affair was an open-and-shut case of ritual murder, Bary remained convinced that he was investigating a criminal case and acted accordingly. Moreover, he was unimpressed with the parliamentary anti-Semites' expertise on ritual murder. "No one in the Diet supported the views of Istóczy and Ónody," Bary recalled, "and everyone condemned them for taking the [Tiszaeszlár] case before the Diet."[25]

Even before the debacle of Tiszaeszlár, Istóczy's views and actions were openly supported by sixteen representatives in the Diet. Their anti-Semitic speeches, in content, style and intensity, conformed to and compared favorably with the distinctive characteristics of Istóczy's established blueprint. There also were undeclared admirers who stopped short of identifying themselves as such. They were content with hiding under the cloak of secrecy and joining the chorus of anonymous voices which often rang out encouragingly during anti–Semitic speeches. The parliamentary base of political anti–Semitism had been established.[26] It was time to move on. By the summer of 1882 the anti–Semites cast their eyes on new horizons. Notwithstanding the enormous publicity and the ever–deepening public support that it generated, the practical utility of the Tiszaeszlár case was waning. The end of Bary's investigation was nowhere in sight, and, aside from the illegally obtained confessions from fabricated eyewitnesses, no concrete pieces of evidence came to light. The anti–Semites realized that the rumors and accusations they had been circulating would neither be corroborated soon nor stand the test of juridical scrutiny.

In addition to the government's effort to contain the spread of anti–Semitic incitement and pamphlets, two formidable obstacles, belated yet predictable, were surfacing. For three months the anti–Semites spread their venomous message, concocted misinformation and tangential evidence in an effort to prove the existence of a ritual murder, and tried Hungary's Jewry before the public without mercy. Their alarming success eventually forced the wealthy and influential leaders of Budapest's Jewish community to abandon the ill–conceived and potentially self–incriminating wait–and–see attitude with which they followed the news of the Tiszaeszlár case. Clearly, no journalistic countermeasures initiated in behalf of the Jews of Tiszaeszlár could retard, let alone discredit, Istóczy's *12 Röpirat*, Verhovay's *Függetlenség* and Simonyi's *Westungarischer Grenzbote*, the principal organs of the anti–Semites. Their unending appeals to base instincts and their persistent charges that the Jews monopolized the press were paying encouraging dividends.

Yet even the most self–confident Jew–baiters felt threatened by the appearance of the first public defender of the accused Jews. In the early 1880s Miksa Szabolcsi (1857–1915) had barely left his years of journalistic apprenticeship. A correspondent of the *Egyenlőség*, a newly founded (1881) Jewish political weekly, Szabolcsi combined youthful enthusiasm, dogged determination and implacable animosity toward the persecutors of his defenseless coreligionists. He planned to initiate a two–front counterattack. He decided to discredit the findings and conclusions which Bary's investigation had yielded by exposing the investigative magistrate's methods of brutal interrogation and obtaining confession under duress. Szabolcsi traveled to

Tiszaeszlár and neighboring towns and began interviewing the victims of Bary's reign of terror. His reports in the *Egyenlőség*, written in the impassioned style of a crusader for justice and with a sleuth's commitment to detail and detached observation, were the first pieces of evidence pointing to the cavalier manner in which the authorities in Nyíregyháza pursued the investigation and prepared for the trial. They alerted Chief Prosecutor Sándor Kozma in Budapest to the need to safeguard the propriety of juridical proceedings. Equally swift was the effect of the reports on the leaders of Budapest's Jewry who reacted with alacrity to the mounting danger signals.[27] As the anti-Semites had transformed the Tiszaeszlár case into a nationwide and international *cause célèbre*, neither the government's handling of the prosecution nor the organization of the accused Jews' defense could be confined to local legal experts. Kozma appointed Ede Szeyffert, a deputy chief prosecutor, and Kálmán Lázár, an assistant prosecutor, to represent the State.[28]

The need to reverse the steadily deteriorating course the Tiszaeszlár case had taken also prompted the Jewish leaders in Budapest to act expeditiously. They were guided by a two-fold consideration: to provide their accused coreligionists with the best and most effective legal representation and to outmaneuver Bary and his superiors. The search, coordinated by József Simon (1844–1915), Secretary of the National Bureau of Israelites and himself a lawyer, ended to the satisfaction of all parties concerned. However, the identity of the person selected caught everyone by surprise.[29]

By the early 1880s the forty-year-old Károly Eötvös had become a nationally known journalist and one of the leaders of the Independence Party in the Diet. The son of Calvinist gentry parents in Transylvania, the patriotic Eötvös was briefly imprisoned for participating in an ill-fated, anti-Habsburg conspiracy in 1863. Although his legal experience was impressive—between 1865 and 1872 he taught law in Pápa, passed the qualifying examination for a judgeship, was chief prosecutor of Veszprém County and practiced law in Budapest—he felt more at ease in the Diet where his eloquent speeches won him numerous admirers. Before undertaking the defense of the accused Jews of Tiszaeszlár, Eötvös requested permission from Chief Prosecutor Kozma, who had been following Bary's machinations with increasing displeasure, to make a tour of Tiszaeszlár and Nyíregyháza and see things for himself. He conducted interviews and visited Móric Scharf, Bary's young star witness. Upon returning to Budapest Eötvös agreed to serve as chief legal counsel for the defense despite the cautionary advice he received from some of Hungary's leading legal experts and his well-meaning friends. He quickly organized a three–member team. With that the legal scale began to balance.[30]

The selection of Eötvös helped allay fears that the Tiszaeszlár case would be tried with a guilty verdict looming over the defendants. He was also viewed as a virtual guarantee against the case being perceived, due to Istóczy's persistent allegations, as one of ritual murder, perhaps the only point in which Eötvös and the Nyíregyháza authorities had a meeting of minds. The stage was thus set, and the next eleven months witnessed an acrimonious tug–of–war between Bary and Eötvös, the effects of which would leave an indelible imprint on both lives.[31]

Chapter VIII

"The Final Solution of the Jewish Question"

Coincidental, mutually complimentary occurrences which exceeded even the most optimistic expectations of the anti–Semites, transformed the month of June into the high watermark of 1882, a year of auspicious developments.

Amid the mystery–shrouded investigation at Tiszaeszlár and the ever–rising waves of anti–Semitic propaganda, Istóczy succeeded in broadening the base of his attack. The text of a petition reflecting the mood of the participants at a public meeting, held in Szatmár County on March 2, had been submitted to the Diet. It was accompanied by a letter from Vice Lord Lieutenant Sándor Újfalussy requesting urgent action. Entitled "Concerning the Curtailment of the Inundation of Jewish Immigrants from Russia through Galicia to the Regions Adjacent to Szatmár County," the petition described the sorry state of affairs in Hungary's northern counties. It attributed the condition to the steady flow of emigrants and the ever–increasing number of poor Jewish immigrants who "settle with the intention of enriching themselves but without making the slightest sacrifice to acquire Hungarian citizenship." Five other counties—Heves, Győr, Somogy, Hajdú and Torontál—and one town, Szatmárnémeti, joined the petitioners as co–sponsors. The debate in the Diet was scheduled to begin on June 7. In the intervening period, representatives of an additional fourteen counties declared their support of the petition. Anti–Semitic speakers and provocateurs turned many a public meeting into an anti–Jewish rally, creating a strong base of support for their spokesmen in the Diet. Neither Istóczy nor any of his followers in the Diet needed to wonder if their speeches generated sympathetic echoes or silent condemnation.

The pressure tactics soon yielded results. The provincial tremors grew into a parliamentary rumble. The Independence Party—among whose members were such anti–Semites as Verhovay and Ónody—held a pre–debate caucus to plot their strategy. With the spectre of Tiszaeszlár looming ominously over the session, for the first time the party automatically took an oppositional stand against any manifestation of anti–Semitism. The members voted to reject both the

Szatmár Petition and the report of the Petitions Committee of the Diet. The latter found the petition lacking the substance necessary to merit parliamentary action and advised against bringing it to the floor. Instead two party stalwarts, Ottó Herman and József Madarász, were commissioned to draw up the text of the party's own motion. In the course of a similar, though less harmonious caucus, the majority of the members of the Liberal Party lined up behind Prime Minister Tisza whose personal distaste for the anti–Semites had become the official policy of the government. A more auspicious opportunity had not been created for the declaration of political independence in Istóczy's decade–long parliamentary career. With the surging hatred among the masses of potential constituents and with his followers in the Diet looking to him for guidance and direction, Istóczy could take but one course of action. He decided to "leave the safe Noah's ark: the Liberal Party." [1]

An anti–Semite professing loyalty to a party of resolute defenders of the objects of his implacable hatred was artificial at best, counterproductive at worst. To outsiders it seemed incongruous, if not irrational. [2] To the Liberal Party, Tisza in particular, Istóczy was an embarrassment–turned–liability. Istóczy's prolonged affiliation with the Liberals and reluctance to switch to the Independence Party which harbored most of his sympathizers posed questions that neither he nor his contemporaries asked, let alone answered. [3] It is unlikely that such a move would have weakened his electoral base because his constituents in Rum voted for him and his political philosophy, not the Liberal Party ticket. That the Independence Party would have served as a more appropriate base of Istóczy's parliamentary activities was demonstrated by the pragmatism of its leaders, Dániel Irányi and Lajos Mocsáry, [4] who recognized and, unlike Tisza, admitted the existence of a Jewish problem. Although they took a firm stand against anti–Semitism, they tolerated expressions of support for Istóczy as long as they were kept discretely muted and their sources officially unidentified. That pragmatism and flexibility were amply demonstrated in a vote by the members to issue a cleverly, and for Istóczy a hearteningly, ambiguous statement concerning the Szatmár petition. It had been drawn up by Ottó Herman, a noted natural scientist and ethnographer, and an intimate friend of the exiled Lajos Kossuth, and József Madarász, a former provincial member of the radical opposition—he had been imprisoned for nine years for his role in the 1848 Revolution—and a representative in the Diet for the electoral district of Sároskeresztúr for nearly seven decades. On 7 June, Herman presented a three–point motion: first, because of its harmful economic and public–health consequences, the mass–immigration of people from Russia must be halted; second, the government of Hungary should persuade other governments to forestall the recurrence of such mass movement of emigrants; and third, the government should turn to the Diet and seek parliamentary sanction of its actions. Although the motion stopped short of endorsing the spirit of the Szatmár petition, Herman's harsh words about the business practices and lifestyle of the "racially pure" and separatist Orthodox Jews had the unmistakable ring of an institutionalized accusation. In his response, Prime Minister Tisza denied both the inherent threat posed by the immigration of Russian Jews and the need for legislation concerning it.[5]

The stage for the official unveiling of the Szatmár petition was set by the deployment of the usual anti–Semitic diversionary tactics. Géza Ónody gave a blood–curling account of the Tiszaeszlár ritual murder case, citing historical precedents and quoting from August Rohling's ever–useful tome of hateful diatribes against the Talmud.[6] The Prime Minister restated his position. On June 9, Istóczy rose to speak on the subject of the petition. The "anti–Semitic prophet"[7] did not disappoint his uncritical followers. He likened the three to four million Russian and Polish Jews to the "Tiszaeszlár lot" and spoke of the increasing Judaization of Budapest; the Jewish offensive against the counties, "the bastions of Magyardom;" the Jews' alien caste system and racial characteristics; and their financial and journalistic stranglehold on the Hungarian people. As always, his words drew a statement of warning from the President of the Diet; and as always Istóczy rambled on undisturbed. The Jews, he noted, have a supranational government, the Alliance Israélite Universelle; preserve their cosmopolitan outlook in an age of rising nationalism; and await the arrival of the Messiah who will lead them back to Palestine, a practical objective in view of the United States' policy of accepting Jews only in limited numbers. "I am convinced that the final solution of the Jewish Question has been reserved for out time," Istóczy declared.[8]

The intemperate words and abusive characterizations notwithstanding, Istóczy never linked the removal of the unacceptable segments of Hungarian Jewry to physical violence even though he did not discourage the sporadic outbursts of violent anti–Jewish demonstrations. Except for launching the menacing phrase, "Final Solution of the Jewish Question," the speech was a surprising oratorical *déjà vu* of tiresome clichés and jaded images. Against the portentous backdrop of Tiszaeszlár and amid the disquieting news of unrest in the countryside, Istóczy should have sounded a forceful, inspiring battle cry instead of emitting a tepid, desultory whimper.

What the speech lacked in fire, content and direction Istóczy more than made up for by becoming entangled in an incident, by far the most unsavory of his political career. Few quirks in parliamentary procedure created a more awkward situation than the seating of the representatives in the chamber of the Diet, a seemingly uncontroversial matter. Members of the different parties and groups within them usually were seated in clusters. However, there were no visible lines of demarcation, separating one cluster from the other, within the rows of two seats occupied by members of the different, often opposing, aggregations. Being the odd man out in the Liberal Party, Istóczy created a climate of tension by his mere presence. For reasons for which no one claimed responsibility or was blamed— whether the representatives adhered to their assigned seats during the sessions of the Diet is an unverifiable detail—Istóczy happened to be seated next to Mór Wahrmann during the debate on the Szatmár petition. The bald, bearded and bespectacled Wahrmann, one of the leaders of Pest's Jewry, was the embodiment of the non–Orthodox Jewish qualities which Istóczy had consistently attacked. He was a respected financial expert, and throughout his entire political career of a quarter century was the representative of Lipótváros, a modern, predominantly Jewish district of Budapest. As if the seating of the two men had not augured ill enough, the speaker immediately following Istóczy was none other than Wahrmann. Yet this significant coincidence was lost on both contemporary observers and later chroniclers of the event.

The oratorical confrontation of the two men transcended the limited scope of the Szatmár petition and became the first salvo that ignited an indiscriminate war of words, at times disguised as legalistic maneuvers, over the Tiszaeszlár case. Contributing to the volatile situation were the facts that Hungarian Jewry closed ranks in the face of the Tiszaeszlár–inspired anti–Semitic offensive, and that Pest's Jewish community, which elected Wahrmann president in 1883, assumed a leading role. An urbane and often witty man who had, however, become taciturn after his wife's death, Wahrmann took more than a perfunctory interest in this latent anti–Semitic ploy. He happened to own thousands of acres in Szabolcs, a county adjacent to Szatmár, whose assembly voted to support the petition. Unlike Istóczy, who preferred vague generalities to tangible specifics, Wahrmann's financially oriented mind operated in the realm of accuracy, substance, and facts. Also, he was not known for concealing his true feelings in the flowery expressions of parliamentary courtesy. "A person who reacts to the killing of a few Jews or the sweeping persecutions in Russia by merely shrugging his shoulders does not deserve to be taken seriously," Wahrmann observed. Like the majority of his assimilated and wealthy coreligionists in Central and Western Europe, Wahrmann was unenthusiastic about the influx and settlement of masses of Russian and Galician Jews whom he treated with benign but aloof condescension, fearing that they could revive the disparaging public view of Orthodox Jews which the assimilationists were laboriously striving to alter. Wahrmann, however, favored granting permits of settlement to certain well–to–do, hard–working and otherwise useful individuals. He reaffirmed the necessity of the Magyarization of Hungary's Jewry, which for him was a life–long pursuit. His defense of the Orthodox Jews, the sole identifiable targets in Istóczy's indiscriminate and obdurate attacks, was cleverly pragmatic, eliciting swift support from the government's spokesman. He cited neither moral compunction nor legal arguments. The Orthodox Jews, Wahrmann noted, displayed adequate signs of interest in accumulating wealth to be considered as economic assets. To members of his audience more comfortable with and easily influenced by religious matters, Wahrmann offered for contemplation passages in Rohling's *Der Talmudjude*, Istóczy's bible of defamation, which were as condemnatory of Protestants as of Jews. In conclusion, Wahrmann spoke confidently of the government and the Hungarian people's ability to thwart the provocateurs' insidious machinations.[9]

In the heat of the debate—and the chamber—the sheer physical proximity of the two hostile bodies was bound to create a tension that went beyond the friction born of a difference in opinion. Because even the eyewitnesses offered differing versions of the incident, the passage of time has only helped it grow even more ambiguous. According to the anti–Semites, Wahrmann's concluding statement contained words which Istóczy justifiably regarded as offensive.[10] In other accounts, Wahrmann merely turned in the direction of Istóczy, who interpreted his opponent's motion as a threatening gesture which he decided not to leave unacknowledged.[11] Still others concluded that Wahrmann "made an oratorical gesture which Istóczy misinterpreted."[12]

The outcome of the incident was determined with no more certainty and clarity than its cause. The anti–Semitic hagiographers created a scenario portraying Istóczy as a passionate hero driven by his need to gain satisfaction. He was said to have sent his seconds, the truculent Ónody and a certain Szuhanyi (another representative whose activities in the Diet were so negligible that contemporary chroniclers could not recall even his first name, let alone his political accomplishments) to Wahrmann to demand satisfaction. Seemingly puzzled, the Jewish representative denied that he had offended Istóczy and refused to accept the challenge. Convinced that he had been wronged, Istóczy persisted. The anti–Semites forced Wahrmann into a confrontation which he could not evade. Although no evidence can be found to support the view that any of the participants of this uncivil episode had a proclivity for transforming rhetorical pugnacity into physical violence, the anti–Semites insisted that after a brief exchange of heated words Istóczy struck Wahrmann, an act that in turn led to an exchange of bullets. In the course of a duel by pistols, fought a few days later outside Ercsi, a small town south of Budapest in Fejér County, neither of the embittered foes found his mark.[13] According to another version the duel took place in the early hours of the following day. By noon the rumors filled the streets and the cafés. Allegedly, Istóczy's shot had struck Wahrmann in the chest just below the left shoulder. By the time the representatives returned from their midday meals, it was determined that the duel had not taken place but was postponed to the following day, then the following week.[14] Eventually, the whole incident simply faded away and was stored in the treasure house of parliamentary anecdotes.

Still, the aftermath of the confrontation was less than amusing. Istóczy and the Liberal Party soon had a parting of ways. Given Istóczy's isolated position in the party and the virtual absence of even a modicum of support for him, only the time of departure was in question. "In June 1882," Istóczy recalled, "I resigned from the Liberal Party and formed a coalition club which then consisted mostly of representatives of the Independence Party."[15] Predictable as his resignation and declaration of political independence were, Istóczy asserted that they were not the direct and immediate consequences of the Wahrmann incident nor were they the result of a sudden realization that all of his followers had long been members of the opposition Independence Party. Such considerations, to be sure, would have been valid and reasonable. It is equally true, as Istóczy observed, that despite Prime Minister Tisza's resolute and unyielding opposition to anti–Semitism, he had spread his hateful message for seven years without so much as a hint from the party's leader to desist, let alone resign.[16] The confrontation with Wahrmann pushed the long–patient Diet too far. At a hastily convened meeting, the Liberal representatives voted to eject Istóczy from the party.[17] To the long–suffering Liberal Party, and Prime Minister Tisza in particular, Istóczy was more than a pesky embarrassment. He had become a heavy burden, a political liability.

Soon after he was forced to abandon the security of his political base and enter the uncertain waters of an unaffiliated political existence, Istóczy was thrown a well–timed life vest. On June 18, the Nyíregyháza authorities were informed that a body had washed ashore by the Tisza River. A group of medical officials was assembled and instructed to perform a preliminary post–mortem. The body was determined to be that of a female, approximately fourteen years old. During a subsequent viewing, members of the Solymosi family failed to identify it as that of the missing Eszter. A more extensive autopsy, which took place shortly thereafter, revealed that the body was that of a sexually active woman of at least twenty years of age. The body had been submerged in water no longer than four days. There was a general sigh of relief, but the anguish continued. Soon, however, the indefatigable Bary zeroed in on a new target: a group of raftsmen who had found the corpse and notified the local authorities. In the weeks of intimidation and torture–filled interrogation that followed, Bary exacted confessions from the raftsmen that implicated two Tiszaeszlár Jews. A new theory replete with numerous inconsistencies and contradictions was fabricated. The leader of the raftsmen, a Jew, and his two accomplices from Tiszaeszlár had the body of Eszter Solymosi in their possession but they substituted for it the corpse of the unidentified twenty–year–old woman, in the hope of deceiving the authorities.[18] The ensuing debate over the identity of the corpse and the circumstances and details of the murder was conducted on the pages of Hungarian newspapers[19] and seemed, in part, to support Istóczy's unwavering contentions and justify the birth of an independent anti–Semitic party.

A battle may have been won by the anti–Semites, but the end of the war was nowhere in sight. In fact, Istóczy's enjoyment of the fruits of his political independence was spoiled by unexpected and embarrassing events. In an attempt to contain the spread of anti–Semitic agitation and demonstrations, Prime Minister Tisza had taken steps that were bound to trample on sensitive toes. No less than four interest groups in the Diet made motions in support of a petition submitted by Heves County. It protested the confiscation of anti–Semitic pamphlets that had been proliferating since the start of the investigation of the mysterious Tiszaeszlár case. Under the guise of righteous outrage over a breach of the constitutional guarantee of the freedom of the press, latent anti–Semitic sentiments began to show themselves. Predictably, the Petitions Committee extended its unblemished record of consistency in judging the merits of such transparent attempts. It rejected outright the validity of the Heves petition. The other three motions, however, indicated an unsupportive consensus. The motion of the Independence Party was made by Géza Polónyi, one of the up–and–coming younger members of the Diet.[20] He characterized the Prime Minister's actions as illegal and belated, even though he perfunctorily admitted that the pamphlets had harm-

ful effects on the population. Similar mild objections were raised in
a motion by Imre Hódossy, representing the Moderate Opposition.
Under the circumstances Istóczy would have been remiss had he let
this promising opportunity pass without testing the weight of his
newly declared political status. The surging waves of the nationwide
anti–Semitic campaign and the presence of his group of noisy and
determined bravos could only enhance his parliamentary reputation
scarred by repeated failures. For reasons that must have angered and
astonished him no more than they puzzled the chroniclers of political
anti–Semitism in Hungary, Istóczy's motion carried only one signature: his own. The motion echoed the criticism of Prime Minister
Tisza's infringement of the freedom of expression and the press and
called on the Diet to issue a declaration attributing the "nationwide
manifestations of bitterness toward the Jews not to the anti–Semitic
publications now under attack, but to the Jews' persistently corrupt
practices and transgressions."[21] The vote in the Diet resulted in an
overwhelming defeat for the makers of the motion, indicating that the
representatives' perceptions of Istóczy's political credibility showed no
improvement.

Although he yearned to be a prophet in his own country—he had
already become a prophet of doom—the most enthusiastic accolades
Istóczy was receiving were sent by his German and Austrian admirers
who had followed with increasing interest his political career since his
first anti–Semitic speech in the Diet on 8 April 1875. The interviews
he was so fond of giving to reporters for foreign, especially German,
anti–Semitic newspapers gave him a measure of international reputation few of his colleagues attained.

On 18 July 1882 at a meeting of the *Soziale Reichspartei*, founded
in 1881 by the youthful Ernst Heinrici, a schoolmaster turned implacably anti–Semitic political activist,[22] a commemorative declaration
was drafted and sent to Budapest to

> the indefatigable protagonist of the European spirit who
> stood up to the power of modern Jewry, the first legislator
> in Europe who had the courage to call attention in parlia-
> ment to the destruction with which Jewry threatens modern
> civilization.[23]

That recognition by his German confederates, of whom he made frequent mention in his later writings, was a great psychological boost
to Istóczy. The roots of modern German anti–Semitism, nurtured
by such theoreticians as Konstantin Frantz, Rudolf Meyer, and Paul
de Lagarde, had been planted deeper and its views expressed with
more sophistication than those of its Hungarian counterpart. Adolf

Stöcker's Christian Social Workers' Party and the *Deutscher Volk-verein* of Bernhard Förster and Max Liebermann von Sonnenberg were founded earlier and attracted a greater following[24] than similar attempts of the Hungarian prophet of anti–Semitism. Yet, Istóczy could boast of a broad range of accomplishments: his unshakable conviction of the Jews' inherent culpability in all aspects of national misfortune—political, social, economic and cultural—that threatened the Hungarian people with exploitation and subjugation, a view he shared with the German anti–Semites; his master plan for the estab-lishment of a Jewish state in Palestine, a political vision he pioneered; and his success in smuggling anti–Semitism into parliamentary pol-itics, an undertaking he tackled virtually alone and one which his comrades–in–arms abroad hoped to duplicate.

Small wonder, therefore, that the German anti–Semites, whose activities were confined largely to Berlin and for whom the 1880s were a period of desperate efforts to extricate their movement from a po-litical quagmire, should redirect their political energy toward uniting the nascent forces of political anti–Semitism. The architect of the plan was Alexander Pinkert, leader of the *Deutsche Reformpartei* in Saxony. He put together a coalition slate of right–wing candidates which won enough votes in the municipal elections in Dresden to dominate the city council. The new power base enabled Pinkert to have Dresden host the "First International Anti–Jewish Congress," the product of his not inconsiderable organizational labors.[25] From the start there was a Hungarian presence lingering over the proceed-ings. Among those whose signatures were expected to lend a visual proof of credibility to the invitations were those of Istóczy and Ónody. The Hungarian delegation, consisting of Istóczy, Ónody and Simonyi, turned the journey to Dresden into a virtual victory celebration.

On September 8 in Pozsony, where anti–Semitism had planted surprisingly strong roots since the middle of the century and where Simonyi's popularity was the greatest, the three delegates were feted amid wildly enthusiastic speeches. Their reception in Dresden was no less exhilarating. The Hungarians were treated with the respect accorded to elder statesmen. On the evening of September 10, Si-monyi gave a lengthy speech on general political conditions, justify-ing the raison d'être of political anti–Semitism. On the following day, the congress officially opened. Simonyi was elected co–chairman—he shared the honor with a certain Bredow, a retired army officer—of the session. One of the main speakers was Istóczy. Both Hungar-ians had good reason to feel at home. Hanging above the rostrum where the dignitaries sat and the speeches were delivered was Si-monyi's gift to the congress: an idealized portrait of Eszter Solymosi,

the missing Tiszaeszlár girl. The *cause célèbre* of Hungarian political anti–Semitism had become the emotional motivating force of the
congress.

It seemed fitting that the "prophet of anti–Semitism," should
write a declaration in commemoration of the gathering. Instead of
releasing it near the end of the two–day congress after all of the
speeches and deliberations were over—as official communiqués usually are—Istóczy's manifesto, entitled "To the Governments and Peoples of Christian Countries Threatened by the Jews," was heard and
accepted by the participants on September 11, the opening day.[26] He
could not have hoped for a more satisfying sign of recognition and
respect. His views had been well known to the participants; they
could hardly have found a more experienced elocutionist of suspicion,
accusation and hate. He needed no time to think things out, he knew
them by heart. The official manifesto of the congress was a synthesis of his well–rehearsed speeches, familiar tunes in an accustomed
sequence.

> After successfully resisting for centuries the attacks of Arabs,
> Tatars and Turks, another no less dangerous alien race is
> threatening the culture, civilization, well–being and future
> of the Christian peoples of Europe. The Jewish monopoly of
> the money market turned the producers in all sectors of the
> economy into financial dependents. . . . The Jews succeeded
> in gaining control of the press. . . . The cosmopolitan
> Jews, preserving the nomadic tradition, are unfamiliar with
> the concepts of nation and patriotism. . . . The final
> anc complete solution of the Jewish Question, like the Arab,
> Tatar and Turkish Questions, can be reached through the
> self–defense of Christian peoples.[27]

Ónony's "expert" lecture on the Tiszaeszlár case was accorded the respect due to the author of the "definitive" study on the circumstances
of the disappearance of Eszter Solymosi. Istóczy capped his series of
performances with a speech at a meeting of the Dresden Reform Association, expressing gratitude for the support he had received from
Germany since his first anti–Semitic speech in the Hungarian Diet.

The Dresden Congress signaled the beginning of a new, violent
phase in the history of political anti–Semitism in Hungary. The end
of September witnessed a resurgence of anti–Jewish demonstrations
in Pozsony and soon spread to neighboring towns. The government
wasted no time in dispatching troops to restore order, and act that
produced a contrary effect. In early October, a month–long martial
law was declared in Pozsony and its environs.[28] Such disturbances

served the useful means of distracting the people of the countryside from the Tiszaeszlár case, which, despite the sensation caused by the discovery of the "Csonkafüzes corpse," was becoming something of an obstacle in the anti–Semites' accelerated quest for political power. Istóczy and his coterie soon realized that Bary's extensive investigation, which under Eötvös's watchful eyes grew even more meticulous and time–consuming, kept them bouncing on the springboard of publicity. The momentum created by their deliberate jump into the pool of national and international fame had to be sustained. The time had come to devise new tactics without decreasing pressure on the Tiszaeszlár affair. The redeployment of the forces of anti–Semitism, however, became a logistical necessity. The benefits that Istóczy and his minuscule parliamentary following gained from the disappearance of the young Tiszaeszlár girl were essentially mass hysteria. The likelihood of legitimizing the actual occurrence of a ritual murder with a guilty verdict against the defendants was, at best, tenuous. In fact, the chances of such a verdict grew increasingly remote as Eötvös's defense team and the sympathetic prosecutor joined forces after they discovered numerous legal irregularities and investigative abuses which undermined and eventually destroyed the inherent interdependence of investigatory and prosecutory procedures and objectives. Thus, the case's short–range usefulness for the anti–Semites had been exhausted. Riding high on the waves of popularity, Istóczy and his collaborators found no shortage of equally promising alternatives to sustain the Tiszaeszlár–inspired momentum and deepen the furrows of hatred.

Chapter IX

The Apogee

Aside from the publicity and the stamp of approval it gave Istóczy, the Dresden Congress helped neutralize the effects of an eloquent message. Its sender still wielded powerful political influences and his words evoked deeply felt emotions in the hearts and minds of many Hungarians. Early in August 1882 Ignác Helfy, one of the stalwarts of the Independence Party and Kossuth's confidant, visited the "Great Exile" in Turin. Kossuth's message was clear and firm. The party that stood for his philosophy should be untainted by the stigma of anti–Semitism. His message, however, had little restraining effect on the party members who were determined to spread hatred of the Jews.[1]

Because of the ambivalent, even tolerant, attitude of the Mocsáry-led majority toward its former anti–Semitic members—a much smaller faction clustered around Dániel Irányi was steadfast in its opposition to Istóczy—the Independent Party became an easy target of criticism by the Liberals.[2] Still, Kossuth's word was sacrosanct, especially to the nostalgic, old revolutionary guard who carried considerable political weight during elections.

In the Diet the anti–Istóczy forces were galvanized by the outspoken and combative Ernő Mezei. In him the Hungarian Jews had found an effective spokesman, their own Tiszaeszlár expert. Thus with Károly Eötvös's spirited leadership of the team of defense lawyers and Miksa Szabolcsi's ever–increasing, almost fanatical, journalistic quest for the truth, the anti–Semites' advances were checked on all fronts. A graduate of the law school of the University of Budapest, the thirty–one–year–old Mezei was a skilled publicist and an eloquent speaker. A native of Sátoraljaújhely, a town in the northern county of Zemplén, and from 1881 the representative of Miskolc in adjacent Borsod County, Mezei matched the anti–Semites' knowledge of the conditions and people of the countryside.[3]

For nearly six months the chamber of the Diet had resounded with charges and countercharges. The anti–Semites objected to the attitude and actions of Sándor Kozma, the chief state prosecutor, and his subordinates who failed to display sufficient zeal in the preparation of the case against the accused Jews of Tiszaeszár. Their opponents, mostly Liberals, denounced Investigating Magistrate József Bary, for employing and the Nyíregyháza court for condoning brutal investigative techniques and for piecing together details to fit the charge of murder. On November 15, Mezei, in the course of interpellating Minister of Justice Tivadar Pauler, whose obstructionist attitude evoked rumors—seemingly well–founded—of his being a latent anti–Semite, stunned his colleagues with a detailed exposé of the investigation in Tiszaeszlár. In an impassioned, lengthy interjection, not unlike Istóczy's favorite tactic of transforming the customarily brief preface of an interpellation into a lengthy, highly emotional speech, Mezei rejected the charge of ritual murder and gave a well–researched and substantiated account of the illegal procedures of which both Bary and the Nyíregyháza court were guilty. "They must come to light," he declared in conclusion, "for it is in the common interest of a nation of laws, the twentieth century, and all humanity."[4]

Mezei's counterattack gave Istóczy and Ónody, his Tiszaeszlár expert, a major setback. It also marked a turning point in the public's perception of the Tiszaeszlár case, theretofore molded by the virtually unchallenged anti–Semitic line of "scientific reasoning." A few days before Mezei's scathingly critical remarks, Eötvös had succeeded in discrediting the autopsy report on the "Csonkafüzes corpse," thereby eliminating the medical evidence that could have been used to support, even substantiate, the charges against the accused Jews of Tiszaeszlár.[5] Sensing trouble, Istóczy reacted quickly to recapture the temporarily stymied momentum and move his parliamentary position away from an anticipated confrontation. For that, however, he needed to solicit a convincing expression of popular support.

Since the formation of the Christian Defense League on 19 September 1882 in Kaposvár, a town in the southwestern county of Somogy, a string of similar anti–Semitic associations had cropped up throughout Hungary. Organized by journalists, affiliated with local anti–Semitic publications, and attractive to landowners, artisans and members of the Catholic lower clergy, such groups adopted the program of the Dresden Congress of the anti–Semites. Although their membership rarely exceeded the low hundreds, the Christian defense leagues could mobilize thousands of sympathizers for a show of political force.[6] For the first time in his career Istóczy proved his detractors wrong and dispelled his own doubts whether his speeches, which had been like desperate cries in the political wilderness, would leave echoes and ignite the fire of nationwide discontent and indignation. His gradual disentanglement from the Tiszaeszlár *cause célèbre* was beginning to pay reassuring dividends at a most opportune time.

The emotional springboard which Istóczy had used to launch his movement and extricate it from the parliamentary quagmire began to crumble, collapsing by the end of 1882. On 23 November the Nyíregyháza court reversed itself and ordered a new autopsy. It also appointed a new team of medical experts consisting of three of Hungary's most prominent pathologists. Their report, made public on 9 January 1883, discredited the conclusions of the local medical examiners and blew away Investigative Magistrate Bary's elaborately constructed house of cards. The vital statistics of the "Csonkafüzes corpse" were found to correspond to those of the missing Tiszaeszlár girl. The cause of death was determined to be drowning. With that the Tiszaeszlár case became a mere legal formality, robbed of the veil of mystery, ignorance, and prejudice beneath which the anti–Semites had pursued their machinations skillfully yet irresponsibly.[7]

There was, to be sure, no shortage of alternative strategies to Tiszaeszlár. Istóczy sought to retain the promising momentum by expending considerable energy on organizational and political efforts. The most auspicious of the new anti–Semitic groups was the one formed in Kecskemét. A thriving agricultural center of the Alföld, an expansive plain to the south of Budapest and known for its cattle and wines, Kecskemét had not developed a tradition that would have foreshadowed its dubious distinction of being a model bastion of anti–Semitism. Except for sharing in the nationwide anti–Jewish disturbances in 1848, Kecskemét's population placed no obstacles in the path of Jewish settlement that began in the middle of the eighteenth century. By the early 1880s Kecskemét's 700–strong Jewry had built an imposing synagogue, developed educational and social institutions, and settled into the economic infrastructure of the city without encountering resistance.[8] Yet within only two months, Kecskemét succumbed to anti–Semitic agitation. The organizers of the proceedings that precipitated the founding of the so–called Hungarian Defense League succeeded in transforming an unpretentious organizational meeting into a citywide celebration. Eleven anti–Semitic representatives of the Diet were sent invitations to attend, and the program of the league—the preservation and furtherance of the interests and well–being of the native Christian society—was finalized. Although the arrival on 21 January of a four–member delegation led by Istóczy himself caused disappointment among the organizers who had anticipated a greater turnout of anti–Semitic dignitaries, thousands of cheering townspeople listened to a barrage of oratorical demagoguery, consumed large quantities of food and wine and took part in a huge torch–lit parade. They gave the activities a resounding vote of approval. Istóczy and Ónody, the two best–known and most active guests, basked in the ribald company.[9]

On 23 June, a noticeably changed Istóczy rose to speak in the chamber of the Diet. The solitary prophet of doom who had feared apathy more than derision and whose words, save the perfunctory parliamentary minutes, were routinely lost on mostly incredulous colleagues existed no more. The Istóczy of 1883, "a year of consecutive convulsions,"[10] had an air of self–confidence about him. He had become the leader of a recognizable group of like–minded politicians, the object of admiration in a steadily growing national movement, and a celebrated pacesetter in an international organization. It was altogether an enviable record of fast–paced achievements capping a ten–year political career, considering the inherently controversial nature of his goal and the seemingly insurmountable obstacles placed in his path.

There was, however, little Istóczy could do to better the odds for the successful resolution of a procedural matter he initiated or sponsored in the Diet. Ignoring the implications of the disquieting reports of the spread of anti–Semitism—they took a considerable, calculated risk in a year preceding nationwide elections—the overwhelming majority of the representatives chose to remain firmly opposed to Istóczy and resolved to thwart his attempts to gain a modicum of support in the Diet beyond the loud encouragement voiced by his die–hard disciples.

The latest round of attacks on the constitutional safeguards of Hungarian Jewry caught no one by surprise. In the summer of 1882, amid numerous anti–Jewish demonstrations, Istóczy's followers acted quickly to link the noisy and often violent outbursts of public hatred to the citizens' attempts to influence the Diet. On 31 July 1882, the participants at a public assembly in Tapolca, a town in Zala County,[11] voted to support the drafting of a petition to the Diet demanding the abrogation of Law 1867:XVII (it granted Jews civil equality), the termination of Jewish religious education and a prohibition of Jewish ownership of tangible property. The instigator of the petition was Andor Vadnay, a local landowner and lawyer and one of Istóczy's most devoted supporters.[12]

At first glance, the procedural sequence and outcome of the debate on the Tapolca petition were a replay of those of the Vasvár petition. Albert Berzeviczy, representing the Petitions Committee, spoke against admitting the Tapolca petition to parliamentary debate. With that, however, the similarity ends. The person responsible for the change was Istóczy. His usual highly charged delivery, undisciplined ramblings and oratorical liberties, for which he frequently drew the Diet President's ire, were notably absent. Instead a pragmatic, calm and self–assured leader of an anti–Semitic faction, sustained by a large and steadily growing constituency, voiced his objection to the recommendation of the Petitions Committee. Although much of what he said had already been heard more than once, Istóczy's new stature gave his words an unaccustomed ring of authority. "I shall be brief," Istóczy declared, recalling the Vasvár petition in support of which he had spoken at length, "the more so since during the debate I will not be alone in defending the anti–Semitic point of view." He chided his colleagues for their unwillingness to perceive the Jewish Question as a political problem and for taking refuge in the misguided notion that it belonged to the realm of social peculiarities which neither the legislature nor the government was authorized or predisposed to address. "We must literally reconquer the country from the Jews for our downtrodden Hungarian society," he warned sternly. He could envision no other course of action against the Jews who had defied integration, learned Hungarian only to become Hungarian–speaking Jews rather than Hungarians, and converted to Christianity so that they could remain professing Jews and practice Jewish traditions without the threat of persecution. "Jews are the most constant of the white races," he noted. "Despite generations of racial intermixing their physical type remains as unchanged as the Jewish spirit which dominates their descendants." The assimilation of the Jews, "whose yoke upon us is more humiliating and dangerous than that of any of our foes in the past," was no more a solution than their emancipation was a success. Istóczy concluded:

> The abrogation of the law of emancipation is the first step that must be taken to restore to the Hungarian nation the favorable balance of power to which it is entitled by historical right and which the Jews have wrested out of its hands since 1867. Only that recaptured favorable balance of power will enable the nation to effect the radical and final solution of the Jewish Question.[13]

To a perennial underdog not all defeats look alike. He accepts some as the inevitable risks of his position; others he views as mere setbacks. He sees still others, especially in the light of peculiar circumstances, as making him look like a winner, not a loser. Following the defeat of his motion on 28 January,[14] a predictable outcome considering the fate of all of his previous legislative initiatives, Istóczy took a ten–month sabbatical from parliamentary oratory. Many a politician, especially one consistently guided by intemperate emotions, would have spent such a respite licking his political wounds, brooding, and contemplating the future. Whatever his feelings may have been, Istóczy took the defeat in stride. Undoubtedly he was hurt and disappointed. His heightened political stature, even if gained from notoriety, held out at least the promise of a prolonged debate. A seasoned loser and a fast healer, Istóczy spent little time recuperating. There were unique opportunities to explore. As preparations for the 1884 elections got under way and the Nyíregyháza court inched closer to the trial of the accused Jews of Tiszaeszlár, Istóczy and his followers plotted a political coup.

By the spring of 1883 Istóczy felt confident enough to consider the practicality of creating an independent political party. The increasing popularity of his views among the steadily widening segments of the population charted a clean path leading him out of the limbo in which he had been confined by the mechanics of dietal proceedings and the priorities of Hungary's political establishment virtually since the beginning of his career. In April, Istóczy sent a circular to his political supporters informing them of his intention to form a political party and have its candidates run in the next general election. However, the feasibility of his plan was first tested sooner than Istóczy had anticipated. Toward the end of May, Istóczy was notified that the entry of an anti–Semitic candidate in a by–election in the district of Szakcs in the southwestern county of Tolna, would not be unwelcome. The identity of a political aspirant to stand for election in Hungary as the first official representative of the Anti–Semitic Party created somewhat of a sensation. Instead of the best–known anti–Semites—the logical choices were Istóczy, Ónody and Simonyi, who founded the party and were in charge of its operations—Dr. Károly Nendtvich, a respected chemist but an inexperienced politician, became the standard bearer, albeit ephemeral, of the anti–Semitic movement.[15] Nendtvich finished a close second to the candidate of the Liberal Party. However, Istóczy wasted no time in transforming the narrow margin of his candidate's defeat into an encouraging sign of popular support.[16] Indeed, one could not overlook the implications of a candidate who had no political experience and represented a socioeconomic program that had consistently faltered in dietal proceedings receiving 625 votes in a minuscule electoral district. Small wonder that plans for fielding other anti–Semitic candidates in the approaching general elections became Istóczy's most urgent priority. He was, however, unexpectedly sidetracked.

Istóczy's almost engrained political reflex that allowed him to create the impression that he could escape unscathed from adversity helped him to extricate himself from one of the most damaging and unsavory episodes of his career. The cloud of an unsettled legal matter, much like the one he faced at the outset of his political career, had hung menacingly over him for nearly a year. However, it caused him little discomfort and did not encourage him to be more discreet in his utterances. Given the similarity between his published writings and his eight years of unbridled oratory, a relentless torrent of unsubstantiated denunciations and accusations delivered in a tone that frequently bordered on the obscene, the episode was predictable, in fact, long overdue. The incident that triggered it was created by the 15 July 1882 issue of the *12 Röpirat* which featured a lengthy article, entitled "The Judaization of Hungary," by a certain Titus Aemilius, an obvious pseudonym. No more pejorative than most of Istóczy's speeches in the Diet or the general tone of other writings in the *12 Röpirat*, the article nevertheless aroused the wrath of Sándor Kozma, the chief state prosecutor who had been one of the anti–Semites' most avowed foes as well as an outspoken critic of the Nyíregyháza authorities, then in the midst of preparing the trial of the accused Jews of Tiszaeszlár.

The author of the article, Emil Szemnecz, a lieutenant in the Hungarian army, was one of Istóczy's most loyal supporters and a frequent contributor to the *12 Röpirat*. His commitment to the cause of political anti–Semitism and his irresponsible dabbling in journalism would force him to resign his commission in 1884. He soon joined Verhovay's *Függetlenség*.[17] Szemnecz managed to duplicate his idol's unmitigated profane style and his accusatory, slanderous rhetorical strategies. He called for the termination of the millennial relationship between Hungarians and Jews, the latter being an

> alien race of harmful traits, dedicated to the destruction of the Hungarian nation through deceit and lies, proliferating and thriving at the expense of Hungarians, bribing lawyers and judges, and monopolizing the professions. They control nearly 450 of the 500 representatives of the Diet, yet are engaged in usury, corruption and unethical business practices. They are the sworn enemies of everything good and patriotic. We do not long for their Magyarization and assimilation, as we do not wish to raise vipers by warming them on our bosoms. It is our conviction that the Jews are an evil people, incapable of changing themselves for the better. Our program: All the Jews out of Hungary![18]

The case produced another round of confrontation between Istóczy and one of the self–disciplining mechanisms of the Diet. In a dramatic display of camaraderie, Istóczy attempted to shield Szemnecz from a predictable punishment by a military tribunal. He assumed full responsibility for the article. Acting on the request of the judicial authorities, the Committee on Parliamentary Immunity found Istóczy guilty and recommended that his parliamentary immunity be suspended and he be brought to trial.[19] On his part Istóczy was more defiant than contrite. On the same day, he issued a combative memorandum defending anti–Semitism as a "political movement" and virtually daring the committee to take action against it. "I cannot believe that the Hungarian Diet will allow the prosecution of a legitimate effort that springs from the purest patriotic feeling," he declared menacingly.[20]

Although the Diet had established a tradition of acting favorably on committee recommendations against everything Istóczy initiated, the tense spring of 1883 tempered that practice with caution and uncertainty. It took the committee eight months to issue a two–page report. Nearly all of it consisted of excerpts from the incriminating article. A brief, concluding paragraph spelled out the committee's decision. Another three months passed before the Diet cleared the way for the court to set the date of the trial.

The juridical authorities acted swiftly, albeit disingenuously. János Kriszt was appointed the presiding judge; Ödön Fekete, an assistant chief state prosecutor, argued the case on behalf of the state; and Andor Vadnay, the newly elected twenty–four–year–old Diet representative of Kecskemét and one of the most active and enthusiastic anti–Semitic politicians, put his brief legal experience to test as Istóczy's defense attorney.[21] The authorities, however, demonstrated an extraordinary lack of sensitivity to the need for careful timing. Avoiding a delay in due process, a virtue in normal circumstances, turned out to be a distressing liability in the summer of 1883, because the trial of the accused Jews of Tiszaeszlár in Nyíregyháza began on June 19.

Judging from the alarming upsurge of anti–Jewish sentiments, especially in the countryside, the anti–Semitic press appeared to have won the opening rounds against the government and the publications supporting it. The proceedings at Nyíregyháza were confined to the small provincial courthouse. Figuratively, the audience was comprised of the whole country, thanks to an office of information set up by the local authorities and the large number of journalists in attendance. In such a tense, highly charged atmosphere, the chances of finding a jury of twelve dispassionate and unprejudiced people for Istóczy's trial were remote. No one denied that Istóczy had intentionally violated Section 172 of the Hungarian penal code which determined that outright incitement to religious hatred was punishable under the law. Because of the prevailing conditions in the country there was unanimity in predicting the outcome of the trial. "I remember," noted

Mór Szatmári, the well-known political writer, "we hardly had any doubt about the verdict that would be rendered."[22] Surprisingly, the jurors were less certain than the oddsmakers.

The verdict was based on the jurors' responses to four questions of unequal importance. There was unanimity in the responses to two questions that implied little or no criminal intent. The jurors agreed that Istóczy was not the author of the incriminating article, but that he was responsible for its publication in the *12 Röpirat*. The other two, more important questions, however, failed to receive a similar consensus. Only three of the twelve jurors felt that the article incited hatred against a religious group, and only two jurors voted yes on the question of whether Istóczy, by publishing the article, was guilty of incitement to religious hatred.

There was, however, no doubt about the verdict itself. Judge Kriszt pronounced Istóczy not guilty. The verdict was greeted by an outburst of acceding shouts from Istóczy's exuberant supporters who filled the courtroom anxiously awaiting the fate of their idol. Although the acquittal cleared Istóczy of any journalistic wrongdoing in only one instance, the anti–Semites took it as a virtual carte blanche to print anything they pleased in their publications.[23] The floodgates of the most vicious anti–Semitic agitation suddenly flung open. The trial of the accused Jews of Tiszaeszlár in Nyíregyháza was engulfed in a torrent of new accusations, threats, and demands for a verdict of guilty.

Chapter X

The National Anti–Semitic Party and the Elections of 1884

By the summer of 1883 Istóczy had good cause to feel optimistic about the prospects of political anti–Semitism's becoming a national phenomenon. There was a marked increase in the number of people, especially in the countryside, who found his views appealing. His acquittal had removed the stamp of illegality from the anti–Semitic publications that thrived in response to their growing readership. There even was a shortage of anti–Semitic candidates standing for election into the Diet. Thus, some were often invited to represent more than a single voting district. Arguably the most potent weapon in Istóczy's hands was the ongoing trial of the Tiszaeszlár Jews at Nyíregyháza. By the actual start of the proceedings, only those who did not want to acknowledge it as a lost cause for the anti–Semites failed to characterize it as such. The trial was expected to release an outpour of parental grief and torrents of xenophobic hatred that could be harnessed for future political gains.

Central to the unfolding spectacle of the anti–Semites' political offensive was Istóczy's conviction that an act of ritual murder had been committed for which the whole of Hungary's Jewry was responsible, regardless of the medical experts' testimonies; the intentionally muted presentation of the charges by a visibly embarrassed prosecutor who sounded more like a defense attorney; the confused testimonies of unreliable witnesses; and the airtight alibis of the accused. He simply ignored both the two principal legal theories—the Nyíregyháza authorities persisted in their view that the young Christian girl had been murdered, whereas the defense contended that no murder had been committed—and all investigative and medical evidence to the contrary.[1] Even Ónody, the resident "expert on ritual murder," wavered, displaying frustration with the proceedings. He accosted the chief prosecutor, accused him of being the "Jews' paid man," and challenged him to a duel. However, he inexplicably backed down.[2] Citing a multitude of biological, moral, and religious proofs, the five–member defense team presented masterfully coordinated summations. They culminated in an historic seven–hour speech by Károly Eötvös, the chief defense counsel. He stripped the charge bare, exposing the untenability of its fundamental contention. The defendants were acquitted.[3]

Considering both the immediate and long–range consequences of the trial, a guilty verdict would have served the cause of political anti–Semitism only slightly better. A mysterious, ominously inconclusive legend was born when shortly after 12:00 p.m. On 3 August 1883 the three-member panel of judges at Nyíregyháza declared that "the fact that the charge of murder against Salamon Schwarcz and his companions [the defendants] could not be proved precludes the concealment of the act of murder."[4] Thus, the verdict of not guilty was merely implied; it was not declared. The three judges, who in the course of the 100–day proceedings had given ample evidence of the distressing inadequacy of the provincial mind to comprehend the historic significance of the trial, also failed to discharge heavy judicial—as well as social and moral—responsibilities. Their concluding statement was in minimal compliance with the instruction of the criminal code that described the mandatory and automatic acquittal of defendants in the absence of incriminating evidence.[5] They, however, stopped short of putting an unequivocal period at the end of an agonizingly long sentence. By not issuing a statement denouncing the absurd nature of the charges and the often patently illegal methods of the pretrial investigation, the judges failed to declare the absolute innocence of the defendants. The shallow simplicity of the wording of the verdict allowed the lingering suspicion of ritual murder and the general anti–Semitic hysteria that gripped the unruly spectators to escape the crowded courtroom and engulf the whole of Hungary. Tiszaeszlár acquired a perpetual ring of unease and uncertainty—even suspicion—undiminished by the passage of time.

"Where is Eszter Solymosi? Who killed Eszter Solymosi?" screamed the headlines of the anti–Semitic publications. Many people felt that not only these questions were unanswered judicially but that Hungarian Jewry had conspired to leave them so. The jubilant editorials in the "Jewish press" threw fuel on the smoldering fire. "The floodgates were open," Bary, the investigating magistrate of Tiszaeszlár, recalled. "The suppressed bitterness exploded with elemental force."[6] Bary's description of the conditions that prevailed in the immediate aftermath of the verdict of the Nyíregyháza court, however, reflect a most cavalier application of the theory of cause and effect in which invisible, impersonal forces, not the relentless accusations of Istóczy, Verhovay, Ónody and other anti–Semitic molders of public opinion, had touched off the fireworks of anger and frustration. Bary's account refused to recognize that the collective sigh of relief, heaved by everyone who felt liberated from the oppressive cloud of medieval fanaticism, ignorance and superstition, was interpreted by the anti–Semites as the "Jews' distasteful and provocative display of joy"[7] and as proof of their "enormous power and influence."[8]

Still, however reproachful and malicious, those were just words. As the course of the flawed administration of justice in Nyíregyháza slowly faded in the memories of the public, the specter of violence rose menacingly. The guilt of the Tiszaeszlár Jews had become a manufactured fait accompli long before the trial began and was perpetuated in the speeches and publications of anti–Semitic activists. Frustration and anger rarely are unexpressed. There had been ample time for the authorities to take the threat of violence seriously and make the necessary preparations. Shortly after the start of the trial Prime Minister Tisza was advised by the high sheriff of Pozsony County, one of the traditional strongholds of anti–Semitism in Hungary, of the likelihood of demonstrations. By the end of June 1882 violent disturbances of such magnitude had taken place that military units, in addition to the local police, had to be called out. Yet the opportunity to diffuse the predictable subsequent explosions of public wrath was allowed to slip by even though the danger signals were clearly visible. The arrival of the defendants in Budapest on 7 August 1883—they had to be spirited out of an already restive Nyíregyháza—touched off rock–throwing demonstrations and violent confrontations with the police. For five days a state of siege existed in the capital. The news of the events in Budapest initiated a chain reaction of violence in thirty–two counties. Jews were repeatedly assaulted, their houses, stores and synagogues vandalized. The well–orchestrated disturbances, exacerbated by the authorities' lack of foresight, extended the poisonous atmosphere of the trial by three months.[9]

The most significant long–range effect of the Tiszaeszlár case was the formation of an anti–Semitic party.[10] As Istóczy's views were rejected outright by the Liberal Party and became the subject of heated debates in the Independence Party, the encouraging signals among the people left only the timing of the decision in doubt. The events of 1883 indicated that both timing and conditions favored the anti–Semites' declaration of political independence. The earlier feelers—the establishment of defense leagues and Istóczy's repeated references in speeches and the *12 Röpirat* to the feasibility of an independent anti–Semitic party—had met no sign of organized opposition.

Less than two weeks after the accused Jews of Tiszaeszlár were acquitted and as the violent anti–Jewish demonstrations were spreading like wildfire, Istóczy triumphantly declared that "the Tiszaeszlár trial had demonstrated to everyone, beyond any doubt, the existence of a Jewish Question."[11] Yet despite the favorable national mood and the state of national emergency which the acquittals had created, Istóczy recognized the need for quick decisions and decisive actions. The devastating surge of hatred, driving a menacing wedge into the Hungarian political landscape, created a unique opportunity for Istóczy to advance his movement into a position of power in the Diet. Left unharnessed, the emotional forces would eventually scatter on the hastily constructed government barriers, receding into the doldrums of everyday concerns, and the cause of political anti–Semitism would suffer a major setback due to indecision and inaction. Istóczy's proposed solution of the Jewish Question would undoubtedly be dealt a deathblow by the "Judaized political parties and the Diet."[12]

The post–Tiszaeszlár nationwide disturbances were contained by police and troops. A bitter residue was felt in the Diet. The government of Kálmán Tisza was criticized for reacting too slowly and only after much delay to the rapidly proliferating acts of violence. As that propitious situation emerged, the anti–Semites made their move. In the September 15 edition of the *12 Röpirat*, Istóczy called for the urgent formation of a national coalition of anti–Semites. Its members would be united by a common goal: the destruction of the Jews' power in Hungary. The identification of the target and the familiar battle cry whetted many a political appetite. Within three weeks the National Anti–Semitic Party came into being. A four–member executive committee, consisting of Istóczy, Simonyi, Ónody, and György Széll, an Independence Party representative from the town of Makó, was elected to plan an organizational meeting. Between October 8 and 10, the first conference of the National Anti–Semitic Party debated and ratified a twelve–point program, a personal victory for Istóczy, the program's principal author.

It was a comprehensive plan with which few anti–Semitic politicians would find fault, basically a synthesis of Istóczy's speeches in the Diet. On October 15—a date that by a strange, then unimaginable, coincidence would mark the beginning of the end of Hungary's Jewry in the Holocaust sixty years later[13]—the final version of the program was published in the *12 Röpirat*:

1. The elimination of Jewish power and the counterbalancing of Jewish influence in politics, society and economy; specifically in the press, finance, commerce, public transportation, industry, and agriculture.

2. Protection of the interests of the landowning and agricultural working class by a new agrarian policy serving the national interest.

3. Restriction of unregulated freedom in commerce by the formation

of compulsory trade associations and the certification of qualifications.

4. Restriction of the extension of credit.
5. Revision of the penal code, now favoring Jewish interests, and the establishment of the jury system in criminal cases.
6. Restoration of the ritual oath before the court in both criminal and civil cases.
7. Community acquisition of the right to sell alcoholic beverages; and the prohibition of Jewish ownership of taverns.
8. The transference of the responsibility of keeping Jewish birth records to the civil authorities.
9. The abrogation of the law ratifying marriages between Jews and Christians.
10. The prevention of the influx of Jews into the country and the modification of the law of naturalization to that effect.
11. The regulation of public finance and national credit structure, leading to the independence of Hungary's financial affairs as well as that of its government.
12. The retention of party members' freedom of action in political and constitutional matters unrelated to the "Jewish Question."[14]

Set against the menacing backdrop of Tiszaeszlár, the initial organizational steps augured well for quick success. The founders of the new party, however, acted impulsively and hastily, ignoring obstacles that stood in their path. Overconfidence was inherent in their calculations. Istóczy brushed aside the feeble reservations voiced by some of the early party members who objected to the name of the party. He "insisted on the word anti–Semitic as he felt it expressed most accurately the objectives of the party as well as the universality of the Jewish Question and anti–Semitism."[15] Another problem emerged in the form of a potentially damaging incident which could not be treated so lightly. Istóczy's jubilant mood turned sour by the embarrassing coincidence of a scandal involving the *Függetlenség*, a principal anti–Semitic publication and the one that had followed the Tiszaeszlár affair most closely. Administered like a feudal domain by Gyula Verhovay and his brother, Lajos, the *Függetlenség*, unlike Istóczy's *12 Röpirat*, frequently evoked interest beyond the narrow confines of anti–Semitism.

One such undertaking of purported patriotism, initiated by the Verhovay brothers, was rumored to have been conducted deceitfully and to illegal ends. The *Függetlenség* started an emotional nationwide campaign to collect donations for the repatriation of the Csángós, a Hungarian–speaking minority in Bukovina and Moldavia, the westernmost provinces of Romania. The Csángós had been appealing in vain to the emperor for permission to rejoin their countrymen. The Verhovays set up the Csángó Fund and thousands of contributors responded enthusiastically. Allegations of financial misconduct, however, were subsequently leveled aginst the Verhovays in the liberal newspapers. They were accused of diverting substantial sums from the Csángó Fund for personal use. Police searched the offices of the *Függetlenség*, arrested the Verhovays, and charged them with embezzlement. Although Gyula Verhovay was not a member of Istóczy's inner circle—there had been areas of disagreement between the two men over the presumed fate of Eszter Solymosi, the central figure of the Tiszaeszlár affair—he had been closely identified with the cause of political anti–Semitism. Hungarians regarded his irresponsible and self–serving conduct as an act of treason, and the *Függetlenség* faced a nationwide boycott. Verhovay countersued and the case dragged on for two years, leaving the National Anti–Semitic Party tainted and in a position of having to refute charges that it was a sanctuary for unpatriotic embezzlers.[16] Despite attempts in the anti–Semitic press to whitewash the Verhovays and accuse the "Jewish press' of conducting a witchhunt, the scandal undermined Gyula Verhovay's political and journalistic career and handed the *Függetlenség* a blow from which it never recovered.[17]

The coup de grace, was delivered by a man whose voice from afar was heard and obeyed by many Hungarians. From his exile in Turin, Lajos Kossuth, the venerated hero of the 1848 Revolution, had often exercised the almost mystical power of his pronouncements by way of letters or through faithful intermediaries. Kossuth's perception of Hungarian Jewry had undergone a significant change since the Diet of 1840 when he spoke of the "dreggy Jewish masses of Máramaros."[18] In light of the Jews' manifold contributions to the Revolution of 1848 and their socioeconomic utility in Hungary's sojourn in the Age of the Industrial Revolution, anti–Semitism was to him an anathema. That it also proved deep–rooted and persistent, nurtured by second–rate politicians who defied his commands to eradicate it, both saddened and angered the "Great Exile."

Kossuth, however, had made up his mind to throw his enormous personal prestige behind his unpopular stance on anti–Semitism. His turned out to be a prolonged effort, his messages of caution and admonition merely thrown into the cauldron of hatred. Ironically the main obstacle was Kossuth's own political mouthpiece: the Independence Party. It was hopelessly divided on the issue of anti–Semitism. One faction led by Dániel Iráni, one of Kossuth's closest collaborators despite some differences of opinion due to his pursuit of moderate, peaceful parliamentary reform, stood steadfast against all manifestations of anti–Semitism and consistently denounced its practitioners. Party members that acknowledged Lajos Mocsáry, an uncompromising foe of the post–*Ausgleich* state system of the Austro–Hungarian empire, as their leader viewed anti–Semitism with a mixture of benign tolerance and outright sympathy. Police investigation of the outbreak and conduct of anti–Semitic incitement and violence implicated many representatives belonging to the Mocsáry faction.

In 1882, twice within a period of three months, a deeply concerned Kossuth spoke out against anti–Semitism. On both occasions his intermediary was Ignác Helfy, one of his most intimate comrades-in–arms, a convert to Christianity, and an Independence Party stalwart. Kossuth was stunned by the rapid spread of intensely anti–Jewish feelings as the investigation into the disappearance of the young Christian girl in Tiszaeszlár began to unfold. When Helfy visited him on August 6, Kossuth expressed his anguish and characterized the Tiszaeszlár affair as a "national calamity."[19] He warned of dangerous consequences unless the Independence Party took a firm stand against the Jewish Question. The party, however, regarded Tiszaeszlár as more embarrassing than dangerous to the Tisza government and took no action. On October 15, the day the National Anti–Semitic Party officially came into being, Helfy read an impassioned letter Kossuth had written four days earlier. By then even the "Great Exile" had lost his immunity to criticism he had enjoyed for more than three decades. He had received hundreds of letters, he complained bitterly. He was accused of having been bribed by the Jews and for not taking part in the defense of Hungary against the Jewish menace. On the other hand the Jews, he noted with surprise, reproached him for not standing up for them. His principal targets, however, remained the anti–Semitic members of the Independence Party. Kossuth exclaimed angrily in conclusion:

> I find it impossible that those who deny to the citizens of the country the principle of equality before the law without regard to differences in race, language and religion should be considered as members of the party.[20]

Oddly enough, the biggest loser, by a contemptuous slap rather than a powerful blow, was Istóczy. As long as Kossuth denounced anti–Semitism in general terms, described it as a national blight caused by socioeconomic inequities, and demanded that its resolution be made a priority by the Independence Party, Istóczy's figure grew steadily larger as the principal manipulator of the forces of evil. It was a role he cherished and cultivated jealously. However, that precariously inflated ego was irreparably punctured not by a sustained and concentrated attack but a casual reference, a belittling afterthought. Kossuth observed:

> It is not advisable to ignore that Istóczy and Co. could never have succeeded, even with agitation imported from Germany (this too, shamefully), had the socioeconomic woes not made the the masses susceptible to incitement.[21]

Although Kossuth's message did not initiate an immediate flurry of activities against the anti–Semites in the Independence Party—the letter was not even made public for a month—a slow, but well-organized effort got under way to rid the party of them. Spearheaded by Gábor Ugron, one of the founders of the party and a spellbinding orator known for his powers of persuasion, a small group of influential leaders managed to gather enough support to bring the party in line with Kossuth's views. On 13 February 1883, Géza Ónody and György Széll, two of the Party's most visible anti–Semites, were removed from the membership. In May, Iván Simonyi and Imre Szalay resigned in protest. However, as the Independence Party made a sharp turn to align itself with the angry pronouncement of its exiled standard bearer on anti–Semitism, the formation of the National Anti–Semitic Party became a virtual certainty.[22]

The wound that Kossuth's letters inflicted on the cause of political anti–Semitism, however, did not diminish, let alone heal, in the aftermath of the traumatic house cleaning in the Independence Party. It continued to deepen, impeding the development of the National Anti–Semitic Party and tainting its reputation. "The greatest blow was struck against us from Italy," Istóczy noted, "but not by the Italian nation. Two preemptory proclamations in the form of instruction . . . came from there."[23] If one subscribes to the notion that the intensity of an attack is usually in direct proportion to the size and power of the object that provokes it, Istóczy's reaction seems justifiable, if slightly skewed. Almost with pride, he recalled that it took two powerfully worded messages from the "Great Exile," who still wielded great influence in Hungarian politics, for the warning to take effect. He almost gleefully took refuge in the confusion they caused. Yet for the full impact of Kossuth's words seemed to escape Istóczy's attention. Istóczy was convinced that he alone was the pioneer and pacesetter of political anti–Semitism, an imitable model for his followers in Hungary and abroad. Yet, Kossuth damaged Istóczy's political career of a decade with embarrassing ease. Kossuth's attacks not only shattered Istóczy's image, inflated by self-importance, but reduced him to a mere imitator and importer of foreign ideas, an opportunist thriving only in times of national turmoil and misfortune. Most importantly Kossuth's anger cracked the foundation of Istóczy's political persona. It would forever defy all attempts to mend it.

At this juncture one can hardly desist from contemplating the position in which Istóczy and the nascent National Anti-Semitic Party might have found themselves had Kossuth chosen to refrain from commenting on the events of 1883. Would guilty verdicts pronounced over the Jewish defendants in the Tiszaeszlár case have molded the course of the 1884 elections and determined their outcome? The severity and extent of the anti-Jewish disturbances pointed in a direction that one may well leave unexplored. For better or for worse, by October 1883 Istóczy and his followers had committed themselves and made their irreversible move. The program of the National Anti-Semitic Party sounded like a defiant, confident battle cry. Still, it is difficult to discern the tangible assets of the party that would have given its founding fathers cause for optimism. Some kind of political fallout due to the outbursts of popular anti-Semitism was hardly in doubt. Such uncontrolled nationwide emotions were expected to pay political dividends. It was suggested that the delegation of unidentified dietal representatives which tried to dissuade Károly Eötvös from undertaking the defense of the accused Jews of Tiszaeszlár by offering him the leadership of a new political party would have used anti-Semitism as a means to win support among the people. The party's proposed anti-Tisza and anti-Austrian program included a list of 133 representatives who stood ready to join such a venture.[24] Istóczy dreamed of storming into the Diet at the head of a force of newly elected anti-Semitic representatives who would number between 50 and 100.[25] Neither of the figures, however, produced a tangible foundation for political anti-Semitism.

Aside from Kossuth's intervention, Istóczy's greatest handicaps were the extreme narrowness of his political philosophy and his miscalculation and inexperience in creating and operating a political organization. In the prevailing atmosphere of anti-Jewish disturbances the former undoubtedly attracted public attention. Yet it was the very nature of the anti-Semitic tradition, the almost mechanical certainty of fluctuation between dormancy and eruption, that inevitably prevented Istóczy's gospel of hatred from acquiring a stable electorate even against the backdrop of uneasy Hungarian-Jewish relations. The pragmatic priorities of the Industrial Age would soon restore a semblance of law and order and allow the socioeconomic utility of the Jews to reassert itself under the watchful eyes of the government. No such fleeting moments of elation could remedy Istóczy's lack of experience in matters of political organization. He had been a lone wolf, fighting his battles against the establishment without the hope of winning even one. At the threshold of opportunity he had the will but not the means to succeed. It was an odd lot that gathered to proclaim the existence of the National Anti–Semitic Party in October 1883: former members of other parties; titled landowners without a modicum of political experience; and provincial officials untested in national politics. None of Hungary's leading politicians had been persuaded to join. Except for a bombastic program, the anti–Semitic party had neither the financial backing nor a network of supporting clubs, the principal requirements for fielding a national slate of candidates. Not even in theory could the party realize Istóczy's fondest dream of seating between 50 and 100 anti–Semitic representatives in the Diet. There were simply not enough members—some candidates were scheduled to run in more than one electoral district—who could sustain the vision of an impressive showing in the elections. None of these handicaps caused Istóczy to modify his stance. Nor did he or his followers give any indication of being unaware of them. On the contrary, Istóczy was only too well acquainted with Kossuth's views; he took pride in his knowledge of the Jews, their history and lifestyle, and often spoke admiringly of the advanced organizational state of foreign, especially Austrian and German, anti–Semitic movements, lamenting Hungary's notable lack of such a structure. Yet Istóczy chose to defy all of them.

Energy was not on the list of appurtenances Istóczy lacked. In addition to his considerable responsibilities in publishing the *12 Röpirat*, the feverish organizational activities of the anti–Semitic party—the latter required time–consuming and fatiguing trips to various parts of the country and attendance at rallies and other support–bolstering functions—and the preparation for his own reelection campaign, Istóczy discharged his dietal responsibilities as conscientiously as ever. Even though there were indications that support in his election district had grown perceptively, making his bid for reelection a virtual shoo–in, Istóczy worked hard to retain the reputation he had labored so long to build in the Diet. On 21 November 1883, Istóczy rose to speak in the course of a five–day debate concerning the ratification of marriages between Jews and Christians and civil marriages contracted abroad, an act that would terminate the mandatory practice of obtaining papal approval. He no longer sounded like a despairing oddity whose lonely whisper in the political wilderness pleaded for attention, but the confident leader of a political movement that commanded considerable, albeit untested, nationwide support. The bill, authored by Minister of Cults Ágoston Trefort and called derisively the "Jew Bill," was introduced at the insistence of Prime Minister

Tisza who decided to override the counsel of those who feared that the debate would only exacerbate an already inflamed situation and others who accused him of insensitivity. Many representatives called for a bill legitimizing civil marriages. Tisza committed himself without caution or restraint.

Demanding that the bill be passed, pro–government speakers lashed out against the manifestations of virulent anti–Semitism which, they claimed, had caused the Jews to feel insecure about their safety and that of their property. With that the battle of the intransigent factions began. Istóczy's speech featured an interesting combination of defensive and offensive tactics. He defended his supporters by claiming that the real instigators were the Jews whose alien lifestyle and duplicitous business practices had caused widespread hatred. As for safety of person and and property, "the Jews and their paid philosemitic lackeys threaten our possessions and the lives of Christians. No Christian parent may rest assured that his child, who has disappeared suddenly, will not fall victim to the ritualistic madness of fanatical Jews that exceeds even that of cannibals . . ." As so often before, Istóczy's undisciplined outburst was cut short by the ever–alert Tamás Péchy, the president of the Diet. He admonished Istóczy for the impropriety of "pouring fuel from this House on a dangerous fire" and instructed him to "moderate his words to fit the objective discussion of the bill." Departing from his established practice, Istóczy resumed his tirade exactly where he had been interrupted without paying the slightest attention to an exasperated Péchy who inexplicably remained silent for the rest of the speech. "For despite all the not guilty verdicts, deep down in his heart, everyone is convinced that that unfortunate Eszter Solymosi met her mournful death in the synagogue of Tiszaeszlár," Istóczy thundered.

Marriages between Jews and Christians, Istóczy warned, were bound to have harmful political and social consequences. Quoting statistical data of the declining number of such marriages in Prussia, Istóczy drew laughter declaring that he "was not concerned that cases of coupling between Jews and Christians would be frequent" in Hungary. He also noted that statistical figures made public in Prussia for the years 1875–1879 indicated that the birthrate in families of Jewish and Christian spouses lagged far behind the number of children born to unmixed Jewish and Christian parents. The reason, Istóczy explained to his visibly bemused audience who somehow failed to be impressed by the unfolding spectacle of racial anti–Semitism, was quite obvious. "Aside from the great psychological differences an irremediable alienation exists between the Semitic and European races," he declared. "The Jewish spouse, taught to hate and despise the *goyim* and, according to the dictate of the Talmud, regard them as inferior even to animals, will always see the Jew, hated since childhood, in a dallying Jewish husband or Jewish wife."

It was, however, the fundamental incompatibility of the Jews with the rest of mankind, one of Istóczy's racial hobbyhorses, that was the source of all evil. Istóczy reasoned:

> Not even by intermarriage have the Jews been able to assimilate with other peoples. Their 3,000-year history, during which they lived as despised outcasts with all the despicable physical and moral peculiarities of pariahs, is proof of that. That pariah-like existence is found intact in Jews even in the present. By being subjugated, or rather suppressing others, and viewing themselves superior rather than inferior to others but never feeling themselves the equal of others, the Jews will never be rid of that liberated slave-like disposition which they inherited from their ancestors in Egypt and have fully preserved even in this present age of legal equality.

Even more threatening were the consequences of intermarriage—waning racial and national characteristics—a forbidding landscape Istóczy was so fond of describing. Ironically, he intended his final remarks to leave the audience pondering their fate, but his words rarely failed to draw smirks and incredulous laughter from his fellow representatives. Istóczy went on undaunted:

> Based on the foregoing conclusions, I do not fear that the passage of this bill will spur an increase in marriages between Jews and Christians. However, the danger of such unions—usually speculative Christians marry Jews—from which amphibians are born, increase the number of Jewish allies, who are also our enemies, does exist. For it is a fact culled from experience that, with rare exceptions, in such cases of intermarriage the Jew will not become a Hungarian but the Hungarian will become a Jew.[26]

Simonyi and Ónody also spoke, much in the same vein.

The bill survived the misgivings of many Liberal Party representatives and the opposition, voiced by the majority of the Independence Party, which called for unqualified compulsory civil marriage. However, because of a combination of the considerably less than enthusiastically supportive majority and an incongruous twist of legislative procedure, the fate of the bill enabled the National Anti-Semitic Party to claim its first parliamentary victory of sorts. Prime Minister Tisza emerged a deserving, albeit tattered, winner from a series of lengthy and bruising polemical confrontations, particularly with Ottó Herman, one of the stalwarts of the Independence Party, and Minister of Justice Tivadar Pauler. Fearing a possible defeat in the Diet, Pauler uncharacteristically let down his guard and revealed a carefully concealed antipathy for Jews by coldly rejecting compulsory civil marriage. The echoes of Tisza's victory were hollow. The bill passed by a comfortable but unconvincing margin in a voice vote at the conclusion of which many a representative, anxious to keep his opinion unrecorded, heaved a sigh of relief.

The spectacle of prolonged and bitter debates that left the floor of the Diet looking like a veritable battlefield was not lost on the Upper House of magnates and high clergy, which until then had given the government no cause to take notice of its existence. The prospect of losing ecclesiastical control over an institution so significant as marriage sent shock waves across the staid rows of the Upper House. On December 11, after a three-day debate, the opponents of the bill won by a precariously slim majority of six votes. To the delight of the National Anti-Semitic Party, the bill was returned to the Diet. It was received by a stunned but unrelenting Prime Minister Tisza. Again he marshaled his forces and insisted on taking a second vote. The bill was passed by a decisive majority.

In the Upper House, whose radical reform had become a matter of priority for the prime minister who hoped to make the Diet the sole forum for the resolution of parliamentary procedure, the opponents of the bill also gathered strength. Its 191 members rejected the bill by a nine-vote majority. Istóczy's influence was noticeable in that most exclusive club of Hungarian politics. Some of the speeches delivered by conservative aristocrats rivaled the venomous outbursts of the representatives of the National Anti-Semitic Party in the Diet. Sensing an unbreakable impasse, Tisza moved to table the bill. In the course of the debates, more so in the Diet than in the Upper House, an atmosphere of mounting acrimony reigned. Verbal duels were frequently interrupted or drowned out by shouts of vehement partisan supporters. In the thick of things Istóczy was in his element. His debating skills—and vocal chords—were severely challenged by his principal nemeses, Károly Eötvös and Ottó Herman, two of the most formidable political orators of the time. However, for the first time in his political career, he did not have to hurl his words against an impenetrable wall of derisive opposition. He cast them into the maelstrom of aristocratic and ecclesiastical conservatism and was convinced that he actually determined their direction,[27] a contention reflecting Istóczy's self-absorbed, unrealistic state of mind.

It was an unfettered and unencumbered Istóczy that rose to

speak on 31 January 1884. He promised to be brief and kept his
word on that occasion. "Now it is our turn to laugh!" he exclaimed
jubilantly, hoping in vain that the customary smiles of derision would
soon disappear from the faces of his opponents. He reminded his audience that the results of the votes in the Upper House had vindicated
the demand of the point in the program of the National Anti–Semitic
Party which called for the removal of the bill from the dietal agenda.
He then attacked the government, describing it as "groaning under
the weight of a deficit–ridden budget and pressured by powerful and
wealthy Jewish interest groups." He criticized the opposition Independence Party for "exceeding even the government in cultivating
friendship with the Jews," thus abandoning its political responsibility. The voters, however, would not fail to express their disapproval
of the prevailing conditions, Istóczy warned sternly.

> Only by electing to the next session of the Diet bona fide
> anti–Semitic representatives or opposition representatives
> who hold anti–Semitic views will the voting citizens of Hun-
> gary be assured of protection against being repeatedly both-
> ered by bills similar to the one concerning marriages between
> Jews and Christians.[28]

Istóczy's concluding remarks sounded like a well–timed and accurately aimed political salvo signaling the start of an anti–Semitic offensive. The defeat of the "Jew Bill," whose fate was not the direct
result of the efforts of Istóczy and his allies, suddenly emerged as a
convenient springboard from which the anti–Semitic candidates would
hurl themselves on the campaign trail. As they pursued their political dream with the same logic with which they ascribed the failure
of the "Jew Bill" to their heightened influence, the election year was
beginning to look more and more promising.

The preparatory events that preceded the national elections in
the summer of 1884, wrapped in an atmosphere of hatred, distrust
and violence, resembled those of a mobilization for war. All other
events in the tumultuous tradition of Hungarian political life paled
in comparison. That Istóczy and his supporters would not even attempt to wage a fair fight was a foregone conclusion. However, the
pre–election activities of the National Anti–Semitic Party candidates
cannot be dismissed as mere random mudslinging and underhanded
infighting. Their public speeches were aimed in three unmistakable
directions. The anti–Semitic candidates added the growing ranks of
industrial workers in the cities to their already growing electorate in
the countryside, where the mounting attacks on Jewish undesirables,
such as high–interest–charging innkeepers, landowners and lessors of

estates, had already assured them a certain measure of success. They demanded sweeping restrictions in the qualifications for manufacturing and commercial licenses, thereby slowing down, if not eliminating, the unrestricted influx of Jews, with their boundless energy and predisposition for accumulating wealth, into most areas of the economy. Because a substantial percentage of the industrial workers was of peasant origin, the presence of loudly cheering and steadily growing audiences at Jew-baiting political rallies was all but assured. That line of attack, constituting the very essence of the platform of the National Anti-Semitic Party, easily advanced.

The second targeted group consisted of the government and two political parties. Prime Minister Tisza, the principal spoiler of Istóczy's parliamentary machinations and the seemingly irremovable obstacle in the path of the National Anti-Semitic Party, was singled out as the object of some of the crudest forms of insult.[29] Ironically, the anti-Semites reserved their most virulent denunciation for the Independence Party from which the majority of them had defected and among "whose members there still were many whose disposition and mind remained resistant to liberalism."[30] The anti-Semites accused the members of the *sakterpárt* (kosher butcher party), the name by which Istóczy and the other anti-Semitic candidates called the party of Kossuth, of the most odious malfeasance: collaboration with Jews. Eötvös, the chief defender of the accused Jews of Tiszaeszlár, especially drew their ire. He was dubbed "King of the Jewish butchers." Because of their ultimate objective, however, the anti-Semites transcended pedestrian name-calling tactics. The solid bloc of gentry voters would inevitably abandon their discredited political leaders and flock to the new standard bearers of Hungarian Christian values, the anti-Semites reasoned.[31]

However, Istóczy's plan of using the momentum of Tiszaeszlár and the defeat of the "Jew Bill" to create maximum national exposure for the National Anti-Semitic Party candidates suffered an unexpected setback. Its cause was Gyula Verhovay, the editor of the *Függetlenség*. He had been an important ally of Istóczy and an indefatigable disseminator of anti-Semitic views and party propaganda. Yet by virtue of his brilliant intellect, nationwide journalistic reputation, and noteworthy yet somewhat erratic parliamentary service, Verhovay was not Istóczy's ideological subordinate. Nor did his *Függetlenség* operate in the shadow of Istóczy's *12 Röpirat.* (The same was true of Simonyi and the *Westungarischer Grenzbote.*) The embarrassment over the Csángó affair had faded. Yet a group of voters in Cegléd, the city that elected Verhovay its representative in the Diet, campaigned hard to switch political allegiance to a more worthy

and less controversial candidate. As a sign of their displeasure with
Verhovay, the organizers of the celebration of March 15, the national
holiday commemorating the outbreak of the 1848 Revolution, invited
Gábor Ugron, one of the founders of the Independence Party and
an implacable critic of the anti–Semites, to be the keynote speaker.
Ugron accepted and traveled to Cegléd in the company of such party
stalwarts as Ottó Herman, Pál Hoitsy and Baron Gábor Prónay.[32]
The anti–Semitic faction scrambled quickly to support Verhovay and
defend the *Függetlenség*. Instead of patriotic speeches and solemn
remembrances of the heroes and ideals of the ill–fated revolution, the
celebration turned into a brawl during which a group of anti–Semitic
townsmen, led by a contingent of *Függetlenség* associates, including
Verhovay, Emil Szemnecz, and Ferenc Persay, beat up Ugron. They
left him stunned and bleeding and went on to create disturbances
throughout the city. Two weeks later Szemnetcz and Vilmos Clair,
one of the writers of the *Függetlenség* and an authority on dueling,
assaulted Ottó Herman in front of the Diet building.[33]

The two incidents set the tone and direction of the campaign tactics of the National Anti–Semitic Party. Mindful of the importance
of retaining the loyalty of those who viewed public disturbance and
physical violence against Jews as the most effective means of resolving personal grievances, communal problems, and issues of national
concern, the anti–Semitic candidates openly encouraged the continuation of hostile and intimidating acts. Rallies organized by non–
anti–Semitic candidates were routinely disrupted and their speeches
drowned out by shouts of profanities. Their supporters were often
assaulted. Not even the gendarmes were safe from the roving squads
of anti–Semitic thugs.[34]

No acts of violence marred the campaigns in the district of Rum.
Istóczy, confident of his own reelection, had no cause for keeping
abreast with his less self–confident fellow candidates. He repeated his
usual anti–Jewish tirades which even after twelve years did not tire
his constituents. His was a matter–of–fact, almost shallow, victory
even though he beat Baron János Mikos, the Liberal Party candidate
by a comfortable—1728–630—margin. There was much jubilation
among the anti–Semites as the nine–day elections ended on 22 June.
Seventeen anti–Semitic candidates were elected: the National Anti–
Semitic Party, no longer a political nuisance, became a parliamentary
aggregation. The editorials of the anti–Semitic papers gloated over
the "sweeping victory over all parties and world–dominating Jewry"
and relayed congratulatory messages from fraternal organizations in
Austria and Germany greeting "the shining triumph of our allies by
the Danube and the Tisza [rivers] over the domination of Israel and

its hirelings." Istóczy savored the election results as the crowning achievement of his much-abused political career. After a twelve-year climb toward the political summit he had reached a point where he could rest, reflect, and plan the next phase of the arduous journey which he would not have to attempt alone. Or had he reached that point?

Despite the anti-Semitic hullabaloo in Hungary and abroad, the reasons for the celebration were deceptively superficial, and the foundations that were expected to sustain the National Anti-Semitic Party appeared even at first glance surprisingly unstable. The political notoriety and parliamentary gains were noteworthy but only in comparison to their absence in the aftermath of the national elections three years earlier. The unique timeliness of Tiszaeszlár was of immeasurable emotional benefit. Yet, its seemingly menacing permanency was deceptive, for its political fallout was more like a light sprinkle than a heavy downpour. The statistics of the elections provided even more sobering and convincing evidence of the basic flaws in the mechanics of the National Anti-Semitic Party and the performance and effectiveness of its candidates. Notwithstanding Istóczy's almost feverish dream of an anti-Semitic avalanche, the executive committee of the party failed to attract qualified candidates in adequate numbers.

In comparison with a mammoth army of 348 Liberal candidates and the impressive but lesser forces deployed by the opposition parties— the Independence Party was represented in 171 election districts and the Moderate Opposition Party in 125—the number of anti-Semitic candidates was decidedly modest, if not discouraging. The intimidation and physical violence perpetrated by anti-Semitic gangs made better headlines than statistical tabulations. The latter proved the anti-Semites' surprising lack of electoral depth, and dispelled their dream of establishing firm foundations of a popular and enduring movement. Of the slate of fifty-five candidates that the National Anti-Semitic Party had managed to assemble and field, only seventeen managed to win.[35] Less than half, including Istóczy, were elected by a decisive majority.[36] Of the electoral districts won by the anti-Semites only two—Cegléd and Hajdúböszörmény—showed an appreciable measure of support among urban voters. The National Anti-Semitic Party had failed to convince the voters in the large cities, the true seats of political power, that its platform contained the cure for all socioeconomic ills and the promise of a better future. The intensity of emotions that had set the country ablaze apparently created only an illusion of powerful, enduring, nationwide support. The voting results indicated that cooler heads and political realities prevailed in most places.

An even more revealing piece of evidence illustrates a virtually insurmountable obstacle that stood in Istóczy's path to political glory, but he underestimated or chose to ignore it. He had directed a disproportionately heavy propaganda barrage against the Independence Party, insisting that powerful Jews controlled and exploited the party's faction that was unsympathetic to the anti–Semites. The number of defections from the Independence Party to the National Anti–Semitic Party did not justify Istóczy's excessive investment of time and energy. The former lost only thirteen of the eighty–eight seats it had won in the 1881 elections. The losses of the Moderate Opposition Party were even more dramatic: its members occupied only sixty seats in the Diet, twenty–four fewer than three years earlier. The real winners of the 1884 elections were Kálmán Tisza and his Liberal Party.[37] When the new session of the Diet convened, the number of Liberal representatives was 242, seventeen more than in 1881. Thus, both losing parties significantly outnumbered the anti–Semitic candidates, whereas the massive Liberal bloc had a virtual stranglehold on all three opposition parties. Because Istóczy had been dismissed as a minor political irritant, the commanding majority of Liberals, to whom he remained an irritant, condemned his sixteen comrades–in–arms to the same fate.[38]

Chapter XI

The Fleetingness of Fame

"The day has hardly broken when the sun begins to set." This line from a folk song aptly characterizes the brief saga of the National Anti–Semitic Party, according to the Jewish Mór Szatmári, an experienced, astute observer of post–*Ausgleich* politics in Hungary.[1] The fraternal movements abroad were declining, the international echo was waning. "At home that ancient Hungarian malady: flash–on–the–pan enthusiasm followed by lethargy and indifference," lamented Zoltán Bosnyák, the anti–Semitic panegyrist.[2] The two comments reveal a strange meeting of minds positioned at opposite poles of the political spectrum. The telltale signs of twilight were clearly visible even at the dawn of political anti–Semitism in Hungary.

One of the most mysterious lacunae in Istóczy's political career is the three–month interregnum between the end of the elections and September 27, the day the 1884 Diet convened. Neither Istóczy nor the chroniclers of the post–*Ausgleich* era paid attention to the inherent significance of this brief span of time let alone shed light on it. Thus, one can only raise questions or reach retrospective conclusions concerning it. What did Istóczy actually do to prepare himself for the unusual experience of sharing the limelight of political notoriety? Did he attempt to coordinate his views with those of the other elected representatives of the National Anti–Semitic Party? Did he map out a common strategy? Did he undertake a post–election nationwide tour to visit the new constituents of the party and reassure them that their political trust would be well served? Was he in touch with the leaders of anti–Semitic movements abroad, soliciting their counsel in matters of party policy in view of the approaching session of the Diet? None of these questions can be answered with certainty, but it is obvious that whatever course he followed, the results of his activities were arguably unsatisfactory and inconclusive.

The weeks following the opening of the 1884 Diet on September 17 saw Istóczy's dream turn into disappointment and eventually a nightmare. The elected representatives of the National Anti–Semitic Party made a false start, stumbled hard in a premature, albeit predictable, display of ineptitude and disunity, and adopted an irremediably erratic course of action which neither they nor the movement would survive. Istóczy himself treaded uneasily in the spotlight of public fame. From the start, he was strangely dispirited and at the finish, he was utterly exhausted. It was not the journey he had dreamed of for more than a decade.

There simply were no signs to follow, no opportunities to explore. Istóczy watched helplessly as the small band of anti–Semitic neophites marched into the parliamentary arena on political quicksand. A hostile atmosphere immediately engulfed them. The ceremonial opening speech the emperor had sent the Diet contained remarks about the new party and the philosophy it represented. The tone of the emperor's remarks was menacingly denunciatory. The huge bloc of Liberal representatives was poised to translate the imperial initiative into political action. Still, bad tidings could be attributed to neither verbal expressions nor the hostile atmosphere. Istóczy knew the sneering faces, intemperate catcalls and verbal slaps all too well and was accustomed to them. Although he had been consistently unsuccessful in his efforts to legitimize his political views, winning only small measures of sympathy, Istóczy clung tenaciously to his self–described parliamentary niche and relished his self–made image as "Hungary's Cassandra." Suddenly he was becoming a stranger among friends. Instead of emerging as the standard bearer of the party he founded, he let others, less experienced and qualified than he, move to the fore. Ónody and Baron Dr. Gábor Andreánszky, a landowner turned politician, were elected co–chairmen of the party.

The initial division of power soon became the source of a steadily growing factionalism. It deprived Istóczy of his preordained right to the leadership of the party and eventually pushed him to the fringes of organized anti–Semitic activity. The anti–Semitic representatives were unable to present even the facade of a united front let alone issue well–coordinated responses to their first challenge in the Diet. They acted as if they belonged to no party. Each voiced his own view on political anti–Semitism. Andreánszky composed and delivered the official party response to the emperor's message. In addition, Simonyi and Imre Szalay submitted their own versions. Uncharacteristically, Istóczy remained silent in face of the first sign of what soon was to turn into a major deviation from his implacable anti–Semitism and unshakable conviction that Hungary's future well–being hinged on the removal of all Jews. Simonyi preferred enacting new laws to reduce the danger of Jewish domination to expelling the Jews. Others merely joined in the loud reaffirmation of the official program of the party and were content to remain its anonymous footsoldiers. The inability of the leaders of the party to impose strict discipline on the minuscule membership and make the principal theses of political anti–Semitism the sole inspiration of their parliamentary activity caused further disorientation and disunity. Istóczy, an admirer of Ferenc Deák, the architect of the *Ausgleich*, had remained a loyal supporter of Hungary's protected ties of cooperation with Austria, a stance which the majority of the anti–Semitic representatives, all erstwhile members of the Independence Party, found unacceptable. Varying views on how to resolve Hungary's socioeconomic problems and chart its political future opened a dangerous chasm between anti–Semites instead of forging a bond among the politically diverse party members. The chasm would deepen and widen with every self–serving speech and uncoordinated action. Clearly this was not the party Istóczy had dreamed of founding and not the political philosophy he had expounded in his solipsistic position.[3]

It was a strange metamorphosis, unexpected and astonishing. Not even Istóczy's most enduring foes could have wished for a more dramatic and complete eclipse of his political star. The speed and duration of his fall were particularly noteworthy. Not only did Istóczy fail to make a single speech on the floor of the Diet in the early months of the 1884 session—a good showing by the anti–Semitic representatives would have given the new party a measure of hope for making an imprint on Hungarian politics—but he persisted in his self–imposed silence for more than a year. It was a rare display of negligence toward the interests of his constituents. He limited his political activity to editing the *12 Röpirat*, itself a pale replica of the once combative mouthpiece of the anti–Semitic movement. He opened a law office in Budapest, but the lack of energy and enthusiasm he displayed in politics seemed to affect this venture into the private sector. His downcast demeanor and legal inexperience were additional hindrances to efforts he may have made to attract clients. His political past apparently went unnoticed by those in need of legal counsel.[4]

Not even the usually reliable sources of support and encouragement in the international anti–Semitic movement gave Istóczy solace. The factionalism that so severely curtailed his association with the National Anti–Semitic Party haunted Istóczy in his relationship with the architects of the Dresden Congress. He had grown impatient with their fratricidal squabbles and was visibly offended by the scheduling of the second congress (Chemnitz, 27–28 April 1883). He considered it premature. He would have preferred that it commence after the conclusion of the trial of the Tiszaeszlár Jews, thus allowing his nascent National Anti–Semitic Party to derive maximum benefit from favorable domestic and external conditions.[5] That none of his German comrades–in–arms should pay him even a modest measure of attention only added to his deepening disillusionment.[6] He was no less chagrined at the congress for the decline in influence of the proponents of racial anti–Semitism, a school of thought that served as one of the cornerstones of his *Weltanschauung.* A promising interlude cheered him briefly. In an act of defiance, Istóczy turned to the leaders of the French anti–Semitic movement; they responded favorably. However, his plan of organizing a rival anti–Semitic congress in Paris came to naught.[7]

Istóczy's political depression was deep and long lasting. His alienation from the National Anti–Semitic Party seemed complete and irreversible. For the first time for more than a decade, the voice that had delighted a few and outraged many was silent. The Diet, the house that unyieldingly resisted the views he proclaimed in private, had been his political home; sharing it with the allies he had dreamed of acquiring turned into quarrelsome cohabitation. Still, the fighter in Istóczy may have only been wounded, albeit nor mortally. Only his pride and feelings were hurt. The lonely years of bitter political conflict had left him battle–scarred but unvanquished. He would hardly surrender to the pressure and disappointment resulting from intra–party strife. Above and despite all, he was a physically and intellectually vigorous man of forty–two, standing exactly midway in his parliamentary career. He needed only to grant himself a brief respite to recover from the shock of a dream gone sour.

It was an ideologically active and fertile recovery, similar to the setting of a stage for the next act. There was little doubt that he would resume his parliamentary duties, only the circumstances of his return were unclear. Would he stand by his convictions and form yet another faction within the party, or surrender the leadership to others and become a loyal footsoldier? The mainstays of his character as a politician—an unbending, contemptuous disposition toward compromise, a combative defiance of authority and tenacious attitude in pursuing his goals even in the most handicapped and isolated of positions—shadowed the course of his actions. He declined an invitation to join the staff of the *Magyar Újság,* an anti–Semitic daily which some of his parliamentary colleagues had started. He was consoled in knowing that he had made the right decision when it turned out to be a short–lived venture. Instead of accepting the dubious privilege of sharing responsibilities with the inexperienced editorial board of an untested anti–Semitic organ, Istóczy unleashed a scathing attack on what he regarded as the principal weakness of Hungary's Christian society: an all too obvious proclivity for indifference, the chief components of which were "moral cowardice, dispassionateness, shortsightedness, unreasonableness, the virtual absence of readiness to make sacrifices, and despair over the failure to achieve instant success."[8] For any politician, lacking self-confidence and standing at the edge of political oblivion, the uttering of such words would have been an inexcusable act of folly. But Istóczy felt invulnerable even though his dream was shattered. He committed an act of near political sacrilege following the chastising words of his declaration. Acknowledging the inherent impermanence of coalition alignments—the National Anti-Semitic Party, he concluded had ceased to perform useful political functions and had become, in fact, an impediment in the path of the future growth and effectiveness of the anti–Semitic movement— Istóczy announced his decision to leave his anti–Semitic colleagues to their devices. On 10 April 1885 he resigned his membership in the National Anti–Semitic Party.

For the next four months Istóczy seemed to be hovering in the murky waters of political anti–Semitism he had helped stir up. Yet for Istóczy, a master illusionist, who could convince a sympathetic audience—and himself as well—that in politics setbacks and defeats were the appurtenances rather than the antitheses of victory, appearances did not necessarily reflect the true state of affairs. Twelve years of swimming against the current of Hungarian politics had taken its toll on him physically and emotionally. The financial strains of keeping the *12 Röpirat* solvent and covering the expenses of a nascent movement had overwhelmed him at long last. In the May 15 edition of the *12 Röpirat*, Istóczy explained the reasons for his decision to leave the party. The prevailing conditions in the Diet, he concluded, had convinced him that he could wage the struggle against the Jews more effectively from the shelter of his legal practice than by charging the swollen ranks of philosemitic representatives.[9] It sounded like a reasonable, albeit self–serving, explanation. Aside from the fratricadal bickering that prevented them from concentrating on the issues and challenges at hand, the anti–Semitic representatives were systematically excluded from all of the committees of the Diet. They were forced to occupy a political no man's land into which both the Liberals and the Independents fired salvos of derisive remarks at will.[10]

Istóczy should have known better. For a practicing anti–Semite, seeking respite in the legal profession was the least promising of ventures. All things considered, he would have been better off returning to his country estate and pursuing the leisurely life of a gentleman farmer. By the mid–1880s the large number of Jewish lawyers, judges, legal scholars and functionaries in the Ministry of Justice isolated anti–Semitic lawyers with as impenetrable a stone wall as the one faced by the anti–Semitic politicians in the Diet.[11] "For us non-

Egyptians [i.e., non-Jews] the legal profession had ceased to be profitable," Istóczy recalled bitterly. "Most of my clients could not afford to pay."[12] It did not take him long to realize that his attempt to strike roots in the legal profession would do both him and his politics a disservice.

Months of anguish and disappointment came and went. Yet Istóczy's will to persist remained. By August he was already planning to make a political comeback. It was a new declaration of resolve, the reaffirmation of the fighting spirit for which his admirers and constituents had been waiting. He resumed his parliamentary responsibilities, ready to fight implacable foes and renounce ideological camraderie with those members of the National Anti-Semitic Party whose heady inexperience and self-serving, undisciplined conduct had become for him a source of disappointment and annoyance. He wasted no time in dwelling on the ironic interlude that sidetracked him in his tumultuous political quest and made him leave, first and alone, the house he had built. He chose not to return to the political wilderness where he had enjoyed more freedom of action and thought than in the illusive sanctuary of the party.

Instead, he embarked on a surprise mission of mediation and limited reconciliation with the National Anti-Semitic Party, then led by Károly Szalay who had attained a measure of fame as the private attorney of the mother of Eszter Solymosi during the trial of the Tiszaeszlár Jews, but could boast only of modest political achievements. It was a mission for the right reasons but for the wrong objective. In deference to his supporters in the party, Istóczy acted correctly in trying to save at least part of the anti-Semitic substratum in the Diet. His struggle in isolation would benefit neither. He also rightly saw that, barring a radical change in political direction, the National Anti-Semitic Party would ultimately lose its identity and merge with the extreme left wing of the Independence Party at best, or fall victim to internecine feuds at worst. Realizing that the majority of party members, notwithstanding their willingness to engage in anti-Jewish activity, were more committed to Hungary's achieving political independence than to its embracing political anti-Semitism, Istóczy concluded that the protracted acrimony could be resolved only by the creation of another anti-Semitic party. One party would revert to the pre-1883 admixture of Independence-Anti-Semitic politics, whereas the other would retain the unadulterated anti-Semitic stance but not intransigently oppose the post-*Ausgleich* political status quo. A loose coalition in which neither party would be hindered in its actions would be formed. The plan would also end the two most debilitating of Istóczy's political handicaps. He would no longer be the founder of a party without a party, and he would make his new party appear less objectionable in the eyes of many Liberal representatives who harbored anti–Jewish sentiments by putting some distance between himself and the anti–Semitic Independence Party loyalists.

In August 1885 Istóczy and three of his followers in the National Anti–Semitic Party, Pál Csuzy, Ferenc Komlóssy, and Ignác Zimándi, formed the Parliamentary Moderate Anti–Semitic Party. The program of the new party incorporated all of the twelve points of the declaration that nearly two years earlier had signaled the beginning of organized political anti–Semitism in Hungary.[13] Istóczy diluted somewhat the excessively anti–Semitic appeal of the program, thereby making it palatable to representatives with less pronounced political taste. Additional objectives, such as guaranteed state subsidy for retirees, new stock exchange taxes, and an independent Hungarian national bank and customs jurisdiction, were included.[14]

The fatal flaw in Istóczy's calculations was that his goals were based on optimistic, albeit unfounded, expectations rather than a rational assessment of the strength of the new party and its potential for growth. Had 50 to 60 anti–Semitic representatives been elected, as Istóczy had hoped, the split would have left each party with an unimpressive but numerically modest membership. However, a party of seventeen looked more like a faction; a party of four must surely have been regarded as a mere fragment. "With that the rupture became permanent at the immeasurable expense of the cause of political anti–Semitism," lamented Zoltán Bosnyák, Istóczy's panegyrist. "The two small party groups would never attain political weight and significance."[15]

Still, there were occasional flickers of a confidence–boosting promise. Verhovay's legal troubles were resolved, allowing him to resume his parliamentary responsibilities. He subsequently was elected to lead the Independence–Anti–Semitic Party. Although a gifted orator, his brief stay in the Diet was quiet and uneventful. Emil Szemnecz, perhaps the crudest and least self–disciplined of anti–Semitic activists, surprisingly won a by–election in the town of Zalaegerszeg. With his election, the number of anti–Semitic representatives in the Diet rose to eighteen of whom only five are remembered for their contributions, exceptions to the otherwise dismal performance of the members of either party.[16]

For Istóczy the path to recovery was slow but steady. The effects of the traumatic experiences of the previous months were noticeable. His first speech in the Diet since becoming a founding member of the new anti–Semitic party—and his first in nearly two years—was a clear indication of how far removed he was from his erstwhile combative self and how short his address fell of the abusive diatribes his audiences had been taught to expect. On October 1 Istóczy interpellated Prime Minister Tisza, in his capacity as minister of interior, and Minister of Justice Tivadar Pauler concerning the procedure of granting liquor licenses. It was a unique opportunity which the Istóczy of old would have turned into a major anti–government offensive, evoking at least once a warning from an anguished president of the Diet. The issue of the granting of liquor licenses was one of the most forcefully enunciated points of the National Anti–Semitic Party's program. The people of the countryside considered this practice the most odious form of Jewish exploitation. Jewish innkeepers frequently advanced loans with interest, the repayment of which often came to be resented by many a financially hard–pressed recipient. Yet except for one intemperate outburst, which Tamás Péchy, the customarily alert and quickly retaliatory president of the Diet, did not even regard as meriting a warning, Istóczy's interpellation was a dispirited, feeble bark in comparison with the defiant roar of his past speeches:

> The Christian innkeepers cannot compete with the Jewish innkeepers, because the latter, as national experience demonstrates, not only make greater profit by serving diluted, even poisoned drinks to their Christian patrons but also view their establishments as merely the comptoir of their usurious financial operations where they prey on the stupefied and demoralized village people. Transferring the liquor licenses into the jurisdiction of the villages with due haste is therefore in the public interest.

His statement petered out in an almost politely worded three–point inquiry to Tisza, as both prime minister and minister of the interior, as to whether the latter would take the matter under advisement, whether the suggestion would be acted on in the near future, and whether only partial remedy might be found until the entire reform plan was implemented.[17]

It took Prime Minister Tisza more than three months to respond to Istóczy's interpellation. Predictably, he dismissed Istóczy's argument but acknowledged the need to reform the procedure of granting liquor licenses. Meekly, Istóczy acquiesced in Tisza's reply and expressed his hope for the passage of a corresponding bill in the not too distant future.[18]

The pre–election year of 1886 witnessed a rare demonstration of parliamentary cooperation among the disparate members of the two anti–Semitic parties. With an eye on the constituents and prospective supporters, together they targeted the Stock Exchange, which the anti–Semites viewed as a stronghold of Hungary's moneyed Jewry. On April 3, the text of a lengthy and detailed motion was read out in its entirety. Signed by Istóczy and all of the seventeen anti–Semitic representatives, it reflected the considerable care and financial expertise of its authors and was—astonishingly—completely devoid of outright anti–Jewish statements. The crux of the motion was the determination of the amount of taxes to be levied on all forms of investment and stock market activity, ostensibly for the purpose of providing Hungary's hard–pressed financial administration a much–needed source of revenue. Only by implication was the motion a well–coordinated attack on the wealth of the "stock–exchange Jews."

The ensuing speech, justifying the rationale of the motion, was delivered by Istóczy with a tone and substance that gave ample evidence of his successful emotional recovery. It was a vintage performance of the days of old, the renaissance of his political vigor, determination and commitment. Istóczy transformed the precise language and legalistic style of the motion into a brutal weapon of near–profane accusations and denunciations with which he punctuated his argument. Istóczy sneered:

> The ever–increasing flood of stocks has created and nurtured in society a mostly Jewish parasitic class, which neither ploughs nor sows, yet harvests most efficiently and whose "productive" work in industry consists, at best, of periodically clipping off the interest and dividend slips, cashing them, and constant wheeling–dealing in stocks.

Anyone engaged in any kind of work—peasant, landowner, craftsman or merchant—"toils and sweats in the service of that parasitic class whose interests are protected by the press and all manifestations of the governing and legislative powers." The goal, as Istóczy saw it, was clearly defined. "We must make sure that we paralyze the Jews' virtually unlimited control of capital and terminate their dictatorship." The achievement of that goal, Istóczy observed, would require fighting to the end.

> The Stock Exchange is the strongest fortress of the Jewish plutocracy. It is on this battleground that the Jewish divisions daily kill or grievously wound hundreds, even thousands, of jobs held by non–Jews.

The introduction in 1881 of a tax law in Germany, Istóczy declared, was the right step in the right direction. Hungary's deficit–ridden economy should do well by following the German initiative.

Istóczy's resurgent combative spirit was matched by the swift counterthrusts of the Tisza government determined to meet the anti–Semitic challenge head on. Minister of Finance Count Gyula Szapáry, one of the most experienced and versatile members of the cabinet curtly dismissed Istóczy's speech.[19] "The anti–Semitic tenets that the sponsors of the motion profess are in direct conflict with all of the ideals on which the Hungarian Constitution rests," Szapáry noted. He described the anti–Semites' motion as an incomplete summary of the German stock exchange law, devoid of the latter's mitigating and exclusionary features. The revenues derived from the implementation of the German stock exchange tax bill, Szapáry said in conclusion, were negligible. Still, he advised that a parliamentary committee study the motion. "We anti–Semites do not regard it as necessary to cover ourselves with some tattered fig leaf of philosemitic phrases," shot back a defiant Istóczy, provoking a ripple of laughter.

> We anti–Semites are in the habit of calling a child by his name and the reason we stress the importance of the anti–Semitic justification of the motion is because the Stock Exchange and the Jew are indivisible entities.

Suddenly and unavoidably the verbal duel between Istóczy and Szapáry was interrupted by Diet President Tamás Péchy who had become a virtually inseparable appendage to Istóczy's parliamentary career. Péchy noted Istóczy's thinly disguised attempt to use the stock exchange tax motion as a subterfuge to spread his hateful anti–Jewish message. He denied the inherent interdependence of the Stock Exchange and the Jews, citing as an example the United States where no connection existed between the two and questioned the propriety of bringing before the Diet a nonexistent matter camouflaged as substance.

Istóczy had no intention of fighting on two fronts. He sidestepped a possibly costly confrontation with Péchy. He welcomed Szapáry's recommendation but not without one last slap. "More can hardly be expected from the finance minister of a state suffering from a chronic deficit," he declared sarcastically.[20]

Through the rest of 1886 Istóczy chased the illusive "stock–exchange Jew." His chances of capturing his prey in the Liberal-controlled Diet were minuscule. Still he persisted, oblivious to the hopelessness of his cause. At long last, Istóczy was given an opportunity to contest the reports of the economic and financial committees which had recommended that his motion be dropped from the agenda of the Diet. On December 4, he made one last desperate attempt to rescue it from certain demise. He defended his calculations of the feasibility and profitability of the stock–exchange tax, noting that only numerous acts of embezzlement and defalcation prevented the German government from realizing the revenues it had hoped to collect from a similar tax program. He expressed doubt that Jewish wholesale wheat merchants would turn their backs on Hungary—a not entirely undesirable eventuality—if such a tax was to be introduced, and he denounced both committees for harboring excessive sympathy toward the "stock–exchange Jews." The speech attracted neither the attention nor the expressions of encouragement that would have convinced him that he had a more secure footing in the Diet than six months earlier or that he was addressing an interested and supportive audience. His chances of pushing the motion through the multiplicity of parliamentary obstacles had grown even more remote. Of the 447 representatives, only 30 supported its passage against an opposition block of 103. Indicating the degree of importance they gave to the motion—or perhaps its defeat was a foregone conclusion—314 representatives did not even bother to show up to vote.[21]

Istóczy's last attempt in 1886 to lead a desperate charge against the financial stronghold of Hungarian Jewry was ill-timed, badly coordinated and ended in a fiasco. The same day that the Liberals' almost casual power play smothered the anti–Semites' tax plan, Istóczy chose to make yet another motion designed to dismantle one of the major, self–governing institutions of the "parasitic Jews' haven": the special courts of the Stock Exchange and the provincial produce and grain exchanges. Seemingly unperturbed by his marked decrease of supporters—in contrast to the eighteen signatories of the stock exchange tax motion, the official text of the special–courts motion had only eleven sponsors—Istóczy bravely scaled the forbidding walls. He described the special courts as being irreconcilable with the existing legal institutions of the nation, calling attention to an 1870 legislative decision that had created them with only temporary jurisdiction. He seemed particularly incensed that the Jews in Hungary had risen to such commanding financial heights in the brief span of time since the Emancipation of 1867. "The special courts consist exclusively of Jews!" Istóczy exclaimed indignantly.

> What kind of elected court is that before which Hungarian–Christian litigants have to choose from Messrs. Pinkeles, Kohn and Levy or Messrs. Rubinstein Galitzenstein, and Karfunkelstein or Messrs. Goldberger, Silberberger and Horebberger or some other Messrs. Erger–Berger to be the judges in their cases?

Such a court, Istóczy reasoned, was none other than the Jewish Sanhedrin. "My motion," Istóczy said in conclusion, "is aimed at termi-

nating the anomaly of the arbitrary verdicts of the Jerusalem Sanhedrin which Christian Hungarians may not appeal and which the
regular courts are forced to put into effect."

Istóczy's venture into the realm of Hungary's legal system was
quickly and effectively rebuffed by a short–tempered Minister of Justice Teofil Fabinyi. With more than three decades of experience as
a judge, including five years on the High Court of Justice, Fabinyi
was clearly unimpressed by Istóczy's demonstration of competence
in judicial matters. As one of the stalwarts of the Liberal Party, he
saw the anti–Semitic leader as easy prey. Fabinyi offered a point-
by–point rebuttal to Istóczy's speech, declaring that the jurisdiction
of the special courts had been carefully defined and their activities
regularly monitored. Fabinyi said sternly:

> These attacks [Istóczy's] on the permanency of our legal in-
> stitutions are attempts to weaken their foundations. They
> will, in my view, cause grievous harm to our economic and
> commercial relations. For that reason I advise the House to
> refrain from putting the motion to a debate.

To Istóczy the vote brought little satisfaction. Although the
number of supporters rose slightly to 36, giving him cause for a brief
cheer, the Liberal–led voting machine of 114 proved to be an insurmountable obstacle. The most noteworthy aspect of the two–part
episode was the astonishing apathy evoked by the anti–Semites' parliamentary struggle. Of the 447 elected representatives, 232 again
found excuses to absent themselves from the proceedings.[22]

The three years that comprised the 1884 session of the Diet left
Istóczy with few pleasant memories to cherish. There were no moments of victory to savor, no promising results to anticipate. Except
for the surprising, albeit negligible, support the two anti–Semitic
motions received—the first received thirteen and the second eighteen votes from officially non–anti–Semitic representatives—the list of
achievements compiled by the two anti–Semitic parties was dismally
short. It was, however, not for the want of trying. The anti–Semitic
representatives made speeches, but they were few and far between.
Frequently lacking in true substance beyond the mechanical recita-
tion of anti–Jewish phrases, the speeches consistently failed to reach
what then was regarded as the lowest acceptable degree of oratorical style and sophistication. Intraparty strife, the massive size and
flawless operation of the Tisza–led Liberal political machine, and the
smaller but more militant Independence Party produced permanent
handicaps. "The group of seventeen representatives occupying such
an exposed position could not resist the attacks of ever increasing

strength coming from all directions," Istóczy recalled bitterly. "Many a dispirited party member found it impossible to engage in productive activity."[23]

The chances of recruiting new converts were minimal. Istóczy could hardly bring himself to attribute that lack of interest to the natural revulsion which men of common decency and political wisdom feel for the hate–filled tenets of political anti–Semitism. Istóczy concluded:

> One of the principal causes of the animosity displayed against us was the fact that virtually the whole of Jewry, fearing anti–Semitism, stood behind the government. There was no chance of the anti–Semitic propaganda developing in the midst of the Liberal Party which leaned so heavily on its Jewish constituency.[24]

Yet neither the inherently resilient and optimistic Istóczy nor the other leaders of the anti–Semitic parties allowed the unequal distribution of parliamentary strength to adversely affect their vision of future political rewards.

Standing at the threshold of a new election year, the anti–Semitic candidates seemed to detect flickering signals of public encouragement in their provincial stamping grounds which they began traversing with increasing frequency and unebbing zeal. They made many speeches that were little more than variations on the familiar, fear–provoking themes ending in tiresome refrains: unless the people elected them into the Diet, within a few years the land of the Hungarians would become the land of the Jews and the children and grandchildren of the Hungarians would be the servants and eventually the slaves of the Jews.[25]

Only illusions supported the anti–Semites' expectations of an improved showing at the polls. The lingering legacy of Tiszaeszlár proved to be less accommodating than its tumultuous aftermath; it had gradually receded into the realm of anti–Jewish phobias and could not be resurrected as a burning and exploitable election issue. The repeated spectacles of infighting between the two anti–Semitic parties and the lackluster performances of their members in the Diet had generated little public approval and interest. The Tisza–led Liberal Party had yielded no ground to the anti–Semites; none of its members were persuaded to defect. The Independents, even without Eötvös and Helfy, two of the most eloquent and bitter foes of the anti–Semites, had held their own. The usefulness of the provincial lower Catholic clergy, once a steady source of support, had diminished. A pastoral letter, made public by Lajos Cardinal Haynald of Kalocsa in 1885, called for the spread of the doctrine of brotherly love and the containment of the destructive spirit of anti–Semitism. It had a sobering effect on many Catholic voters.[26]

The anti–Semites campaigned in sixty election districts, ignoring the danger signals. The plans for fielding twice as many candidates as in 1883 had to be abandoned due to the lack of qualified political hopefuls. Istóczy sighed in exasperation:

> Hungarian intelligentsia! Whatever became of you? You, if not your children, deserve to become the bootblacks of Jews who are sitting in your ancestral domains, and to go bankrupt, financially and morally.[27]

The results of the elections dealt the anti–Semites a crushing blow. Only eleven of the eighteen representatives the two anti–Semitic parties had fielded won re–election. Of the stalwarts only Istóczy, Ónody, and Vadnay were returned to the Diet. Verhovay and Szemnecz, the most controversial and litigation–ridden anti–Semitic pundits, lost their constituents' support. There was growing apprehension over the much–diminished parliamentary base as the full scope of the anti–Semites' defeat was revealed. Not only did whatever political weight their small number had managed to sustain dissipate, the election results gave the anti–Semites' principal foes even broader and firmer mandates. The Liberals increased their commanding influence in the Diet, adding 19 to their total of 242 in 1884, whereas the Independence Party seated 81 representatives, a gain of six.[28] Still, few politicians could entirely dismiss the disquieting implication of the post–election statistics. Nationwide, thirty thousand voters cast their ballots for the eleven anti–Semitic representatives who won elections.[29]

Next to the party's dramatic loss of political support and its corresponding diminution in parliamentary presence, it was Istóczy's belated realization that the Liberals had regarded the anti–Semites as more dangerous foes than the larger and politically less compatible Independence Party that caused him the most anguish. Somewhat illogically Istóczy convinced himself that because he had avoided expulsion from the party after making his first anti–Semitic speech in the Diet on 8 April 1875, the Liberals had looked upon his activities with benign complacence. He also reasoned that his relationship to the party remained unaffected by his decision to leave its ranks eight years later. He was especially dismayed by Tisza's decision to push through the Diet, before the 1887 elections, a motion that muzzled the anti–Semites and effectively restrained their participation in legislative debates. Istóczy responded by putting the Prime Minister on notice that the anti–Semites would, in retaliation, adopt the tactics of strikers, keeping themselves aloof from the parliamentary proceedings and assuming positions of defiant passivity. No evidence in the annals of contemporary Hungarian politics can be found to support the contention that Istóczy's decision to boycott the Diet elicited expressions of concern, let alone regret.

Not even a surprising change of names caused a respectable modicum of acknowledgement in the Diet. For reasons known only to its eleven members and without altering its philosophical outlook or political stance, the recognizable National Anti–Semitic Party became the indistinct Hungarian People's Party. The anti–Semites broke their self–imposed code of silence only in rare exceptions.[30] For the first time in nearly twelve years the prophets of doom, to almost everyone's relief, were uncommunicative.

The principal and sole victims of this curious political strategy were the anti–Semites themselves. Neither they nor the party they represented managed to regain their lost status or initiate any meaningful legislative action. Traditionally, the anti–Semitic views in the Diet were presented by noisy and undisciplined interlocutors. The anti–Semites' policy of advancing the cause of political anti–Semitism through passivity and silence was counterproductive in the extreme.

For nearly three years, an extraordinarily long lacuna in the career of an active politician, Istóczy kept his silence. In his later writings he chose to shed no light on his frame of mind during this period. The much–diminished anti–Semitic contingent under his command was headed toward oblivion. Their political disengagement only hastened the process.[31] By an ironic and unexpected twist of events, however, the man who was "the most stubborn and determined foe of Hungarian anti–Semitism"[32] unwittingly gave Istóczy and his coterie a reprieve.

The fifteen–year tour of duty of the "General," as Prime Minister Tisza was often called because of his unwavering insistence that the Liberal Party observe an almost military discipline, was drawing to a bitterly contested close. His alliance with the increasingly powerful leaders of the industrial bourgeoisie and the charges against him of improprieties in government conduct—Tisza was accused of giving his hand–picked "Mamluks" the most important posts—enraged the pro–agrarian critics in the Liberal Party. Their mounting opposition to Tisza strengthened the Moderate Opposition Party whose leader, Count Albert Apponyi (1846–1933), one of the most notable and durable figures of his time, had been the Prime Minister's severest detractor. The last offensive against the beleaguered Tisza came in the course of a prolonged and unusually acrimonious debate over two government–sponsored motions. One called for removing from the jurisdiction of the Diet the procedure for determining the annual conscription figures in Hungary. The other motion required that reserve military officers be proficient in the German language. Both motions passed, partly out of deference to a grieving Francis Joseph— his son and heir, Rudolf, had committed suicide shortly before—and partly because they had been modified somewhat. Still Tisza's reputation and credibility were tainted beyond repair. Only quick police action extracated him and some Liberal representatives from a crowd of aroused street demonstrators. He was a fallen man, and the Austrian government, viewing him as a political liability, made no effort to save the "most hated man" in Hungary. On 9 March 1890, Tisza resigned, ending an epoch of relative calm and stability.[33]

The new government, led by Count Gyula Szapáry with whom Istóczy had had at least one confrontation, avowed priorities that did not include Tisza's unbending opposition to anti–Semitism. The approaching demise of political anti–Semitism received little attention from Szaáry or the rest of the cabinet which included such luminaries as Minister of Public Transportation—and subsequently Commerce— Gábor Baross; Minister of Religious and Public Instruction Count Albin Csáky; Sándor Wekerle, the most influential financial expert of the Age of Dualism who headed the Ministry of Finance; and Dezső Szilágyi, the tireless minister of justice who initiated numerous reforms in civil and criminal law and began charting a course of fast–paced industrial and social development that would later ensure Hungary's untroubled entry into the twentieth century. It was from behind the protective curtain of oblivion that Istóczy made a sudden move to extricate himself from the political no man's land and salvage his cause. He fell short of reviving the National Anti–Semitic Party, achieving only modest results. Communication among former party members was reestablished, an agreement on broad ideological issues was reached, and a pre–election strategy was worked out.

On 19 March 1890, ten days after Kálmán Tisza's resignation, Istóczy spoke on the floor of the Diet. The bill which Istóczy chose to address related to the development of domestic industry. He was on familiar ground and demonstrated that his three–year, self–imposed silence had not adversely affected his determination to preside over the "final solution of the Jewish Question." To Istóczy, Hungary's incipient factory system, which he regarded as the principal beneficiary of the bill, was the third stronghold of the unscrupulous and exploitative wealthy Jews. He moved against it with the same determination and vigor he had displayed in attacking the other two areas of Jewish privilege and profit: the sale of alcoholic beverages in the countryside and the Stock Exchange. He criticized the bill's privileging of heavy industry at the expense of agrarian mechanization and small industry, the ever–diminishing and neglected areas of refuge accessible to non–Jewish toil and enterprise.

> This one–sided economic policy will have fatal effects, resulting in the destruction of the class of principally Christian–Hungarian small craftsmen and artisans. They will be degraded to hapless industrial workers at the mercy of Jewish factory owners who will grow richer and richer by securing loans from their coreligionists in banking and receiving government support. These small craftsmen and artisans, along with the small landowners who constitute the bulk of the nation, and the patriotic bourgeoisie of our towns, who, for reasons of state and national interest, must not be thrown prey to the Jewish factory owners from Galicia, Moravia or God knows where.

The socioeconomic well–being of the nation, Istóczy declared, depends on the termination of the Liberal–Jewish economic policy which clashed with the traditional Hungarian approach to agrarian and industrial production. Istóczy concluded:

> When I speak as an anti–Semite, I reserve the right, as do the proponents of the anti–German or anti–Slav policy in this House or in the press, to emphasize and declare the legitimacy of the anti–Semitic school of political thought.[34]

Istóczy's abandonment of his policy of disengagement in the Diet proceedings was a clear signal that political anti–Semitism had not entirely lost its capacity to stage yet another comeback. Would Istóczy, its only true standard bearer, be able to seize the momentum and breathe life into the fading movement? Tisza's departure and the vision of expanding the constituency of thirty thousand voters who had supported the cause of political anti–Semitism in the 1887 elections were sufficiently strong incentives for a renewed drive. By maintaining visibility through consistent attendance of the sessions of the Diet and delivering inflammatory speeches on controversial matters in which he excelled, Istóczy utilized the most effective tactics for keeping the anti–Semitic program within striking distance of the mainstream of Hungarian politics. The possibility of an anti–Semitic renaissance born of personal leadership was promising. Istóczy seemed ready to again throw himself into the whirlpool of parliamentary debates.

In many a group effort, ultimate success hinges on the performance of a key individual. A missed opportunity or one acted upon in a crucial moment could lead to decisive short or long–range results.

In many ways, the spring of 1890 presented such an opportunity to Istóczy. His actions present one of the most baffling riddles of his checkered political career and seemingly defy all efforts to unearth a reasonable explanation. His brief speech on March 19 marked the resurgence of anti–Semitism. The speech had fallen short of Istóczy's pre–1887 vintage in substance and style, particularly the anti–Jewish imagery constructed from a virtually inexhaustible reservoir of pejorative phrases. It sounded much like a clarion calling the troops to prepare for battle. The order to commence fighting, however, was not issued.

On 28 May Istóczy rose to speak in defense of a twelve–point motion he had made the day before. The topic, the regulation of the sale of movable property for payment by installments, meshed smoothly with his long–time interest in economy and finance, the bastions of Jewish power and influence. Instead of the anticipated torrent of wildly accusatory statements about the multiplicity of Jewish abuses, which President of the Diet Tamás Péchy would have attempted to stem with his curt but eloquently worded warnings, Istóczy's speech was built on a pedantic, disciplined enumeration of innocuous explanations which could have been made by any one of the more than four hundred representatives in the Diet. Aside from observing that "the exploitative practices of greedy businessmen and their agents have destroyed, or at least weakened, the livelihood of countless people," the veteran coiner of some of the most elaborately worded and abusive phrases in the vocabulary of anti–Semitism spoke like a politician stricken with a sudden attack of amnesia. The search for clues to explain this unique transformation in character is complicated by Istóczy's proclivity for consistency. During the next five months there was ample opportunity for a change of heart. Yet on October 30, when Istóczy resumed his explanation of the feasibility and timeliness of his motion, he continued speaking in the same disciplined manner and moderate tone. He even found an unexpectedly sympathetic ally in Minister of Commerce Gábor Baross who endorsed the spirit of the motion and called on the government to present the Diet with a practical solution of the problem.[35] Neither Istóczy nor any of his comrades–in–arms ever offered posterity the slightest hint of how the substance and delivery of these speeches were supposed to advance the cause of political anti–Semitism.

Istóczy's last recorded speeches in the Diet charted the evolution of a new approach to—or departure from—the anti–Semitic conception of a Christian Hungary freed from its Jewish shackles. The purpose and rationale of the new approach, barring the discovery of relevant sources of information, remain unfathomable secrets. There are, however, a number of plausible, albeit incomplete, answers. Causes attributed to matters of a personal nature may be discounted. Nearing his fiftieth year, Istóczy appeared to be in full control of his faculties. No trace of any physical disability or mental disorder was detectable. If anything, there was a noticeable improvement, a theretofore unknown and untapped reservoir of confidence and versatility, that enabled Istóczy to skillfully navigate his political vessel built to battle the elements of controversy. His dramatic disengagement from the mechanical and indiscriminate application of anti–Semitic illogic and profanity in his speeches reflected the reluctant yet unmistakable realization by a twenty–year veteran of parliamentary infighting of the need to come to grips with the political reality that enveloped and smothered his cause. The most important causes of national concern in fin–de–siècle Hungary did not provoke anti–Semitic initiative or involvement.

The ambitious and in many ways productive program of the Szapáry government—it could boast of such impressive achievements as revolutionary improvements in public transportation, the balancing of the national budget, the adoption of the gold standard, the easing of working conditions by the designation of Sunday as a day of rest and the introduction of health insurance, and the long–awaited legislative triumph which recognized Judaism as a legally accepted religion—made the anti–Semites' political platform look antiquated and hollow. The sudden and unexpected rise in popularity of the Apponyi–led Moderate Opposition, which under the new name of the National Party accentuated the Hungarian national spirit and stressed the theoretical equality of Austria and Hungary within the structural confines of the Dual Monarchy, weakened the secessionist group which harbored a number of anti–Semitic representatives. The sweeping changes envisioned by the reform–minded, urbane Sándor Wekerle, who in November 1892 became prime minister, diverted attention from the real and imagined ills of Hungarian society for which the anti–Semites claimed to possess the cure–all, and revealed the national well–being and confidence in the jubilant expectation of the 1896 celebration of the millennium of the Magyar state. Not even the growth of socialism in the early 1890s, which touched off turbulent demonstrations by industrial workers and agricultural laborers who had been receptive to the anti–Semites' denunciation of Jewish exploiters, opened new avenues of promise to Istóczy's renascent drive to revitalize the old ties of camaraderie and form new ones.

However, the greatest obstacle to the growth of political anti–Semitism remained Lajor Kossuth, in both life and death. The emotional fealty which the majority of Hungarians had sworn to their revolutionary hero did not diminish with the passage of time. His repeated words of warning reduced the anti–Semites' prospects in the 1884 elections and helped keep their political philosophy on a collision course with his convictions, thus creating an emotional tug–of–war in many an anti–Semitic voter. Still, the exiled Kossuth, however intertwined with the heartbeat of the Fatherland, was more an idealized example than a daily reminder of everyday politics. However, the very mention of his name could evoke powerful surges of support and sympathy. Istóczy's decision to rescue his movement from the parliamentary oblivion to which it had been condemned by his self–imposed passive resistance happened to coincide with the beginning of a five–year upsurge of Kossuth mania. Shortly before he resigned as prime minister, Kálmán Tisza caused a sensation by making an uncharacteristic gesture of solidarity with the Hungarian people's deep emotional attachment to Kossuth. The turbulent circumstances of his resignation, which transformed him into one of the most hated individuals in the country, was not the kind of legacy the man who controlled virtually all aspects of political life for fifteen years would have wished to leave. For him Kossuth was the return ticket back to the good graces of the people. Tisza chose to commit a well–prepared and self–serving political faux pas by attempting to modify a law passed in 1879 that required, under the penalty of forfeiture, every Hungarian living abroad to renew his citizenship at an Austro–Hungarian consulate. Kossuth, that quintessential Hungarian, was nearing the ominous deadline which he had no intention of meeting. Emperor Francis Joseph rejected Tisza's proposal. Tisza's political fate was thus sealed but not before it was linked with Kossuth's loss of citizenship. It was a stunned nation that started an anguished vigil and awaited a change of the imperial heart. It was a futile wait. Less than two weeks later Kossuth's body, defiantly draped in black, was returned to a grieving nation.[36]

The national preoccupation with Kossuth and Kossuth's implacable animosity toward anti–Semitism kept Istóczy in a political limbo from which he was unable to extricate himself. It also diffused his movement, making its hate–filled messages sound irrelevant and unpatriotic. Istóczy's last recorded speeches in the Diet—all of them delivered before the 1892 elections—amply document his irremediable predicament. On 5 November 1890, he made a motion with detailed justification and recommendations calling for the implementation of the homestead exemption. It was arguably the longest and most detailed and documented initiative—and possibly the most constructive—of his entire political career.[37] Istóczy had made an extensive study of the homestead–exemption administration of the

United States, in his words "a most liberal and democratic institution," and the *Heimstätten-Gesetzes,* its German counterpart.[38] In a lengthy speech on 25 April 1891 he urged the adoption of the homestead exemption in Hungary.[39]

Istóczy's remarkable self–restraint—an almost complete turnabout from his usual political direction—held firm. On 23 June he spoke in favor of the modernization and expansion of the Hungarian railway network. He made one self–serving remark, citing the need to remedy the lamentable conditions of public transportation in his native Vas County.[40] His last parliamentary contribution on record (9 December 1891) was a swan song of sorts. His presence, like the ghost of a bygone age, would linger on for another five years. The speech charted a course of socioeconomic policy he felt Hungary would follow into an uncertain future. It was a rambling discourse, filled with pessimistic observations and prophecies of doom and running counter to the prevailing buoyant hope with which most speakers greeted the topic of the discussion: the plans for the national exhibit to be held in the millennial year of 1896. Istóczy lamented the increased cost of running the government, the oppressively high taxes, and the growing number of emigrants to the United States. "No cure to any of these ills is in sight!" he exclaimed dejectedly.

Toward the end of the speech there was a sudden relapse into what years earlier had been a bitter denunciation of the Jews' exploitive machinations and a defiant call to resistance. The government, he advised, should put an end to the entry of masses of harmful elements from Russia and Galicia and promote the growth of a healthy agriculture. Istóczy observed almost perfunctorily:

> If need be obstacles will have to be raised to the mass influx of Jews from Russia and their settlement here in order to prevent these people, wanted by no country on earth—even by England and Turkey—from choosing Hungary as their new home and pushing the lareadyhard–pressed native population from its living space. Only he who has declared war on common sense will object.

In conclusion, he called on his fellow representatives to resign from their respective parties and run for reelection as independents on the platform of socioeconomic changes he had envisioned.[41]

Few politicians have been as ill–served by the views they expounded as Istóczy. Most of his speeches and writings, the objects of substantial mockery, were tiresomely narrow, consistently profane, and largely unsubstantiated. They condemned him, save for the notoriety he acquired, to the ranks of the second–rate. The cloak of anti–Semitism in which he wrapped himself was both a means to gain public attention and an impediment to personal growth. From his last speeches in the Diet a theretofore unknown and unappreciated Istóczy emerged, sporting a new image he had so successfully concealed. Stepping out of character and temporarily abandoning hate–filled refrains, Istóczy's attempt to practice the politician's craft yielded surprising, positive results. His speeches were delivered with the discipline and confidence of a man who had worked hard at gathering data and marshaling them into a cohesive and credible argument. His observations sounded accurate and his conclusions reasonable. Only in the light of these speeches would the otherwise inexplicable statementsmade by the Jewish Mór Szatmári, the reliable Istóczy–watcher and knowledgeable political editorialist of the *Egyetértés*, the mouthpiece of the Independence Party, acquire the ring of credibility. Szatmári recalled:

> Győző Istóczy, the leader of the anti–Semites, towered like a mast above them. He was perhaps the only one among them guided by sincere conviction; he was a truly correct and honorable man.[42]

Still, no explanation can be offered for the devoted and uncritical support which the constituents of the election district of Rum had given their anti–Semitic representative in the Diet. Istóczy's unpredictable political moods, his oscillation between stubbornly persistent discursive outbursts and extended periods of sullen silence, appeared to elicit not the slightest demonstration of bewilderment or displeasure from his supporters. Neither the declining fortunes of political anti–Semitism nor the demise of the National Anti–Semitic Party caused them to waiver in their allegiance or loosen their personal bonds of attachment to the man who lost his ideological raison d'être. In 1892, they reelected him and he returned to the political wilderness from which he had risen.

The last four years of Istóczy's parliamentary career were as apolitical as they were silent. Aside from occasional cryptic remarks in his memoirs about the destruction of the National Anti–Semitic Party, Istóczy left no clues as to why he chose to reduce his role in parliamentary politics to that of a spectator or what he hoped to accomplish by doing so. Recurring references to his frame of mind, however, allow the disparate pieces of a mosaic to fall into place. The political wilderness that had been his stamping ground before 1883 had become a constant reminder of a failed dream. The results of the 1887 and 1892 elections, following the surprisingly rapid disintegration of the National Anti–Semitic Party, devastated Istóczy. The ever–tightening web of opposition maneuvers rendered him and his steadily diminishing comrades–in–arms inactive if not purposeless. Against such an unyielding backdrop a final lesson had to be learned. The political system of fin–de–siècle Hungary was ready neither to tolerate the existence, let alone the growth, of organized political anti–Semitism nor take its prophets of doom seriously.[43]

The end came in the form of a platitudinous announcement: a quarter–century of public service abandoned in self–pity and for self–serving reasons. In the autumn of 1896, on the threshold of national elections, Istóczy informed his constituents of his decision to withdraw from parliamentary politics. He acknowledged the unswerving loyalty of his supporters that had assured his victory in seven consecutive elections and enabled him to extricate himself from the legal entanglements which haunted the early years of his political career. The prevailing conditions underscored the wisdom of his decision. Baron Dezső Bánffy, a Transylvanian nobleman who on 14 January 1895 succeeded Wekerle as prime minister, was a heavy–handed executor of the emperor's orders, an unyielding protector of social and political tranquility, and uncompromising champion of the theory that Hungary's eventual succession to a central European power depended on its increasing the strength and influence of Magyardom at the expense of other nationalities. He cracked down on his critics hard, calling them unpatriotic, and was determined to reduce and eventually root out all forms of opposition, a prospect not altogether lacking in interest to Istóczy in a preelection year.

Bánffy's efforts were aided by the emerging nationalistic and religious fervor. Even opposition politicians muted their voices in deference to "Treuga Dei" (God's Peace), the leitmotiv of the millennial year. The anti–Semites took refuge in two parliamentary shelters of slightly promising possibilities. After doing poorly in the previous two elections, the Independence Party, to which most of the anti–Semitic representatives belonged at one time or another, was reorganized and gathered strength. Ferenc Kossuth, the eldest son of the great revolutionary hero, who after accompanying his father's body to the solemn funeral subsequently settled in Budapest, entered politics and took over the leadership of the party. The Kossuth name worked magic, albeit for a short time. The younger Kossuth soon showed his true political colors: he became a staunch defender of the dualist system and eventually accepted the post of minister of commerce. In 1896, the Catholic People's Party came into being. Led by Nándor Zichy, a prominent economist–politician, the party's program of "defending religion" by seeking to abrogate laws which had diminished the influence and jurisdiction of the Church found quick and growing support among the conservative aristocracy and the clergy.[44] Unlike his surviving anti–Semitic colleagues, Istóczy showed no interest in considering the possibility that his declining political fortunes could be linked with either party.

The reasons Istóczy gave for his decision sounded petty coming from a man who was accustomed to earning a modest livelihood, and initiating and receiving some of the most unrestrained and pejorative remarks in the annals of modern Hungarian politics.

> Having covered the constitutional expenses of seven elections . . . and in deference to my loved ones, I resigned from active politics. I believed that silence would bring me and my shunned loved ones tranquility.[45]

His political rationale sounded no more convincing:

> Having gradually withdrawn [from active participation] I finally pulled out of parliamentary politics at the end of the millennial year. I concluded that after bearing the expenses of seven elections I would not run for an eighth time. In view of the changed conditions in the House my continued membership had no meaning and purpose anyway. So I told myself, "All right, I'm going; let the flood come in my wake""[46]

For a man who had made a thriving career of the vicissitudes of his protracted stay in the political wilderness, the sudden display of such bristled sensitivity can hardly be justified, let alone regarded with sympathy. Istóczy's departure from the Diet proved to be a multifaceted miscalculation. It left one of the most supportive and devoted constituencies in the Hungarian electorate without counsel, leadership, and direction; it helped give political anti–Semitism, staggering on the brink of oblivion, the final push; and it failed to protect him and the members of his family, whom he had thus far protected to the point of anonymity. Vengeful foes would continue to vilify or condemn him to the life of a nonentity.

Chapter XII

Alone Again

Unlike the athlete, who usually marks the end of his career with voluntary or forced retirement, a politician need not end his career by stepping into the quicksand of oblivion. A politician's decision not to seek reelection or to actively pursue his craft may be reversed because of a change of heart or circumstance. However dejected or affected by controversy, Istóczy had that option to reverse his decision. As he charted the future course of his political life he made an error in calculation, one that was to prove irremediable. Despite the rapid disintegration of the National Anti–Semitic Party and the steady diminution in the number of its elected representatives in the Diet, Istóczy's conviction in the timeless relevance, popularity, and utility of anti–Semitism remained unshaken. Equally unswerving was his belief in his ability to rekindle the enthusiasm of his loyal supporters, a not entirely unreasonable conclusion in view of his remarkable string of seven victories at the polls. He could have become the hidden imam of his movement, outriding an era of adversity and reappearing with renewed vigor and a spirit of vengeance. However, Istóczy did not recognize or ignored the fundamental limitations of a monotonous doctrine of implacable hate to which his own political career had been a monument.

Anti–Semitism had failed in the form of an independent political movement. Although it was a persistent personal common denominator of varying intensity, beneath the facade of nineteenth–century Hungarian politics, anti–Semitism neither attracted first–rate political minds nor succeeded in establishing a well–structured, durable organization. The members of its parliamentary faction bickered among themselves more often than they attacked their foes and eventually resumed their previous party affiliations, established new ones or left politics altogether. Moreover, the voters who had elected practicing anti–Semites as their representatives in the Diet and found their performance dishearteningly inadequate threw their support to the Catholic People's Party and helped seventeen of its ninety candidates win parliamentary seats in the 1897 national elections. Their switch of allegiance paid satisfactory dividends. Well–financed and well–organized, the party's program vowed to "protect the Christian character of our society, heal the wounds that Christianity sustained, and fight the bills and laws in conflict with the doctrine and spirit of Christianity."[1] Although the leaders of the party acknowledged the right of all religious associations to freedom of worship, they did not prevent the majority of the ninety candidates from engaging in anti–Jewish polemics.[2] Istóczy, however, evinced no interest in seeking shelter in the Catholic People's Party. He remained the lone wolf he had been much of his political career. Under the changed circumstances it was a luxury he could ill afford. Less and less did people heed his fading cry in the wilderness.

One of the most intriguing—and puzzling—aspects of Istóczy's retirement from parliamentary politics was his decision to settle in Budapest permanently. Buoyed by the steadfast support and protection it had been given by the progressive post–*Ausgleich* governments, which it had earned and reciprocated, as well as by the much–improved official status accorded its religious beliefs in 1875, Budapest's Jewry had grown into an influential, prosperous, and productive segment of the capital's population. Jews were highly visible in all sectors of Budapest's vibrant social, economic, and cultural life. Efficiently run by two successive secretaries, József Simon and Ferenc Mezey, the National Bureau of Israelites, the nerve center of the community, coordinated the manifold communal activities. It also maintained an ever–alert watch on the political scene, especially the parliamentary proceedings, drawing on the considerable influence and financial strength of the community, to react swiftly and effectively to danger signals, which since the advent of Istóczy and political anti–Semitism, were numerous. Istóczy's parliamentary career had necessitated that he establish residence in the capital within easy access to the building of the Diet. But it remains a bewildering puzzle why an implacable foe of Hungarian Jewry, upon the demise of his career, voluntarily chose to permanently settle, as a defenseless target, in the stronghold of his adversaries. Undoubtedly Istóczy was not short of alternatives. He could have returned to his native Vas County and live among friends and wellwishers, practiced law or held a position in the local administration and occasionally dipped his venomous pen into a hate–filled ink bottle—or settled anywhere in Hungary. No allusion, let alone direct reference, can be found in his later writings to the circumstances of his retirement from parliamentary politics, which some of his unswervingly loyal and patient constituents may have viewed as an act of ingratitude or even desertion. Judging from his subsequent actions, it never crossed his mind that his unexplained withdrawal from politics could be viewed as such.

Istóczy chose literature as the means by which to extricate himself from his penurious existence; however, it offered him no more promise than a twig thrown to a drowning man. It was a peculiarly disingenious decision for one who for nearly a quarter century managed to keep an unpopular and discredited view from disappearing in the maze of parliamentary politics but failed in all of his journalistic ventures. Yet for a fifty–four–year–old retired politician, Istóczy's options were exceedingly limited. His estate, virtually consumed by the expenses of political life, was by then only a symbol of a carefree childhood and a reminder of his disinterest in the petrified lifestyle of a country squire, not an incentive to begin a new life. Still, despite the fact that his brief attempt to practice law in Budapest met with financial failure, practicing law in Vas County, his stamping ground, should certainly have merited his consideration. A similarly promising alternative could have been a decision to return to local public service. Istóczy showed no interest in pursuing either alternative. Instead he chose to transform avocation, an appendage of his political life until his retirement from the Diet, into the single source of both his livelihood and intellectual reward. Although his literary activity was of interest to a limited readership, it could have become a new and even profitable basis of a productive existence anywhere in Hungary—anywhere except in Budapest where, as Istóczy himself had concluded, Jewish influence was most pronounced in the press and publishing.[3] Yet he entered the lion's den virtually unprotected, seemingly oblivious to the risks of failure. He had done little preparation for his transition from public to civilian life or toward his quest for financial success. Although intellectually, especially linguistically, he was firmly established and unusually well–informed on domestic and foreign affairs, Istóczy's literary style had been inextricably interwoven with his political obsession and made to serve its narrow function. His numerous, lengthy speeches that also appeared in the *12 Röpirat* and other publications merely served as one–way communication. The irreversible diminution in the number of subscribers that had eventually forced Istóczy to stop the publication of the *12 Röpirat*, the best–known of anti–Semitic mouthpieces, failed to convince him of the correspondingly declining market for his obsession. The professional practice of anti–Semitism had ceased to be a politically and financially profitable enterprise.

Between 1896, the year he announced his decision not to seek re-election, and 1915, the date of his last published work, Istóczy worked as diligently and persistently as at any time during his political career. In addition to the volumes of the *Legal and Administrative Guide*, of which a total of twenty–two would be published, Istóczy translated from Latin *The Jewish War* and *Jewish Antiquities*, the two major works of Flavius Josephus, the famous first–century Jewish historian; and the fifth volume of Tacitus's *Histories* which describes the destruction of the Second Temple in Jerusalem by the Romans. The last phase of Istóczy's literary career revealed an unmistakable change in direction and purpose. Neither the meager livelihood he had eked out as a writer–editor–translator nor his political obsession assured him tranquility and contentful retrospection. He wasted no time in shifting into a higher gear. Within the next seven years and in a carefully paced sequence, Istóczy published four works intended to be both monuments to his political career and the means by which he hoped to rekindle the smoldering embers of hatred.

The voluminous collection of his parliamentary speeches, resolutions and bills serves as a permanent reminder of the indelible imprint that his unswerving advocacy of political anti–Semitism left on Hungarian politics of the last quarter of the nineteenth century; the brief pamphlet–like but equally combative work on the destruction of the National Anti–Semitic Party gives an embittered account of his unending tribulations in the Diet; and *A magyar nemzetet megillető hely az európai népcsaládban* [The place befitting the Hungarian nation in the family of European peoples], is a confused, rambling historical–ethnographic–linguistic polemic "against the attacks leveled internally and externally against the Hungarian nation."

The last and most revealing of Istóczy's literary trial–balloons, *Emlékiratfélék és egyebek*, is a self–pitying epitaph as well as an impassioned plea for support, interspersed with random denunciations of Jews and some of the most profane paraphrasing of biblical passages and illogical conclusions found in the annals of anti–Semitic mud–slinging. "The Egyptians," the name Istóczy bestowed on Jews, "were a leprous and scabious people. The askew, flap–eared Jews of our time are their direct descendants." Because of the mass influx of Jews, everyone calls "Hungarians Judeo–Magyars and Hungary New Judea." The emergent theme and persistent tenor of these writings clearly indicate that Istóczy regarded his retirement as a well–earned sabbatical rather than a final act and clung to the hope that his time would again come sooner or later.

Istóczy, however, had more success with Jew–baiting as a literary ploy, than as a financial venture.[4] Unlike other writers and politicians of lesser notoriety—and even talent—who left the marketing of their works to the publishing houses, Istóczy found only closed doors in his desperate search for a courageous intermediary. No respectable publisher in Budapest showed interest in helping Istóczy achieve his goal; no agent ever carried any of his works to raise the number of

subscribers and buyers Istóczy needed to defray the cost of printing and maintaining a modest lifestyle. His penance, which began
with the completion of his first tome in retirement, was a lonely and
frustrating circle he would repeatedly travel for fifteen years. Buyers, however, were rare. His unshakable willpower and equally strong
physical constitution kept him on the go, chasing the elusive chimera.
He traveled by train at night so that sleeping would not slow down the
pace of his frantic search of readers. Yet the people in the towns and
villages of the countryside where he had won support as a politician
proved to be less responsive than he had anticipated. "Everyone who
could afford it and was not afraid of the 'Egyptians' ordered from
me," he noted. He should also have excluded those who had grown
disinterested or become disillusioned by his shallow performance in
his last years in the Diet and the circumstances of his retirement.

At any rate, the lack of financial reward for his literary labors
caused him anguish. His tiring nationwide travels turned out to be an
inadequate source of steady income; he was compelled to constantly
replenish his income with his dwindling inheritance. Only once did
Istóczy step completely out of character. If the works which he filled
with the frightening imagery of Jewish domination and exploitation
proved to be largely unsalable, he reasoned, perhaps one entirely devoid of anti–Semitic jingoism might bring financial success. However,
without the accustomed shield, Istóczy sounded unconvincing, insin-
cere, and amateurish. The reception of *A magyar nemzetet megilletö
hely az európai népcsaládban* was as chilly as that given the rest of
his literary ventures. Istóczy admitted:

> I was disappointed. The newspapers to which I sent copies
> of it remained, with a few exceptions, silent and boycotted
> it. Thus the reading public, uninformed of its existence,
> could not respond to my work.[5]

The plain truth, which Istóczy was unwilling to face, was that few
people shared the optimism and logic that had prompted him to write
l'art pour l'art. Furthermore, because the author had been inextricably fused with anti–Semitism, even fewer readers were attracted to a
study of the history and language of the Hungarian people that also
included "a new theory of the structure of Hungarian folk songs which,
due to their charm, had become world famous." This setback pushed
him to a level of disappointment which he had not yet experienced.
Not only were his hopes of finally being spared the exhausting door-
to–door peddling dashed, he was deeply hurt to learn that his only
literary effort based on history, linguistics, and music, the three topics
which had interested him since his youth, should meet such a disheart-

ening fate.[6] Equally disappointing—and far more irritating—was his
desultory contact with the leaders of foreign anti–Semitic movements.
Within a few years their respect for him had evaporated, and they
treated his entreaties with an indifference that bordered on hostility.
Istóczy translated the "Palestine Speech," which he regarded as the
most authoritative pronouncement of his political career, into German and French and mailed the appropriate translation to Berlin
and Paris. "Not even four Germans who wanted to order copies of
it could be found," he noted bitterly.[7] Edouard Drumont, the French
anti–Semitic leader who had become rich from the royalties of his
writings—an achievement not entirely lost on an obviously envious
Istóczy—neither acknowledged the receipt of the French translation
of the "Palestine Speech" nor returned it. Istóczy fumed:

> Yet it was on account of the resounding echo in France of my
> parliamentary agitation that Monsieur Drumont is what he
> is today: a modest newspaper reporter turned parliamentary
> deputy, anti–Semitic party leader, and a wealthy man to
> boot.[8]

It was yet another jolt to the man who had yearned for camaraderie
among anti–Semites but come to despise it.

However bitter and disillusioned the vicissitudes of fifteen years
of ill–fortune had made him, Istóczy never lost hope in his eventual
triumphant return to politics and the full vindication of his views.
Like a tired wrestler with one shoulder pressed to the mat but struggling to avoid being pinned, Istóczy found new reserves that enabled
him to regain his emotional balance after every seemingly disastrous
setback. First he had to mobilize and inspire his lethargic troops before he could lead them to battle, not with rousing speeches but with
persistent pleas for compassion, good will, and support.

> Don't be afraid of contacting me, the object of the Egyp-
> tians' boycott, and don't help them boycott me. It is shame-
> ful that Hungarians, who had courageously stood up to
> Tatars, Turks, Germans, and other foes, should humble them-
> selves before a people whose reputation among the ancient
> historians I have already exposed. Remember that what has
> happened and is happening to me now may happen to you
> and your children. For that reason, help me!

Hungary, Istóczy pleaded, must not be conquered by the Jews and
become the New Judea.[9]

Gradually the thin line between illusion and reality, never sharply
defined in Istóczy's mind, disappeared altogether. He believed that
his supporters numbered in the millions. He implored them not to

wait for him to knock on the door of every one of them but subscribe to or order copies of his works in which the titles and prices, ranging from one to ten crowns, were listed in order of publication date.[10] He remained convinced that the discrepancy between the presumed number of supporters and the number of copies sold—less than four thousand—was due either to fear of the "Egyptians" or lethargy. The possibility that he had greatly overestimated the numerical strength of anti–Semites in Hungary never occurred to him. He looked to the miraculous appearance of a maecenas—or preferably more than one— who would order a thousand copies of his translation of Josephus's *The Jewish War*, ten crowns apiece, or underwrite the expenses of an anti–Semitic daily. He called on imaginary legions of support- ers to contribute funds that would enable him to publish 50,000 to 100,000 copies of the second and third editions of his memoirs. Given the fact the first edition sold less than 4,000 copies, Istóczy seems to have definitely entered the realm of the irrational. Conversely, even the numbers he anticipated are inexplicably low estimates by one who believed his supporters to be in the millions. However, the most astonishing phantasm of his tormented mind revolved around his lifelong foes.

> This work of mine is fundamental to the understanding of the full dimension of the Jewish Question. For that reason even the Jews may benefit by reading it and learning what's what with them. As a source of self–knowledge, I have done the Jews a greater service with it than, for instance, the daily *Világ* (World) that wanted to make them believe that they occupy a truly privileged position [in Hungary] or the "P.H." [the initials of *Pesti Hírlap* (Pest Gazette)] which wanted to make them believe that they are *Übermensch*-like beings.[11]

Second to his indefatigable labors to attract a large readership that would enable him to become self–sufficient and secure him ad- equate funds for printing costs—because of the publishers' repeated rejection of his manuscripts this expense remained a permanent drain on his meager resources—Istóczy's most persistently recurring dream was of founding an anti–Semitic daily. Without such an organ, he concluded, political anti–Semitism had no chance of making headway in Hungary. The thriving anti–Semitic publications in Austria, Ger- many and France, where his name and views had become forgotten relics, made him envious and bitter. However, they also heightened his sense of urgency and determination with which he pursued the elu- sive dream. The fact that among the nearly two thousand newspapers and magazines published in Hungary, only a handful still paid a limited and largely ignored homage to the Jewish Question, should have given him an easy clue to the feasibility of such an enterprise. However, Istóczy never felt better than when he hurled himself against an unyielding barrier. To him Hungarian newspapers, particularly the ones in Budapest, had long been the strongholds of Jewish influence. They, he contended, enable the Jews to conquer Hungary and make plans to transform it into a New Judea.

Istóczy believed that Jewish influence could be broken only by establishing a state monopoly—in the form of state–controlled and operated supplement—of advertisements through which the Jews held their powerful grip on the press. "I will shake the nation out of its lethargy and make it realize the grave threat," Istóczy vowed. "Then I will be able to rest and enjoy a life of tranquility which I have more than earned."[12]

During the last four years of his life Istóczy became an embittered recluse, abandoning the public pursuit of his lifelong dream and limiting his activities to the distribution of his *Legal Guide*. While living quietly in a public housing project in Budapest's Tenth District, the death of his son Imre devastated the prophet of doom. A daughter and a longtime housekeeper remained his only companions.[13] He had been an obsessively private man and had chosen to keep the members of his family out of the political turmoil that engulfed him. His wish, respected by friend and foe alike, leaves a one–dimensionally political personality to posterity.

On 7 January 1915 Istóczy died, a sad, embittered and disillusioned man. No visual reminders of the founder of political anti–Semitism in Hungary, even in the district of Rum which he represented in the Diet for a quarter century, exists. No statues preserve his likeness, no streets bear his name, no plaques identify the houses in which he lived. He was laid to rest quietly and without ceremony. Ironically, his death was reported only in some liberal Jewish newspapers.[14] He owes posterity but one answer. To what end did those thousands of "leprous and scabious Egyptians" enlist in the Hungarian army in 1914; give life and limb in the bloody battles of World War I; elicit the highest praise from field commanders and generals; and help the war effort by praying fervently for victory and making huge financial contributions? The recognition—let alone the acknowledgement—of the obvious and the simple had never been Istóczy's forte.

Chapter XIII

The Fascist and Zionist Connections

A virtually uninterrupted series of setbacks was Istóczy's constant companion in the last four years of his life, but he was not in the habit of walking away and giving up all he had struggled for. A supplement, written in 1909, to his memoirs attests to his unshakable faith in the timeless validity of his political philosophy.

Entitled "Sociálpolitikai pártszövetkezet" (Sociopolitical party alliance), the nine–page document was intended to be the ideological cornerstone of a renascent anti–Semitic movement. The faint echoes it generated, combined with Istóczy's death six years later, give the document the appearance of a codicil to a political testament. However, it is an extraordinary bridge, linking the ultimate objectives of the political anti–Semitism of Istóczy's time not only to the program of the right–wing aggregations that emerged in the decades following his death, but to the goals of political Zionism as well.

Much of the ideological ammunition Istóczy fired in retirement was left over from earlier political battles. He continued to decry the alarming increase in the number of emigrants, calling it a national catastrophe. Within decades, he concluded, there were bound to be more Hungarians in the United States than in the Fatherland. He took issue with Austrian politicians whose repeated references to Hungarians as Judeo–Hungarians solidified that image among the non–Hungarian nationalities of the empire and caused the whole world to regard Hungarian and Jew as synonymous. He purported that Jewish achievements in agriculture, commerce and industry were exploitative and placed Christian Hungarians in a limbo in their own homeland.

The destruction of the National Anti–Semitic Party, Istóczy claimed, had no adverse effect on its sweeping program of socioeconomic and political reforms. Many bills which anti–Semitic representatives, himself in particular, had introduced in the Diet, only to be voted down, were subsequently resubmitted by others and were accepted by the government and became law. Political anti–Semites were thus vindicated and able to view themselves as pioneers in the Hungarian politics of the sociopolitical movement that repudiated the philosophy of Social Darwinism. Hungarians had been pacesetters in the evolution of political anti–Semitism in Europe, yet in the end lagged behind their Austrian, German, and French comrades–in–arms in numerical strength, parliamentary representation and public relations.[1]

"He preceded his time by at least half a century," concluded Zoltán Bosnyák, erroneously and unflinchingly, adding yet another insupportable declaration to the already bulging corpus of his inaccurate and undocumented generalizations.[2] Indeed, Istóczy correctly sensed the start of a new, inevitable upswing in the cycle of anti–Semitism. He may have even detected the coming storm itself. For despite the steady flow of deeply appreciative statements which the political and military leaders of the Dual Monarchy issued in recognition of the varied contributions of Hungarian Jewry, the waves of anti–Semitism gathered strength soon after the outbreak of World War I. Analyses of statistical data led to predisposed conclusions and clouded the pictures of conspicuous heroism and grateful acknowledgement. The citations, decorations, and promotions which numerous Jewish officers and soldiers received and the outpour of patriotism in rabbinical sermons and parental sacrifices—some Jewish families gave seven, eight, even nine sons to the war effort—stood as eloquent testimonies, complementing the civilian awards given to communal leaders and prominent Jews in finance and industry. Still, the anti–Semites cited statistical disparities and other unrepresentative data as proofs of the Jews' disloyalty, indifference and opportunism. The number of Jews killed and wounded in action, constituting 1.1 percent of Hungarian Jewry, they alleged, compared unfavorably with the losses sustained by the Christian population of the country, 2.8 percent of the total. The difference between the figures inevitably led to makeshift and unjust, albeit intractable, conclusions. Jewish soldiers were accused of pussyfooting at best, cowardice at worst. Because Jewish manufacturers and suppliers of war materiels and other necessities earned large profits and occasionally delivered products of substandard quality, they were charged with profiteering and sabotaging the nation's heroic struggle. The recognized and oft–rewarded service record of Jewish army officers, doctors and nurses as well as the less dramatic but equally significant work of Jewish men and women on the home front went unnoticed and unmentioned.[3] With that the pattern was set, and Istóczy's legacy became the cornerstone of the emergent Hungarian Fascist movement.

In the midst of the war an ill–conceived idea, which exposed Istóczy's favorite hobbyhorse, the Jewish Question, to yet another round of public discussion, backfired. In 1917 the *Huszadik Század* (Twentieth Century), a Budapest weekly, conducted a poll among selected Jewish and non–Jewish notables of Hungary's intellectual and religious life. The editor–in–chief of the *Huszadik Század*, the Jewish Oszkár Jászi (1875–1957), was a well–known advocate of bourgeois radicalism and a prolific author of sociological works. The whole project was as ill–timed as it was unwise and unnecessary, including questions such as: Does the Jewish Question exist in Hungary, and if yes, what do you think its manifestations are? What are its causes? What do you think is the solution of the Jewish Question, and what social and legislative reforms do you think are needed to achieve it? One had to be virtually deaf and blind not to respond in a predetermined manner. Thirty–seven of the fifty respondents who had agreed to participate answered the first question in the affirmative. With respect to the causes of anti–Semitism the opinions ran the entire spectrum of reasonable possibilities, ranging from the manifestations of atavism through economic competition and differences in education and traditions, to ignorance and clerical antagonism. The suggestions offered as the solution of the Jewish Question were no less varied. Alternatives to the two conventional conclusions— sociocultural assimilation and emigration—included abandonment of the Jewish religion, intermarriage, prohibition of immigration, complete reform of the dogma–based religions, enlightenment through education, and elimination of the numerous ills of peasant life.[4]

The lopsided results of *Huszadik Század*'s poll engendered further debate on the Jewish Question, kept it in the foreground of anti–Semitic activities and assured it unwanted publicity. The clashes of opinions were inevitably transformed into a veritable struggle for existence in the aftermath of the short–lived (21 March to 30 July 1919) Hungarian Soviet Republic, of whose thirty People's Commissars seventeen were identified as Communists of Jewish origin. To the odious image of Jews as exploiters and profiteers the new charge of antinationalist Bolshevik was added and used as justification for the atrocities committed by the counterrevolutionary army officers of the White Terror. Although the Regent of Hungary, Admiral Miklós Horthy, was fond of describing himself as Europe's first anti–Semitic head of state, he managed to keep the emergent forces of Fascism at bay. However, Istóczy's heirs never lost sight of or altered their objective.

In 1921 Gyula Gömbös (1886–1936), an influential right–wing army officer turned politician of the interwar era and a future prime minister, sounded a keynote that was to become the official policy of Hungarian Fascism on the Jewish Question.[5] The solution to the Jewish Question, he wrote, lay in the "removal from the country of hundreds of thousands of Jews holding Hungarian citizenship." Gömbös's view was shared by Ferenc Szálasi (1897–1946) and his

Arrow–Cross Party,[6] the most violently anti–Jewish aggregation in Hungary. Despite the rhetorics of non–violence—both Gömbös and Szálasi envisioned eliminating the Jews' harmful influence without resorting to physical means—Szálasi's brief tenure as prime minister and the short–lived rule of the Arrow–Cross Party (16 October 1944–4 April 1945) contributed some of the most horrifying pages on extermination in the annals of the Holocaust.[7]

The ease with which Istóczy's legacy was transformed into a blanket justification of anti–Jewish acts demonstrates the fallacy of his belief in the natural interdependence of incitement and non–violence. Istóczy was a pacesetter in blaming the omnipresent Jewish influence and self–centeredness for social injustice and economic inequality in Hungary. The seemingly unending line of his enthusiastic imitators and loyal admirers institutionalized both the predictable recurrence and violent manifestations of anti–Semitism. They were particularly effective in times of disorder and their intensity was in inverse proportion to the degree of control exercised by the law enforcement authorities. The two most violent occurrences of anti–Semitism in twentieth–century Hungary were the "cleansing" activities of counterrevolutionary officers in the wake of the collapse of the Hungarian Soviet Republic in 1919 and the Arrow–Cross takeover in 1944, when Szálasi's phantasmagoric utopia of a new Europe dominated by Germans and Hungarians in a mutually complementing partnership had dissipated. In both instances, the implementation of the solution of the Jewish Question legitimized atrocities. Anyone carrying a weapon claimed to be both judge and executioner.

Istóczy would have been gratified to learn that his ideological descendants retained his zest and persistence. However, even he might have been amazed at the inexhaustible capacity to find reasons to believe that the Holocaust had not sufficiently fulfilled the expectations of everyone harboring ill–feelings toward Jews. Indeed, one stands bewildered before the spectacle of the quickly suppressed atrocities in the summer of 1946 when pogroms that swept the towns of Kunmadaras, Miskolc and Diósgyőr ended in the death of five Jews.[8] Unsavory incidents also cast a dark shadow on some phases of the Revolution of 1956. When émigré and foreign critics denounced "Anti–Semitism and Anti–Jewish Violence During the Hungarian Counterrevolution," a propagandistic, slogan–ridden, yet disturbingly accusatory exposé published by János Kádár's Soviet–protected Revolutionary Workers' and Peasants' government, they could advance no more convincing argument than the statement that "none of the alleged anti–Semitic outrages related in the White Book refer to the capital and its environs."[9] The statistical data speak clearly for themselves and suggest conclusions that need no explanation.

"It is a short path that leads from the provincial Jewry of 200,000 to 12,000," lamented József Schindler, who until his death in 1962 was rabbi of Szeged and a reliable observer of the post–war reconstruction of provincial Jewish life. "Hardly fifteen years."[10] Of the fifty–nine Orthodox religious slaughterers that functioned before October 1956 only ten remained, according to Jenő Schück, Chief Rabbi of Hungary's Orthodox Jewry.[11] Even more revealing are the brief studies of László Harsányi, the knowledgeable chronicler of the fate of provincial Jewish communities. With minor variations—and changes of names—this terse but ominous statement is repeated almost as a matter of course:

> In Hajdú County, due to the anti–Semitic excesses during the 1956 counterrevolution, from the Jewish remnants numerous families emigrated; others Debrecen and the capital absorbed.[12]

Thus, within half a century Istóczy's dream of ridding the counties of Jews had come near realization.

Istóczy's legacy has also been reverently cultivated outside Hungary. The surviving members of the Arrow–Cross Party and other extreme right–wing political groups incorporated Istóczy's views on the Jewish Question and his proposals for its solution, partly to retain the historical continuity of anti–Semitism, thereby legitimizing the anti–Jewish aspects of the Hungarist *Weltanschauung*, and partly to justify their own ideological raison d'être. These surviving members had left Hungary when the Red Army occupied it or were released from jail during the 1956 Revolution and joined their comrades–in–arms abroad. They lament the shattered world of Hungarism, recount past grievances and wait for the end of Communist rule in Hungary. Their political and literary activities revolve around such themes as the "infamous" Treaty of Trianon (1921) that deprived Hungary of two–thirds of its prewar territory; the emergence of Hungarism and the voluminous literary legacy of its principal theoreticians; the brief rule of the Arrow–Cross Party and the premiership of Ferenc Szálasi, its standard bearer; and the execution or death in prison of Arrow–Cross leaders captured by the new Communist masters of Hungary. The latter has spawned an emotional literature of political martyrology.

Woven into the fabric of Hungarism are Istóczy's words and ideas. Lajos Marschalkó and Ferenc Fiala, two of the most prolific Hungarist writers, preserved Istóczy's memory and paid homage to the timeless validity of his views on the solution of the Jewish Question. Since Istóczy, "the Hungarian program has always been that of peaceful separation, not Eichmann's program of extermination," Marschalkó concluded.[13] Fiala, Szálasi's press secretary, provides a brief glimpse into the bizarre, self–contradicting mind of the Hungarist *Nemzetvezető* (Leader of the Nation): "I am not an anti–Semite. Never have been," Fiala stated Szálasi during a press conference in November 1944. "I am an a–Semite. The Jew is just as much a human being as we are. This question cannot be solved by brutal means."[14] Still, Marschalkó, Istóczy's most devout disciple and tireless promoter, made a literary career out of discovering an ever–increasing body of evidence proving the existence of an omnipresent conspiracy to dominate and exploit a helpless mankind.[15] He and the surviving remnant of the Hungarist movement have been the only preservers and transmitters of Istóczy's political legacy.

Istóczy's most lasting and utilitarian contribution was the belated realization that the Zionists would ultimately—and perhaps to the greatest degree—profit from his political program and views on the solution of the Jewish Question. It came to him not as a sudden, illuminating flash of lightning but as faint flickers of uncertain origin that were to take a definite shape within five formative years. In comparison to the evolutionary stages through which the Nazis' version of the Final Solution of the Jewish Question passed and the horrible images of the Holocaust, Istóczy's solution sounds like a reasonable, even compassionate, proposal. However, when it was first made public in 1906—by a strange coincidence the Central Bureau of the Hungarian Zionist Federation was moved from Pozsony (Bratislava) to Budapest in the same year—its echo among Hungarian Jewry reverberated with a ring of promise as faint as his ideas and speeches in the Diet. If they had bothered to listen, the overwhelming majority of Istóczy's audience would have been the fervently assimilationist Neologs or the passionately traditionalist and exclusivist Orthodox Jews. Both groups viewed the rise, tenets and proponents of Zionism with apprehension and hostility. The fact that Theodor Herzl and Max Nordau, the founder of Political Zionism and his earliest disciple, were Hungarian born only exacerbated the situation.

Istóczy declared:

> We anti–Semites want nothing different than the Zionists, i.e., the restoration, with the mediation of European diplomacy, of the Jewish state anywhere—except in Hungary—preferably in Palestine, as I proposed in my 24 June 1878 speech in the Diet during the sessions of the Congress of Berlin. Let those Jews who are unwilling or unable to assimilate and feel ill at ease among us—the way we feel having

them among us—return to their homeland along with our incorrigible philosemites. This anti–Semitic party program, which the development of the Zionist movement has made entirely legitimate, is the most radical anti–Semitic viewpoint. We, anti–Semites, declare ourselves to be non–Jewish Zionists.[16]

Istóczy found the new avenue created by the Zionist connection intriguing, and he became absorbed in exploiting its potentials. Within three years he learned enough of the tenets and objectives of political Zionism to discuss them with nearly as much ease and fervor as those of political anti–Semitism. The reciprocal utility of the two ideologies, however, was tempered by a formidable obstacle.

In his 1909 proclamation to voters Istóczy stated that the Young Turks had overthrown the autocratic Sultan Abdul Hamid II with the support of influential and wealthy Turkish and European Jews. He quoted comments of Ahmed Riza Pasha, the President of the Turkish Diet, on foreign Jews being welcome in Turkey and declared that Zionism was no longer a mere utopian aspiration.[17] However, two years later he saw things differently. As soon as the Young Turks perceived the Zionists' ultimate goal, the expropriation of a portion of the empire, they balked. "If the Young Turks have been unwilling to grant autonomy to the Albanians, who are fellow Muslims, they will certainly not grant the Jews autonomy in Palestine," Istóczy concluded. With the avenue of their first preference thus blocked, Istóczy reasoned, the Jews, in order to establish themselves as the dominant race, would search for a country in Europe. "Except for Hungary, no such country exists in Europe," he declared.[18] Only the Young Turks' realization of their inability to rejuvenate Turkey by themselves—the principal obstacle being Islam, "a grotesque version of Judaism,"—would save Hungary from a new onslaught of Jews.[19]

These ideas and utterances are attributable to Istóczy's awareness of the common ground shared by political anti–Semites and Zionists and the practicality of their joint effort. By 1911 Istóczy had come to the conclusion that he was personally responsible for the advent of political Zionism and its emergent philosophy. Admitting that the Young Turks' change of heart had given the Zionists a temporary setback and chagrined him the most, Istóczy declared that the cause of those feelings was his seminal contribution to the Zionist movement. Istóczy concluded:

It was I who caused a worldwide echo in both Jewish and non–Jewish circles with my speech delivered on 24 June 1878 in the Diet, on the subject of the restoration of the Jewish

state in Palestine. My subsequent motion to that effect gave
the Zionist movement a decisive push.[20]

The idea that the ideologies and goals of political anti–Semitism
and political Zionism intersect turned out to be much more than
a fleeting chimera. In 1921, two years after he began his political career and became chairman of the right–wing, fascist *Magyar
Országos Véderő Egylet* (Hungarian National Military Association),
Gyula Gömbös suggested that "the Hungarian government get in
touch with the Central Bureau of the Zionists concerning the removal
of hundreds of thousands of Jews holding Hungarian citizenship."[21]
After his Arrow–Cross party seized power and he became prime minister on 16 October 1944 and subsequently *Nemzetvezető*, Ferenc Szálasi
rejected the demands of SS General Winckelmann concerning the de-
portation of Budapest's 200,000 Jews, declaring that "If we win the
war, the Jewish Question will have to be solved in accordance with
the basic principles of Zionism."[22]

Istóczy often took credit where credit was not due, presented
figments of his imagination as facts, and used facts in reaching illusory conclusions. However, with respect to political Zionism he was
advancing an essentially credible argument. On a first reading the argument borders on the irrational. However, the evidence supporting
it is so intriguing, albeit circumstantial, that it justifies consideration.
It links Istóczy to the seminal phase of Zionism on a more personal
basis than he assumed. The nature of the circumstances transcends
the barriers of uncertainty and incredulity which the searchers of historical truth, encountering lacunae in documentation, automatically
erect. It is hoped that the prudent pursuit of probabilities will point
in the direction of both reason and truth.

The "Palestine Speech" was both the cornerstone of Istóczy's political philosophy and the source of ideas that fueled his obsession with
finding the solution of the Jewish Question. Delivered on 24 June 1878
on the floor of the Hungarian Diet, it established Istóczy's reputation
in European anti–Semitic circles and thrust the minuscule leadership
of the emergent Hungarian anti–Semitic movement into a position
of international prominence, particularly in Austria, Germany and
France. The distinctive, combative style and the obsessively anti–
Jewish rhetoric, the most characteristic features of his demagoguery,
however, were formed in the course of three earlier speeches, delivered between 1875 and 1878. Although still a one–man movement,
the presence of a number of sympathizers notwithstanding, Istóczy
succeeded in laying the foundations of political anti–Semitism in Hungary. There was little, if any, fanfare. Still, few speeches made on the
floor of the Diet fell on deaf ears or simply dissipated in the august

chamber.

In 1875 a fifteen–year–old Jewish boy lived and attended school in Budapest, virtually within a stone's throw of the building of the Hungarian Diet. His name was Tivadar. The members of his family and friends affectionately called him Dori, his nickname. Twenty years later, Theodor Herzl became the founder of political Zionism.

Research into Herzl's youth has discovered no evidence to support the hypothesis that he knew of Istóczy or heard of any of his speeches. The likelihood of finding corroborating evidence appears unpromising. However, as neither the facts of Istóczy's political career nor Herzl's youth are common knowledge, the unique intersection of their paths justifies the pursuit by inference of an intriguing allusion.

For nearly seventy years after his death in 1904 few particulars of the life of Theodor Herzl were as indistinct as his youth in Budapest and the origins of the principal theses of *Der Judenstaat,* the book that stimulated in him the dormant emotional forces of Jewish nationalism and triggered the start of political Zionism. Much of the vagueness regarding his youth has been due to his biographers' unwillingness to investigate behind the veil of obscurity. The first eighteen years of Herzl's life have been extricated from the confines of a few perfunctory observations in brief opening chapters of biographical works.[23] The inception of Herzl's political ideas, however, remains clouded, if not obscured, mainly due to his peculiar and uncharacteristically careless habits as a diarist.[24] His *Diaries* contain dramatic descriptions of his startling transformation from a sophisticated Viennese feuilletonist and playwright and an assimilated Jew into an imaginative and driven formulator of the doctrines and goals of Jewish nationalism. They constitute no history. The scattered pieces, however, both delighted and chagrined scholars who first found them, but they characterized them as too fragmented. The entries "were not intended to be literature but a frank account of his day–to–day struggle for the movement, of his meetings, plans and actions, and of the ideas and ideals that motivated him."[25] Yet it is the qualities of incompleteness and impreciseness that have made the prospect of entering and exploring the realm of allusions all the more intriguing. Of the numerous possibilities, only two led in the direction of reasonable probabilities regarding the Istóczy–Herzl connection: Herzl's formative stages in both his awareness of the existence of the Jewish Question and his emerging political views of Jewish nationalism. With respect to the former, Herzl recalled reading Eugen Karl Dühring's anti–Semitic book, *Die Judenfrage also Frage der Rassenschödlichkeit für Existenz, Sitten und Kultur der Völker* (The Jewish Question as

a Question of Racial Damage for the Existence, Morals, and Culture of the Nations) in 1881, the year of its publication, or 1882.[26]
Herzl's biographers portray him as out of touch with Jewish realities
and culture, trapped in a protracted limbo of assimilationism; however, the powerful emotional reaction caused by his reading of only
one such book indicates otherwise. Herzl was unable to point to one
identifiable event or experience—or even a firm date—which marks
the origin of his ideological stance. "It took at least thirteen years for
me to conceive this simple idea," he noted in an entry dated 7 June
1895. "Only now do I realize how often I went right past it."[27]

Some creative minds pay little attention to antecedents. Their biographers, however, do or should. By the start of those thirteen years,
constituting a period of emotional and political incubation, Herzl had
already stood at the crossroads of four major strains of influence, any
one of which was strong enough to trigger in him a surging sensitivity
to anti–Semitism and the Jewish Question. His paternal grandfather,
Simon Loew, to whom he was very close, was a disciple of Rabbi Judah
Hai Alkalai, the spiritual leader of the Jewish community of Zemun
(Zimony), a town in Hungary's southernmost county of Szerém, a
prominent proto–Zionist.[28] His father, Jacob Herzl, was a supporter
of Rabbi József Natonek, another proto–Zionist who had alienated
the assimilationist leaders of the Jewish community of Székesfehérvár,
whose spiritual leader he was, by suggesting that Erez Yisrael, not
Hungary, was the Jewish homeland.[29]

The other two influences were loud and undistinguished harbin-
gers of anti–Semitism. Between 1875 and 1878, Istóczy laid the
foundation of political anti–Semitism and sought supporters for his
solution of the Jewish Question. During those years, the last ones he
would live in Budapest, Herzl was the president of a small literary society composed of relatives and close friends, and was a prolific writer
of essays, stories, sketches, and critiques. His early writings included
at least one bitingly sarcastic political essay; a brief composition of
Girolamo Savonarola, the ill–fated fifteenth–century Dominican friar
of Florence; an historical study, entitled "The Conspiracy of Cati-
line"; and a biographical essay on Napoleon.[30] Neither the school he
attended nor the demands of his position as president of the literary
society isolated Herzl from the world around him. After spending four
years as a student in the Jewish Elementary School of Pest, Herzl
was enrolled in a *főreáltanoda*, a science–oriented secondary school
in 1870 and subsequently in the Evangelical High Gymnasium of the
Augustan Confession, where familiarity with the classics and subjects
of Magyar interest were stressed. Although a parochial institution,
the high gymnasium accepted Jewish students in gratitude for the

financial help the Jewish residents of the district had given for the construction of the building that housed it.[31]

Herzl was a precocious youngster who became interested in the Ferdinand de Lessep's venture at Suez, while a student in *fóreáltanoda*. He "developed an idea for the cutting through of that other isthmus, the Panama,"[32] and pursued studies in Hungarian history and literature in the high gymnasium. The presumption—a self–perpetuating consensus holding firm for nearly a century—that he remained oblivious to the boisterous anti–Semitic declarations in the Diet virtually within hearing distance, is not a credible one. Neither could he have been unaware of the last of the influences on him. In 1882 the Tisza-eszlár case made headlines in Hungary and throughout Europe. Although by then Herzl was a resident of Vienna, information there about Tiszaeszlár was readily available. In addition, he traveled to Budapest at least once a year on the anniversary of his sister's death and visited her grave.[33] Herzl could hardly have stepped in and out of the caldron of anti–Semitism unscathed.

In Herzl's lifetime, assimilationist and Hungarocentric Jewish leaders dominated and guided the political and cultural outlook of their coreligionists in Budapest and through them influenced Jewish thought in the rest of the country. They felt the less said and written about the Zionist movement and its founder, the better. Still, even the last nine years of Herzl's life (1895–1904) remained intertwined with assorted representatives of the country of his birth. Some of them were either active participants in Hungary's post–1867 political structure and familiar with Istóczy and his movement or well–informed chroniclers of the personalities, issues, and events of that period. Ernő Mezei (1851–1932) was Kossuth's personal friend and an impassioned dectractor of Istóczy both in the Diet, into which he was elected by the voters of Miskolc in 1881, and on the pages of the daily *Egyetértés*, the official organ of the Independence Party. Soma Vison-tay (1854–1925) who, like Mezei, was an Independence Party representative, was elected in 1892 and was thus an eyewitness to Istóczy's last four years in the Diet. Adolf Ágai (1836–1916), Baron Lajos Dóczi (1845–1918), and Sámuel Róthfeld (1857–n.d.) were sharp–eyed and prolific publicists who were well acquainted with political issues.

The most convincing link between Istóczy's political anti–Semitism and Herzl's political Zionism was provided by Iván Simonyi (1836–1904). A somewhat eccentric[34] lawyer turned publisher and politician, in 1875 he founded a German–language daily, *Westun-garischer Grenzbote*, with the help of the Jewish Ede Horn and the popular writer and liberal politician Mór Jókai. After his partners' interest in the paper had waned, Somonyi took control and turned

it into an unabating disseminator of his anti–Semitic views. He also
became one of Istóczy's earliest supporters and closest collaborators,
although the bond of their ideological partnership gradually loosened
in the aftermath of the 1887 elections. Simonyi was the first Hungarian anti–Semite to discover the common bond between Herzl's
Zionism and the solution of the Jewish Question. In February 1886
he wrote a glowing review of *Der Judenstaat* in the *Westungarischer
Grenzbote*, to Herzl's surprise, albeit undisguised delight.[35] A month
later Simonyi called on a perplexed Herzl. Herzl observed:

> A sexagenarian, a mercurial loquacious man with an aston-
> ishing amount of sympathy for the Jews. His conversation
> is a mixture of the sensible and the nonsensical; he believes
> in the ritual murder lie, but along with it has the brightest,
> most modern ideas. Loves me![36]

Herzl, however, neither gave details of Simonyi's ideas nor did he
write down anything about the conversation in which Simonyi expressed those ideas. It hardly seems possible that during the entire
conversation with a fellow Hungarian Herzl should leave unmentioned
such subjects as his childhood in Budapest, his familiarity with Budapest and his knowledge of the Hungarian language. Similarly, there
are no compelling reasons to expect that Simonyi, in the course of
expounding the Hungarian anti–Semitic solution of the Jewish Question, would make no reference, if only to impress his incredulous host,
to Istóczy and the National Anti–Semitic Party, its showing in the
national elections and the participation of its representatives in parliamentary debates.

Despite the documented incidents of their indirect contact, the
environment they shared—the sounds and sights of Budapest—and
the similarities in their dreams, plans, and goals, neither Istóczy nor
Herzl is on record as alluding to, let alone admitting to, knowledge
of each other. It is at this point that the historian must stop lest
he, attempting to pursue a hypothesis when reasonable evidence of
its probability is unavailable, violate one of the cardinal rules of his
craft. He is, however, allowed to hope that the evidence will be found
someday. For nearly eighty years it had been assumed that Herzl's
path to Zionism passed through two phases of evolution: his awareness of anti–Semitism in Vienna and his emotional reaction to the
Dreyfus Affair. The documentable experiences of the first eighteen
years of his life in Budapest can now be identified as constituting a
distinct phase which precedes both phases. As Istóczy emerges from
oblivion and the full scope and significance of his political career become discernible, Herzl's tenuous query, "When did I actually begin

to concern myself with the Jewish Question?" remains unanswered. One is tempted to give a hypothetical answer: "Between 1872 and 1878 in Budapest and in the course of subsequent visits there." Given the probable circumstances, that answer sounds neither presumptuous nor unreasonable.

Notes to Chapter I

1 Péter Ujvári, ed., *Magyar zsidó lexikon* [Hungarian Jewish lexicon] (Budapest: Magyar Zsidó Lexikon, 1929), s.v. "Antiszemitizmus" (Anti-Semitism). Even in the countryside, relations between Hungarians and Jews were not based only on feelings of mutual mistrust, suspicion and hatred. Jews often appear in Hungarian proverbs in a favorable light. They are called "neighbors" or "one of our people," and respected for their intelligence and business acumen. However, Jews at times were also called "pagans" and "as trustworthy as unmanured soil." See Ármin Flesch, "A zsidó a magyar közmondásban" [The Jew in the Hungarian proverb] in József Bánóczi, ed., *Évkönyv* (Budapest: Izraelita Magyar Irodalmi Társulat, 1908), pp. 176–194. Similar feelings are expressed in jokes popular among the inhabitants of cities. See György Gracza, *Nevető Magyarország* [Laughing Hungary] 2 vols. (Budapest: Robert Lampel, 1901), 1:326–50. Whenever permitted, Jews were prepared to contribute to the development of mutually profitable, even amicable, relations. See Ignác Acsádi, "A zsidók a magyarság multjában" [Jews in the Hungarians' past], in *Évkönyv* (1902), pp. 7–20; Fülöp Grünwald, *A magyar zsidó mult historikusai* [Historians of the Hungarian Jewish past], in *Évkönyv* (1934), pp. 208–222; József Balassa, "A magyar zsidó dialektus" [Hungarian Jewish dialect], in *Évkönyv* (1898), pp. 114–117; Sándor Büchler, "A magyar nyelv terjeszkedése a zsidók közt" [The spread of the Hungarian language among the Jews], in *Évkönyv* (1905), pp. 259–264. Still, arguments have been advanced to show the fundamental incompatibility between the customs, traditions, and lifestyles of Hungarians and Jews. See István Bogdán, *Régi magyar mulatságok* [Old Hungarian pastimes] (Budapest: Magvető, 1978); János Makkai, *Urambátyám országa* [My uncle's country] (Budapest: Singer & Wolfner, 1945).

2 Of an unnamed town of the Alföld—the expansive plain in the middle of Hungary—Izabella Gyujtó, a well-known nineteenth-century writer penned the following description: "There is no trace of public life. Social life reveals a ridiculous caste sys-

tem. The women are trapped in cafés and gossip groups, and the men are the slaves of wine and cards. Culture is represented by troupes of wandering thespians who come to town from time to time only to depart due to the lack of patronage." Quoted in László Tarr, *A délibábok országa* [The country of mirages] (Budapest: Magyar Helikon, 1976), p. 178. Still, the traditional way of life among Istóczy's social peers was showing a discernible change as "the stereotypic Hungarian nobleman who farmed on a small homestead, merrily hunted, read the classics, the Bible, or the handbook of Hungarian civil law by the fireside on long winter evenings, and entertained whenever a suitable occasion presented itself, became obsolete." See Lóránt Czigány, *Oxford History of Hungarian Literature* (Oxford: Clarendon Press, 1984), p. 233.

3 Antal Papp, ed., *Magyarország* [Hungary] (Budapest: Panoráma, n.d.), pp. 635–641; László Szabó, *Magyarország földrajza* [The geography of Hungary] (Budapest: Művelt Nép, 1954), pp. 85–87.

4 Ernő László, "Hungarian Jewry: Settlement and Demography 1735–1738 to 1910," in Randolph L. Braham, ed., *Hungarian Jewish Studies*, 3 vols. (New York: World Federation of Hungarian Jews, 1966–1978), 1:119.

5 The center of Jewish life in Vas, Zala and Somogy Counties for over a century, Rohonc (today the Austrian city of Rechnitz) declined markedly by the middle of the nineteenth century. See Ujvári, *Magyar zsidó lexikon*, s.v. "Rohonc." However, the Jewish community of Vasvár entered a period of conspicuous progress from the early 1860s. *Ibid.,* s.v. "Vasvár."

6 Béla Bernstein, chief rabbi of Szombathely (1892–1909) and a prominent historian, wrote an exhaustive study of the Jewish community of that city in *A zsidók története Szombathelyen (1687–1909)* [History of the Jews in Szombathely] (Budapest: n.p., 1914).

7 Quoted in Tarr, *Délibábok országa*, p. 255.

8 Among the many excellent studies describing the evolution of the capital of Hungary into one of the principal cities of Europe, the following contain perhaps the best combinations of data and description: László Solymosy, *Hogyan épült Budapest? (1870–1930)* [How was Budapest built?] (Budapest: Fővárosi Közmunkák Tanácsa, 1931); Károly Vörös, *Egy világváros születése* [The birth of a metropolis], *Budapest társadalmának és gazdasága- nak száz éve (1872/3–1972)* [A hundred years of Budapest's society and economy] (Budapest: Kossuth, 1972).

9 Tarr, *Délibábok országa*, pp. 125–129.

10 Ferencz Eckhart, *A jog és államtudományi kar története, 1667–1935* [History of the faculty of law and political science] (Budapest: n.p., 1936), pp. 464–475.

11 Zoltán Bosnyák, *Istóczy Győző élete és küzdelmei* [The life and battles of Győző Istóczy] (Budapest: Könyv és Lapkiadó Részvénytársaság, 1940), pp. 21–22. Hereafter cited as *Istóczy*.

12 Sándor Büchler, "Zsidók a magyar egyetemen," [Jews in the Hungarian university], in *Évkönyv* (1897), p. 168.

13 Technically Fleischer was the first Jewish student ever to enroll officially at the university (*Ibid.*, p. 170). However, as no law prohibiting the admission of Jewish students had ever been passed, the policy of the faculty of law with regard to Jews was set by preference and tradition. Since Fleischer was known to have been preparing to convert, his prospective status was apparently accepted as a suitable precondition for admission.

14 Eckhart, *A jog és államtudományi kar története*, pp. 370–371. Sources are at variance concerning Vízkelety's tenure as dean. According to the entry about him in Ágnes Kenyeres, ed., *Magyar életrajzi lexikon* [Hungarian biographical lexicon] 3 vols. (Budapest: Akadémiai Kiadó, 1982, 2:1010), Vízkeleti was dean from 1824 until 1826. He was professor of canon law at the University of Pest between 1829 and 1862.

15 The involvement of Istóczy and other leading Hungarian anti-Semites in the case, virtually from the start of the legal proceedings and long after the verdict had been pronounced, is described in detail on pp. 68–74.

16 Zsigmond Groszmann, "Mezei Mór és kora" [Mór Mezei and his times], in *Évkönyv* (1936), pp. 199–200.

17 A colorful picture of the extent and manifestations of the Jews' integration emerges from Péter Hanák, "Polgárosodás és asszimiláció Magyarországon a XIX században" [Bourgeois status and assimilation in Hungary in the nineteenth century], in *Történelmi Szemle* (1974/4), pp. 513–536; Idem., ed., *Zsidókérdés, asszimiláció, antiszemitizmus* [The Jewish Question, assimilation, anti-Semitism] (Budapest: Gondolat, 1984); László Erőss, *A pesti vicc* [Pest joke] (Budapest: Gondolat, 1982); Ferenc Hont, ed., *Magyar színháztörténet* [History of the Hungarian theater] (Budapest: Gondolat, 1962).

18 Some of them were his grateful patients. See István Csillag, "Hirschler Ignác ifjúkori arcképéhez" [To the portrait of the young Ignác Hirschler], in *Évkönyv* (1979/80), pp. 92–100; Zsigmond Groszmann, "Hirschler Ignác," in *Évkönyv* (1941), pp. 143–158. Hungary's Progressive Jewry, led by the Jewish commu-

nity of Pest and inspired to a great extent by the Czech–born, German–speaking and fervently patriotic Chief Rabbi Benjamin Zeev Meisel (1816–1867) (see Zsigmond Groszmann, "Meisel pesti főrabbi kora" [The times of Chief Rabbi Meisel of Pest], in *Évkönyv* (1933), pp. 100–113, espoused the tenets of the Industrial Age and supported the dynamic changes that were gradually transforming the essentially static, often backward–looking, Hungarian lifestyle into one more compatible with and appreciative of the spirit of the nineteenth century. Count Miklós Zay, a nobleman whose grandfather had opposed the emancipation of the Hungarian Jews, wrote admiringly about Jewish contributions ("Zsidók a társadalomban") [Jews in society], in *Huszadik Század*, (July–December 1903). He noted that modern Budapest was, to a large extent, built by Jews (p. 959) but also pointedly observed that the economic woes of the provincial gentry tended to keep anti–Semitism alive (pp. 963–964).

[19] Although all Jews in the countryside were vulnerable to varied manifestations of hatred by the general populance, the Jewish types consistently singled out were the opportunists in quest of noble titles (Zay, "Zsidók a társadalomban," p. 960), the buyers of debt–ridden estates (*Ibid.*, p. 964), the usurious innkeepers and the uneducated (*Ibid.*, p. 965). The tenuous position of Jews in villages and the peculiarities of peasant life are colorfully portrayed in Margit Luby, *A parasztélet rendje* [The structure of peasant life] (Budapest: Centrum, 1935); Kálmán Eperjessy, *A magyar falu története* [History of the Hungarian village] (Budapest: Gondolat, 1966); and Gyula Ortutay, *Kis magyar néprajz* [Small Hungarian ethnography] (Budapest: Gondolat, 1966). For useful statistical data on the various non–Hungarian minorities and immigrants, see László Kővágó, *Nemzetiségek a mai Magyarországon* [Nationalities in today's Hungary] (Budapest: Kossuth, 1881); Ferencz Székely, "Számok és tanulságok" [Numbers and lessons], in *Évkönyv* (1900), pp. 43–49.

Notes to Chapter II

[1] *A magyar antiszemitapárt megsemmisitése és ennek következményei* [Destruction of the Hungarian anti–Semitic party and its consequences] (Budapest: n.p., 1906), p. 2. Hereafter cited as *Magyar antiszemitapárt.*

[2] Iván Bertényi, *A magyar korona története* [History of the Hungarian crown] (Budapest: Kossuth, 1980), pp. 118–120.

[3] Until 1889 when the hereditary disease of the princely Wittelbachs claimed her mind, the Empress had been a loyal and much–

loved friend of Hungary. No doubt the disease was accelerated by the suicide of her son, Crown Prince Rudolf on January 30 of that year. See Tarr, *Délibábok országa*, pp. 110–111. Rudolf, himself a friend of the Hungarians, had been offered the Junior Kingship of Hungary by Prime Minister Kálmán Tisza. See Judith Listowel, *A Habsburg Tragedy, Crown Prince Rudolf* (London: Accent Books, 1978), pp. 85–89.

4 Bosnyák, *Istóczy*, p. 21.

5 Istóczy, *Magyar antiszemitapárt*, p. 1.

6 *Ibid.*

7 Lajos Venetianer, *A magyar zsidóság története* [History of Hungarian Jewry] (Budapest: n.p., 1922), p. 99. Hereafter cited as *Magyar zsidóság*.

8 *Ibid.*, p. 100.

9 *Ibid.*

10 The location of such estates and the names of their owners are listed by Venetianer, *Magyar zsidóság*, pp. 107 and 113.

11 Childhood experiences enabled József Nagy to recreate the lifestyle of Jews in the countryside in "Falusi zsidó–élet Vasmegyében" [Rural Jewish life in Vas County]. *Évkönyv*, (1904), pp. 174–205.

12 László Fayer, *A magyar búnvádi eljárás mai érvényében* [Contemporary Hungarian criminal procedure] (Budapest: Franklin, 1887), p. 46.

13 The fabled exploits and picturesque lifestyle of the *betyárs*, the most famous of whom were Sándor Rózsa and Gyurka Babaj, are described in colorful detail in Tarr, *Délibábok országa*, pp.110–111.

14 Only two primary sources are extant. Istóczy later offered a rare, albeit brief and partial, glimpse into the circumstances of the trial years later in the course of a libel suit initiated against him. He also penned a malevolent, cryptic account of the event.

15 The actual amount of the difference is at variance. Istóczy (*Ibid.*, p. 1) recalled 45,000 forints, whereas Bosnyák (*Istóczy*, p. 23) put the figure at 60,000. In either case, the figure is astronomic in view of Istóczy's financial worth.

16 Istóczy, *A magyar antiszemitapárt*, pp. 2–3. Bosnyák (*Istóczy*, p. 23) expanded the conspiracy theory to include the Jews of neighboring Zala County as well.

17 *Magyar antiszemitapárt*, p. 4.

18 Bosnyák, *Istóczy*, p. 24.

19 *Ibid.* Vas may have been one of the more reform–minded of counties (Béla K. Király, *Ferenc Deák* (Boston: Twayne, 1975),

p. 92. The enlightened Deák—he leased his house in his native town of Sojtor in Zala County to the local Jewish community to be used as its official house of worship, yet accepted no money in return (*ibid.*, p. 117)—could hardly have sponsored the political career of an anti-Semitic upstart.

20 *Magyar antiszemitapárt*, p. 4. Regarding the intrigues of the *kahal*, Istóczy chose to remain conveniently and mystifyingly cryptic: "I do not wish to discuss its details here. I should tell it all—the space for that is inadequate—or nothing."

21 Alarmed by the seemingly unending waves of Jewish immigrants from Galicia in the 1840s, some of Hungary's most respected politicians, including Count István Széchenyi and Lajos Kossuth, spoke out against the presence of uninvited aliens who, they claimed, served neither the interest nor the future of Hungary and the Hungarian people. See Venetianer, *Magyar zsidóság*, p. 101.

22 Bosnyák, *Istóczy*, p. 24. Inexplicably, neither Deák's name nor his political influence is cited in any of Istóczy's terse autobiographical accounts.

23 Although it enjoyed a good reputation nationwide, the Deák party was not without critics. "There has never been a more dissolute, maladjusted and hatefully fratricidal government party in the country," observed one Imre Visy. "Its members have greater confidence in their political opponents than in one another." Quoted in Tarr, *Délibábok országa*, p. 49.

24 The candidates put up a portion of the cost of wining and dining the electors. Istóczy complained ruefully of sliding near the edge of bankruptcy. However, he justified his expenses as an effort to neutralize the well-financed and well-organized Jewish opposition to his candidacy.

25 László Tarr's tongue-in-cheek description of Hungarian counties (*Délibábok országa*, pp. 51–60) is a useful source of information for the often ribald election process of the late 1860s and early 1870s. For a more detailed, albeit chronologically slightly earlier account, see Andor Csizmadia, *A magyar választási rendszer 1848–1849-ben* [The Hungarian election system in 1848–1849] (Budapest: Közgazdasági és Jogi Könyvkiadó, 1963).

26 Rum was not one of the thirteen cities in Vas County where Jewish communities existed between 1723 and 1929. See László, "Hungarian Jewry," p. 119. Individual Jews, however, were known to have been residents of the city.

Notes to Chapter III

1 György Kiss (*A budapesti várospolitika 1873–1944* [City politics of Budapest], 2nd rev. ed., Budapest: Közgazdasági és Jogi Könyvkiadó, 1958, pp. 25–26) gives a sobering description of Pest–Buda's woes in the early 1870s.

2 Tarr, *Délibábok országa*, pp. 64–71, 187–189; Vörös, *Egy világváros születése*, pp. 190–199. By the end of the nineteenth century, the Hungarian capital had more houses of prostitution, ranging from cheap brothels to elegant salons, than any other European city. See Mme. Endre Tóth, ed., *Budapest enciklopédia* (Budapest: Corvina, 1981), s.v. "Prostitúció" [Prostitution].

3 An impressively large number of studies describe the character and more notable features of Budapest in the latter half of the nineteen century. For an interesting, almost contemporary account, containing many useful pieces of information, including photos, sketches and advertisements, see Joseph Kahn *An Illustrated Guide of Budapest* (Budapest: Légrády, 1891).

4 Vörös, *Egy világváros születése*, pp. 190–199; Tóth, *Budapest enciklopédia*, s.v. "Budapest neve" [Budapest's name].

5 Following the emperor's approval on 26 August 1865 of the plans designed by Miklós Ybl (1814–1891), the famed architect of many of Budapest's public buildings, churches, spas and palaces on the aristrocrats' country estates, construction began on September 11 and was completed on December 9 of the same year. See Tóth, *Budapest enciklopédia* s.v. "Képviselőház (Régi)" [House of Representatives (old)].

6 Tarr, *Délibábok országa*, p. 46.

7 Kenyeres, *Magyar életrajzi lexikon*, s.v. "Tisza Kálmán."

8 Tarr, *Délibábok országa*, pp. 49–51; András Gergely and Zoltán Szász, *Kiegyezés után*, [After the compromise] (Budapest: Gondolat, 1978), pp. 51–66.

9 *Istóczy*, p. 24.

10 *A zsidókról* [On the Jews] (Budapest: Nándor Tettey and Co., 1875). It is difficult to gauge the interest with which the fifty-three page pamphlet was received. That it was not limited to a handful of readers is indicated by the curious fact that one of the few existing copies, now in the possession of Hungary's prestigious Széchényi Library, had been acquired by Lajos Kossuth, the exiled leader of the 1848 Revolution. It is marked by the bookplate of his personal library and numbered 1966.

11 *Ibid.*, p. ii.

Notes to Chapter IV

1 Kenyeres, *Magyar életrajzi lexikon*, s.v. "Sennyei Pál."
2 For additional details, see I. T. Berend and G. Ránki, *Hungary, A Century of Economic Development* (London: David and Charles, 1974).
3 Extensive accounts of the cholera epidemic of 1872–1873, the second in fifty years to sweep across Hungary, may be found in F. Fodor and I. Vedres, *A közegészségtan és járványtan alapjai* [Foundations of public hygiene and epidemiology] (Budapest: Medicina, 1975,), and Geyza Halász, *A Budapesten uralgott járványos betegségek történelme, különös tekintettel a cholerára* [History of contagious diseases prevailing in Budapest with special attention to cholera] (Budapest: Magyar Királyi Tudományos Egyetem Könyvtára, 1879).
4 György Szabad, *Forradalom és kiegyezés válaszútján (1860–1861)* [At the crossroads of revolution and compromise] (Budapest: Akadémiai Kiadó, 1967), pp. 359–366.
5 On 29 July 1849 the revolutionary Diet, having fled to Szeged, performed one of its last legislative acts when it passed the emancipatory "Bill Concerning the Jews." It was subsequently abrogated by the Austrians. The second bill of emancipation was passed on 25 November 1867.
6 George Barany, "Magyar Jew or Jewish Magyar" (To the Question of Jewish Assimilation in Hungary), *Canadian–American Slavic Studies* (Spring 1974), p. 27. János Széchy chronicles the manifold attempts of Hungarian Jews at assimilation and identifies the areas of their conspicuous achievements in *Az ittfelejtett nép* [People left here] (Budapest: Magyar Enciklopédisták Társasága, 1945).
7 Paul Ignotus, *Hungary* (London: Ernest Benn, 1972), p. 91.
8 *Ibid.*, p. 93.
9 Not all Orthodox rabbis stood for separatism. Eizik Taub (1751–1821), one of the founders of Hasidism in Hungary, spoke Hungarian flawlessly and was respected by his Christian neighbors with whom he mingled freely and frequently. For additional details, see Andrew Handler, ed. and trans., *Rabbi Eizik: Hasidic Stories About the Zaddik of Kálló* (Cranbury, N.J.: Associated University Presses, 1978). Similar flexibility was displayed by Izrael Hildescheimer (1820–1899), the German–born rabbi of Kismarton. A man of uncommon intellectual qualities, he moved easily in both the world of the Talmud and secular learning, distinguishing himself in mathematics and classical languages. He

received a doctorate in Oriental Studies from the University of Halle in 1844. Hildescheimer was repelled by the rigid combativeness of the Orthodoxy and founded the Cultured Orthodox, a small group of followers dedicated to both the preservation of tradition and the cultivation of the spirit of enlightenment and progress. Ujvári, *Magyar zsidó lexikon*, s.v. "Hildescheimer Izrael Azriel."

[10] Ernest (Ernő) Marton presents a sweeping overview of the composition of the immigrants in "The Family Tree of Hungarian Jewry" in *Hungarian–Jewish Studies*, 1:1–59.

[11] Ignotus, *Hungary*, p. 105.

[12] The *Magyar zsidó lexikon* contains the full list of such dignitaries under the entry "Nemesek" [Nobles].

[13] As punishment for participating in the 1848 Revolution, General Baron Julius Haynau (1786–1853), the heavy–handed military governor assigned to oversee the implementation of Austrian absolutism, levied a fine of 2,300,000 forints on Hungarian Jewry which Francis Joseph subsequently annulled. In its place he decreed the collection of 1,000,000 forints for the purpose of setting up a school and educational fund. The latter financed the construction of Jewish schools, teachers' institutes and the National Rabbinical Seminary. See Ujvári, *Magyar zsidó lexikon*, s.v. "Iskolaalap," [School fund].

[14] Venetianer, *Magyar zsidóság*, pp. 306–308.

[15] *Magyar antiszemitapárt*, p. 4.

[16] Judit Kubinszky's detailed study of the contemporary movements is included in her *Politikai antiszemitizmus Magyarországon (1875–1890)* [Political anti–Semitism in Hungary] (Budapest: Kossuth, 1976), pp. 5–19. Hereafter cited as *Politikai antiszemitizmus*. She, however, stops short of acknowledging the chronological precedence of Istóczy's first anti–Semitic speech.

[17] *Magyar zsidóság*, p. 324. Venetianer's reputation as an expert on late nineteenth–century Hungarian Jewish history (Ujvári, *Magyar zsidó lexikon*, s.v. "Venetianer Lajos") lends his ominous words particular weight and credibility. In 1871 a certain Pater Sasinek set off an outbreak of anti–Semitic agitation in the Croat–dominated town of Túrocszentmárton. In sermons and in articles that he wrote in the *Narodne Noviny*, a Croat–language newspaper, he denounced the Jews of the area for being patriotic Magyars and making Magyar the language of instruction in their schools. Venetianer also noted that the "ultimate causes of Judeophobia in Hungary may be found not only in the vengeful craze of one man, but also in the decades of nationwide economic

problems preceding it. Istóczy was merely the spark that ignited the flammable material. Sooner or later, it would have reached the point of combustion and exploded on its own," (*Magyar zsidóság*, p. 325). Lastly, Venetianer cited a financial scandal, involving a certain Count Langrand–Dumonceau, a Belgian–born financial manipulator of the early 1870s. His preposterous plan of "Christianizing capital" and his warnings against the Jewish menace attracted and subsequently ruined numerous unsuspecting investors of modest means whose bitterness could easily be turned into a political asset by the newest scourge of the Jews (*Ibid.*, pp. 338–339).

[18] Istóczy claimed that he requested to speak in connection with a naturalization bill which included the proposed granting of citizenship to foreign Jews residing in Hungary. See *Istóczy Győző országgyűlési beszédei inditványai és törvényjavaslatai 1872–1896* [Győző Istóczy's parliamentary speeches, resolutions, and bills] (Budapest: F. Buschmann, 1904), p. 1. Hereafter cited as *Beszédei.*

[19] *Ibid.*, pp. 1–8.

[20] Trained as a lawyer, Ghyczy (1808–1888) had a fifty–five–year political career. After a decade spent in local public service, he entered national politics as the representative of his native Komárom County. Because he was state secretary in the ministry of justice in the short–lived government of the ill–fated Count Lajos Batthyány, the Austrians sentenced him to forced retirement on his estate. Subsequently, he resumed his career in politics and was elected president of the Diet in 1861 and leader of the Left Center. He was minister of justice (1874–1875) in the cabinet of Prime Minister István Bittó. He resigned that position and in 1875 was reelected president of the Diet, a position he held for four years. In 1885, he was named to the House of Magnates. See Kenyeres, *Magyar életrajzi lexikon* s.v. "Ghyczy Kálmán."

[21] The parliamentary record, reproduced by Istóczy, shows two instances of the representatives voicing approval of Ghyczy's remarks.

[22] Istóczy, *Beszédei*, pp. 8–12.

[23] *Ibid.*, pp. 12–14.

[24] *Ibid.*, pp. 14–16.

[25] *Ibid.*, pp. 15–16.

[26] *Ibid.*, pp. 16–17.

[27] Istóczy, *Magyar antiszemitapárt*, p. 4. That opinion, ironically, was not shared by Istóczy's slavish hagiographer. According to Zoltán Bosnyák (*Istóczy*, p. 25), Istóczy's first speech did not

evoke a loud echo. By then, directly and indirectly, the press was primarily in Jewish hands. The Jews preferred to keep quiet about the matter rather than call attention to it. Bosnyák also reduced Istóczy's imaginary European fame to Austria and Germany where the incipient anti–Semitic organizations were greatly heartened by the first reports of the speech.

[28] Berend and Ránki, *Hungary*, pp. 28–39; Tarr, *Délibábok országa*, pp. 87–89.

[29] *Beszédei*, pp. 18–21.

[30] Venetianer (*Magyar zsidóság*, p. 316) was aware of the stock-exchange portion of the speech but inaccurately characterized it as having been presented "with the appropriate undertone, of course." Istóczy's style in public speaking left nothing to imagination. He spoke his mind; allusion was not a technique he employed.

[31] Du Mesnil–Marigny, *A zsidókról*, pp. 27–31.

[32] A journalist by training, Csernátony (1823–1901) was Kossuth's secretary during the revolution of 1848. He spent nearly twenty years in exile, living in France, England and Italy. He contributed articles to many prominent newspapers. After returning to Hungary in 1867, he won election into the Diet and remained active in both politics and journalism until his death. See Kenyeres, *Magyar életrajzi lexikon*, s.v. "Csernátony Lajos."

[33] Istóczy, *Beszédei*, pp. 32–37. A writer with an entertaining but offensive style with which he set a new tone for political journalism in Hungary, Csernátony penned a number of articles about Hungarian Jews in the *Ellenőr,* a Budapest daily which he edited briefly. Although he denounced anti–Semitism, his description of the so–called negative Jewish traits were eventually exploited by anti–Semites to bolster their own arguments. György Száraz skillfully incorporated Csernátony's articles into his account of the development of anti–Semitism in modern Hungary, *Egy előítélet nyomában* [In pursuit of a prejudice] (Budapest: Magvető, 1976).

[34] Venetianer (*Magyar zsidóság*, p. 316) inaccurately reported Istóczy's attack on "Jewish usury." Bosnyák's description (*Istóczy*, pp. 25–26) was more in keeping with the contents and spirit of the speech.

[35] Istóczy, *Beszédei*, pp. 38–41.

Notes to Chapter V

[1] The name of Edouard–Adolphe Drumont (1844–1917) and anti-Semitism became synonymous in late nineteenth–century France.

Fighting against the alleged Jewish subjugation of France was the leitmotif of his book, *La France juive* (1886); the anti-Semitic League which he founded in 1889; and *La Libre Parole*, the newspaper which disseminated his views and fueled the anti-Semitic hysteria during the Dreyfus Affair.

2 Istóczy, *Magyar antiszemitapárt*, pp. 4–5.

3 Győző Istóczy, *Emlékiratfélék és egyebek* [Memoirs of sorts and other things] (Budapest: F. Buschmann, 1911), p. 15. Hereafter cited as *Emlékiratfélék*.

4 Istóczy's misplaced faith and narrowness of vision appear even more glaring in light of the date of his claim (1911). He made it in *Emlékiratfélék*, a slim volume of garbled reminiscences. Astonishingly, he was unaware of the proto–Zionists and made no mention of the Budapest–born Theodor Herzl, the founder of political Zionism who had been dead for seven years; the work of the World Zionist Organization; or the profound anti–Zionism of the Hungarian Jews—the Progressives' exaggerated nationalism and the presumed incompatability of the Messiah–centered beliefs of the Orthodox and Zionist secularism. No more enlightened was Zoltán Bosnyák. He called Istóczy the "virtual forerunner of Zionism, the subsequent Jewish nationalist movement." (*Istóczy*, p. 26).

5 For further details on the difficulties presented by accepting Herzl's statement at face value, see Andrew Handler, *Dori: The Life and Times of Theodor Herzl in Budapest (1860–1878)* (University, Alabama: University of Alabama Press, 1985), pp. 26–27 and 32–34.

6 For a comprehensive study of the Hungarians' likes and dislikes of other nations, see István Diószegi, *Nemzet, dinasztia, külpolitika* [Nation, dynasty, foreign policy] (Budapest: Magvető, 1979).

7 Istóczy, *Beszédei*, p. 42.

8 Zsigmond Tieder, author of the comprehensive entry, "Magyarország zsidósága" [Hungary's Jewry], in the *Magyar zsidó lexikon* and a prominent sociopolitical writer, disputed the accuracy of census figures prior to 1869, the year authoritative statistical data were made available. The figures support Istóczy's conclusion —but only retroactively. The numerical increase of the Jews in the next thirty–year period—553,641 in 1869 and 846,254 in 1900—fell short of his prediction.

9 On 29 August 1526 the armies of the Ottoman Sultan Suleiman II routed the forces of King Louis II at this town in southern Hungary. The victory led to a 150–year Turkish occupation of Hungary. Klára Hegyi describes life in Hungary under the role of the

Muslim Turks in her informative *Egy világbirodalom végvidékén*
[At the borderland of a vast empire] (Budapest: Gondolat, 1976).

[10] As if anticipating the need to allay the incredulity this preposterous, albeit oft–heard, theory would evoke, Istóczy lined up a
contemporary corroborator. He cited the *Revue de France*, whose
31 October 1875 issue contained an article, "De la race juive,"
by a botanist identified only by the initials A. L. Istóczy believed
him to be a Hungarian. The author contended that available statistical evidence on the cholera epidemics through the centuries
supported the conclusion that Jews were far less susceptible to
the disease and succumbed to it in significantly lower numbers
than non–Jews. See *Beszédei*, p. 47.

[11] Istóczy's attitude toward the veracity of details was as cavalier
as his unshakable belief that anyone born a Jew or to Jewish parents remained, even if converted, a Jew for life. Of the "five Jewish statesmen" only Eduard Lasker (1829–1884), an influential
politician in Berlin, was a practicing Jew. Like Disraeli, Julius
Anton Glaser (1831–1885), and Joseph Unger (b. 1828)—the former a professor of jurisprudence at the University of Vienna and
subsequently minister without portfolio, the latter professor of
criminology at the same institution and subsquently minister of
justice—were converts to Christianity. Leon Michel Gambetta
(1838–1882), the French statesman, was the son of practicing
Catholic parents. His Jewish descent, first rumored by Drumont
in *La France Juive*, was deduced from his "Semitic" nose and
dark curly hair but never substantiated.

[12] The text of the "Palestine Speech," as well as Ghyczy and Trefort's remarks, are reproduced in Istóczy, *Beszédei*, pp. 41–63.

[13] Bosnyák, *Istóczy*, p. 30. Bosnyák's allegation that by the summer of 1878 Istóczy's views had won him considerable following
among the lower Catholic clergy, the gentry and university students is not backed by evidence. By 1880, however, they formed
the basis of Istóczy's emergent popularity.

Notes to Chapter VI

[1] Berend and Ránki, *Hungary*, p. 86. The development, goals
and organization of the workers' movement in Hungary have attracted numerous chroniclers. For useful information on Istóczy's
burgeoning attention to the workers of his time see the follow-

ing studies: Erzsébet Andics, *A magyarországi munkásmozgalom az 1848–49-es forradalomtól az 1917 nagy októberi szocialista forradalomig* [The Hungarian workers' movement from the revolution of 1848–49 to the Great October Socialist Revolution of 1917] (Budapest: Szikra, 1956); Iván T. Berend and Miklós Szuhay, *A tőkésgazdaság története Magyarországon (1848–1944)* [History of the capitalist economy in Hungary] (Budapest: Kossuth, 1978); Klára Dóka, *A pest-budai céhes ipar válsága (1840–72* [Crisis of the guild industry of Pest–Buda] (Budapest: Akadémiai Kiadó, 1979); László Felkai, *A munkásság művelődési törekvései a dualizmus korában* [The cultural endeavors of workers in the age of dualism] (Budapest: Tankönyvkiadó, 1980).

2 A lifelong advocate of the rights of workers everywhere, Frankel (1844–1896) was one of the most active and feared organizers of the international workers' movement. For years he lived in Germany, France, Switzerland, England, and Austria. Although he spent only seven years (1876–1883) as an adult in the country of his birth, the Hungarian authorities kept a close watch on him. He was imprisoned twice during his stay in Hungary. He died and was buried in Paris. The son of a Jewish physician in Óbuda and a true internationalist, Frankel appeared particularly odious in Istóczy's eyes. See Kenyeres, *Magyar életrajzi lexikon* and Ujvári, *Magyar zsidó lexikon*, s.v. "Frankel Leó."

3 Erik Molnár, Ervin Pamlényi, and György Székely, eds., *Magyarország története*, 2 vols. (Budapest: Gondolat, 1967), 2:123.

4 Istóczy, *Beszédei*, pp. 64–66.

5 *Ibid.*, pp. 67–71.

6 Like Kálmán Ghyczy, his predecessor, József Szlávy (1818–1900), commanded respect and admiration for his fervent patriotism and political pragmatism. A mining engineer by training, during the 1848 Revolution Szlávy directed the reorganization of factory production of everything from civilian goods to war materiel. He was subsequently tried by the victorious Austrians and sentenced to five years in jail. After serving two and a half years he was released. Elected into the Diet in 1867, Szlávy rose quickly in various government posts (state secretary for the interior, 1867–1869; minister of agriculture, industry and commerce, 1870–1872; prime minister, 1872–1874; and minister of finance, 1873–1874). His presidency of the Diet, a position he held in 1879–1880, capped his distinguished career as a representative. In 1882 Szlávy was named to the House of Magnates, and later became its vice–president (1885–1894) and president (1894–1896). See Kenyeres, *Magyar életrajzi lexikon*, s.v. "Szlávy József."

7 *Statuten–Entwurf des Central–Vereins des Nichtjuden–Bundes von Ungarn* (Berlin: n. p., 1880).

8 Istóczy, *Beszédei*, pp. 72–75.

9 For additional details, see Kenyeres, *Magyar életrajzi lexikon,* s.v., "Verhovay Gyula"; Andrew Handler, *Blood Libel at Tiszaeszlár* (East European Monographs—New York: Columbia University Press, 1980), p. 31. Hereafter cited as *Tiszaeszlár.* In addition to a talent for inflammatory journalism, Verhovay displayed a burning zeal to leave his mark by means of a more lasting literary vehicle. His books, *Az álarc korszaka* [Age of the mask] (Budapest: F. Buschmann, 1889), and *Az ország urai* [Masters of the Country] (Budapest: F. Buschmann, 1890), are monuments to his painfully offensive style and implacably hate–filled mind.

10 Jews were expelled from the city in 1360 and 1526. Following their gradual return in the early eighteenth century, huge gates enclosing a part of the city where Jews lived in large numbers were installed. Although the gates of the ghetto of Pozsony were removed in the early 1840s, the Jewish quarter was the scene of anti–Jewish violence during the revolution of 1848 and the trial of the Tiszaeszlár Jews in 1883. See Ujvári, *Magyar zsidó lexikon,* s.v. "Pozsony"; Andor Sas, *A koronázó város* [The coronation city] (Bratislava: Madách, 1973); Bertalan Fabó, "A pozsonyi gyászos húsvét" [The mournful Easter of Pozsony], in *Évkönyv* (1913), pp. 276–280.
   Despite the consistency of his anti–Jewish views, Simonyi was the most reasonable of the leading anti–Semites of his time. He called for patience in face of the gradual transition of Hungarian Jewry from disenfranchised isolation to constructive citizenship. That spirit pervades his books, *Nemzeti tragikomédia* [National tragicomedy] (Budapest: n. p., 1880) and *Mentsük meg a magyar földbirtokot* [Let's save the Hungarian manor] (Pozsony and Lipcse: n. p., 1882).

11 Kubinszky, *Politikai antiszemitizmus,* pp. 65–66.

12 Istóczy, *Magyar antiszemitapárt,* p. 5.

13 Supra, p. 32.

14 Istóczy, *Beszédei,* pp. 76–81.

15 Kubinszky, *Politikai antiszemitizmus,* p. 66. The event was reported by Istóczy in the February 15 edition of the *12 Röpirat.* Most of the 234 signatures also identify places of permanent residence outside Budapest. The number of law students (148) is nearly twice the number of students from other fields of specialization.

16 Venetianer, *Magyar zsidóság,* pp. 342–343.

17 The Jewish communities of Pásztó and Losonc were formed early in the nineteenth century. It is a matter of record that the Jews of Losonc were represented in the revolutionary armies in 1848, suffered with the townspeople from the ravaging Austrian and Russian forces, and witnessed the punishment of their spiritual leader Rabbi Moshe Hőgyész for his support of the cause of independence. A further proof of the patriotism of Losonc's Jewry may be deduced from the consecration ceremony of its first synagogue in 1863 during which the guest speaker, Rabbi Salamon Braun of Putnok, delivered his sermon in Hungarian. No documentation of the patriotism of the Jews of Pásztó exists. However, circumstantial evidence leads to a similar, albeit inferential, conclusion. Public opinion and policy–making decisions in a Jewish community customarily mirrored the views and preferences of respected spiritual leaders or the wealthiest members of the community. The most prominent of Losonc's Jewish families, the Wohls, the first Jews allowed to settle in the town in the late eighteenth century, were also the founders of the Jewish community of Pásztó, where they owned a sizeable estate. See Ujvári, *Magyar zsidó lexikon,* s.v. "Losonc" and "Pásztó" For a detailed account of the participation of Jews in the 1848 Revolution, see Béla Bernstein, *Az 1848/49-iki magyar szabadságharc es a zsidók* [The 1848–49 Hungarian war of independence and the Jews] (Budapest: Franklin, 1898).

18. Like his predecessors, Tamás Péchy (1828–97) basked in the afterglow of the 1848 Revolution. He had fought with distinction and was promoted to major. Upon leaving the Austrian army, into which he had been forcibly conscripted after the revolution, Péchy launched a career in politics in Abaúj County. In 1868 he ran a successful campaign on the Liberal Party ticket and was elected into the Diet. He was appointed minister of public works and transportation in the Wenckheim and Tisza governments (1875–80), and in 1880 became president of the Diet, a post he held until 1888. See Kenyeres, *Magyar életrajzi lexikon,* s.v. "Péchy Tamás."

19. Istóczy, *Beszédi,* pp. 82–100.

20. *Ibid.,* pp. 100–101.

21. In the spring of 1881 the *Berliner Ostend Zeitung* featured a lengthy interview with Istóczy. The reporter described him as the person "whom Europe could thank for causing the Jewish Question to resurface." Reiterating one of the arguments in the interpellation, Istóczy disputed the assertion of Adolf Stöcker, the founder of the Christian Socialist Workers' Party and a fellow

inciter of students, that converted Jews could be embraced as trusted members of Christian society and accorded equal rights. "[Buda] Pest suffers of Jews and Europe suffers of the Jewish pest," he noted with callous facetiousness. See Bosnyák, *Istóczy*, pp. 38–39.

Notes to Chapter VII

[1] The election was held on June 24. The results reconfirmed Istóczy's popularity. Of the 1,816 votes cast he received 1,419. Only 397 people wanted Béni Tulok, a district judge, to replace Istóczy. The winner's acceptance speech put his supporters in a curious light which may have made some of them feel uncomfortable. "May the district of Rum remain the impregnable bastion of anti–Semitism," Istóczy delcared confidently. See Bosnyák, *Istóczy*, p. 38.

[2] Jenő Zsoldos, "Két elfelejtett Mikszáth–karcolat" [Two forgotten Mikszáth sketches] in Sándor Scheiber, ed., *Évkönyv* (1970), p. 191. Mikszáth was one of the few nineteenth–century Hungarian writers in whose works Jews appear more clearly defined than the customary incidental, faintly drawn characters, and it may be said developed a firm outlook on Jews. Intimately familiar with the people of the countryside, Mikszáth often wrote of the lifestyle and character of the Jews, honestly yet at times sharply. See Jenő Zsoldos, *Magyar irodalom és zsidóság* [Hungarian literature and Jewry] (Budapest: Országos Izraelita Tanítóegyesület, 1943), p. 87; István Radó, "Zsidó vonatkozások Mikszáth műveiben" [References to Jews in Mikszáth's works], in *Évkönyv* (1913), pp. 166–195.

[3] Planning to attract readers outside Budapest, however, he ran the risk of confronting the opposition. The most spirited and durable campaign against the *12 Röpirat* was conducted in Nagyvárd where Márton Hevesi, an Independence Party representative in the Diet, edited the *12 Ellenröpirat*. Although its contributors were progressive intellectuals residing in the city, the *12 Ellenröpirat* also attracted outsiders, including Kálmán Mikszáth who wrote two anti–Istóczy sketches. After a little more than a year of operation the journal fell on hard times and ceased publication in October 1882. A less successful undertaking, the *12 Telefon* in Kaposvár, lasted but a few editions. A similar effort in Győr did not even get beyond the planning stage. See Kubinszky, *Politikai antiszemitizmus*, pp. 86–87.

[4] *Ibid.*, p. 85.

5 A similarly receptive climate developed among the mostly Slavic and German–speaking Lutheran ministers and Greek Orthodox priests ministering to the spiritual needs of Hungary's Romanian and Serbian nationalities.

6 As he accepted the watered–down version of the Hungarian government's disapproval of the declaration of papal infallibility at the 1869–1870 Vatican Council, Pope Pius IX's alleged words to the members of the prematurely departing delegation of Hungarian bishops were: "You are much too wealthy." Quoted in Tarr, *Délibábok országa*, p. 101.

7 Venetianer, *Magyar zsidóság*, p. 344.

8 Remarkable achievements highlighted the brief career of Gábor Baross (1848–1892), a lawyer turned politician and one of the most influential economic reformers and innovators of his time. A member of the Diet from 1875, Baross was a loyal supporter of Prime Minister Kálmán Tisza in whose government he served as minister of public works and transportation (1886–1889) and as minister of commerce (1889–1892). His name became synonymous with the modernization of Hungarian economy.

9 In February 1882, Albert Berzeviczy (1853–1936) was still a virtual, albeit promising, newcomer. A lawyer turned politician, Berzeviczy got his start in his native Sáros County. In 1881 he was elected into the Diet on the Liberal Party ticket. The various positions in which he served in his career of fifty years indicate an uncommonly broad spectrum of interests. He was state secretary in the ministry of cults (1887–1894), a vice–president of the Diet (1895–1898), minister of cults (1903–1905), president of the National Council on Physical Education (1913–1923), a member of the House of Magnates (1927), and president of the Hungarian Pen Club (1932). See Kenyeres, *Magyar életrajzi lexikon*, s.v. "Berzeviczy Albert."

10 From the Hebrew *shochet*, meaning slaughterer, i.e., the authorized slaughter of animals, according to the rules governing kosher food. In this instance, however, the expression was used by Istóczy as a euphemism for killing humans, possibly alluding to the absurd rumors of the blood libel.

11 Istóczy, *Beszédei*, pp. 104–113. Nearly contemporary data and analysis testify to waves of large–scale emigration of Jews from Hungary. See Dávid Kohn (Pap), "Zsidó népmozgalom statisztika" [Jewish demographical statistics], in *Évkönyv* (1895), pp. 35–47; Idem., "Zsidók vándorlása" [Wanderings of Jews], *Ibid.*, (1896), pp. 46–51 and (1903), pp. 22–28.

12 *Ibid.*, pp. 114–117.

[13] József Bary, *A tiszaeszlári bűnper. Bary József vizsbálóbíró emlékiratai The criminal case of Tiszaeszlár. The memoirs of Investigating Magistrate József Bary,* 2nd ed. (Budapest: Magyar Élet Kiadása, 1941), p. 30. Hereafter cited as *Tiszaeszlári bűnper.* In the Preface, members of the Bary family voice their hope that the new edition will "set the record straight" about Tiszaeszlár, which had been distorted by Károly Eötvös in his three–volume work, and remove the stain caused by the *Magyar zsidó lexikon* from József Bary's reputation.

[14] Handler, *Tiszaeszlár,* pp. 36–47. For a detailed study of the stubbornly enduring legacy of Tiszaeszlár and other anti–Jewish traditions, see Ilona Dobos, *Tarcal története a szóhagyományban* [History of Tarcal in oral tradition] (Budapest: Akadémiai Kiadó, 1971).

[15] *Ibid.,* p. 202, n. 5.

[16] The author of the report was József Adamovics, the Catholic priest of Tiszaeszlár. See Handler, *Tiszaeszlár,* pp. 32 and 218, n. 4.

[17] Jews had settled in growing numbers and prospered in Ónody's political base since the end of the eighteenth century. There is no evidence of strong anti–Semitic feelings in the town that would have justified Ónody's election purely on those grounds. See László Harsányi, "Adalékok a hajdúvárosok zsidóságának történetéhez" [Addenda to the history of the Jews in the hajduk towns], in *Évkönyv* (1970), pp. 116–165.

[18] As a participant in the politics and battles of the 1848 Revolution— he acquitted himself with distinction in both—and subsequently one of Lajos Kossuth's closest collaborators in exile, Dániel Irányi (1822–1892) laid a firm emotional foundation for his post–*Ausgleich* political career. Upon his return to Hungary he was elected chairman of the Forty–Eighters Party, and after its demise he assumed the leadership of the Independence Party. See Kenyeres, *Magyar életrajzi lexikon,* s.v. "Irányi Dániel."

[19] Investigating Magistrate József Bary was convinced that the disappearance of Eszter Solymosi was a criminal case. He accused József Adamovics, the Catholic priest of Tiszaeszlár and author of the implicating report in *Magyar Állam,* of persuading Ónody to speak of ritual murder in the Diet. "A fatal error," Bary observed (*Tiszaeszlári bűnper,* p. 154). The speech, however, caused no uproar. Only Verhovay's *Függetlenség* reported it on the following day, noting that Ónody seemed hurt by the indifference with which his speech had been received. In general, Bary was critical of Ónody and Istóczy for blowing the Tiszaeszlár

case out of proportion and exploiting it for political advantage. He characterized Ónody's speech and tactic of quoting Talmudic passages, which Ónody claimed, encouraged Jews to kill Christians, in an effort to prove the Tiszaeszlár case a ritual murder, as "possibly the most unfortunate things." He called Ónody a "Tiszaeszlár anti-Semite" as opposed to Istóczy whose anti-Semitism "stood on a higher ideological plane" (*Ibid.* p. 199).

20 Istóczy, *Beszédei*, pp. 118–127.

21 Mór Szatmári, *Húsz esztendő parlamenti viharai* [Parliamentary storms of twenty years] (Budapest: Amicus, 1928), p. 24. Hereafter cited as *Húsz esztendő.*

22 Bary, *Tiszaeszlári bűnper*, p. 160.

23 The most convincing proof of the lack of cooperation between Bary and the parliamentary anti-Semites was that on May 23 and 24, the days Ónody and Istóczy spoke in the Diet about the Tiszaeszlár case, neither speaker was informed of the most damaging piece of evidence which had been obtained. On May 21, during a brutal interrogation session, Bary exacted a confession from an exhausted and intimidated fourteen-year-old Móric Scharf, the elder son of the man whose words of consolation to the mother of the missing girl had put the rumor into circulation. According to Bary's report, Móric watched through the keyhole of the synagogue door as two ritual slaughterers slashed the girl's throat and let her blood drip into a pot. The boy's confession was discredited during the trial. See Handler, *Tiszaeszlár*, pp. 50–57.

24 Kubinszky, *Politikai antiszemitizmus*, pp. 95–96.

25 *Tiszaeszlári bűnper*, p. 163.

26 At long last the anti-Semites' star seemed to be on an ascending course. In the early 1880s there were rumors—a letter containing promises of support was alleged to have been circulated by 133 representatives—of the formation of a political group in the Diet. Its initial declaration criticized Prime Minister Tisza's "increasing dependence" on Austria and denounced the high visibility and pervasive influence of the Jews in Hungary. See Handler, *Tiszaeszlár*, p. 84.

27 Szabolcsi's reports actually confirmed the experiences of Ignác Heumann, a well-known Jewish lawyer in Nyíregyháza, who had been hired by the accused Jews of Tiszaeszlár. Heumann, whom the local authorities had harassed and prevented from consulting his clients, was accused of murdering Eszter Solymosi. He eventually traveled to Budapest in search of a more effective means to fight back (*Ibid.*, p. 64).

28 *Ibid.*, p. 95.

29 According to Mátyás Eisler, a prominent Orientalist and chief rabbi of Kolozsvár (today the Romanian city of Cluj), Simon had all the symptoms of *horror publici*, and was aloof, reclusive, and anti–social. Yet he was an efficient and indefatigable administrator and a fearless defender of Jewish rights. See "Simon József," in *Évkönyv* (1916), pp. 227–228.

30 *Ibid.*, pp. 65–66 and 84–86; Kenyeres, *Magyar életrajzi lexikon*, s.v. "Eötvös Károly."

31 Tiszaeszlár affected the two arch–rivals differently. Eötvös would spend the rest of his life basking in the triumphant afterglow of the trial as a champion of human rights, a respected politician and a prolific author. In 1904 he published *A nagy per mely ezer éve folyik s még sincs vége* [The great trial that has lasted for a thousand years and still is not over] (Budapest: Révai Testvérek), hereafter cited as *Nagy per*, a monumental three-volume account of the Tiszaeszlár case. Bary, portrayed as the manifestation of evil, was one of the main characters imprinted with the stigma of everlasting infamy. The publication of the *Nagy per* spurred Bary to start writing his *Tiszaeszlári bűnper*, a massive 850–page embittered and impassioned self–defense and counterattack. The two literary sparring partners not only provide unique, albeit often exasperatingly contradictory, pieces of documentary evidence of the investigation of Eszter Solymosi's disappearance, the interrogation of the defendants and the trial, but also offer rare glimpses into the lives of both the major and minor characters of the great drama that became the epitome of the age–old struggle between injustice and hatred and the quest for truth.

Notes to Chapter VIII

1 Istóczy, *Magyar antiszemitapárt*, p. 7.

2 Before he transformed his *Függetlenség* into an enthusiastic disseminator of anti–Semitic propaganda, Gyula Verhovay thought that Istóczy was not quite sane. See Szatmári, *Húsz esztendő*, p. 25.

3 Istóczy's reminiscences, at times bordering on the incredible, shed some light on the causes of his misplaced loyalty. A Deákist turned Liberal, Istóczy left the parliamentary caucus of his party in the uneasy aftermath of his first anti–Semitic speech in the Diet lest he compromise the party. Upon Tisza's goading—he is alleged to have said, "Don't be pigheaded, Győző, and come back"—Istóczy changed his mind. Until Tiszaeszlár, recalled

Istóczy, the Prime Minister had given him free reins to pacify the opposition representatives among whom Istóczy suspected were his earliest, still undeclared, followers. After Tiszaeszlár, quoting a statement attributed to one of the leaders of the Paris Commune—"I must follow them, after all, I am their leader"— Istóczy decided to join the ranks of his new comrades–in–arms already in the opposition parties. See Istóczy, *Magyar antiszemitapárt*, p. 7. In light of Tisza's consistent denunciation of anti–Semitism, such retrospection appears to be more a self–serving and misleading analysis than a reasonable assessment of the atmosphere which Istóczy's intemperate and foul–mouthed tirades had created.

4   A former member of the Liberal Party, Lajos Mocsáry (1826–1916) had been one of Tisza's early supporters. Following his declaration of opposition to the *Ausgleich*, he switched to the Independence Party which he served as its long–time chairman. Although he counseled Eötvös against accepting the offer to defend the Tiszaeszlár Jews, Mocsáry at times expressed a distaste for anti–Semitism. He was a fair–minded and egalitarian politician who, in deference to Hungary's non–Magyar speaking minorities, disapproved of the increasingly chauvinistic Magyarization of the 1880s, a conviction for which he would pay dearly. The declining years of his political career found him in virtual isolation, forcing him to retire, a disillusioned man, in 1892. See Kenyeres, *Magyar életrajzi lexikon* s.v. "Mocsáry Lajos"; Handler, *Tiszaeszlár*, pp. 84 and 108. The members of the party professed widely disparate views on anti–Semitism. Verhovay and Ónody were anti–Semitic stalwarts; Eötvös held radically opposing views.

5   Bosnyák, *Istóczy*, pp. 48–49.

6   His graphic description of the details of ritual murder caused considerable discomfort among the faint of heart in the crowded galleries. Some visitors complained of the excessive heat in the chamber which contributed to the surge of emotions. Despite repeated warnings from the Diet President, Ónody completed his speech, leaving nothing to imagination. See Kálmán Mikszáth, *Cikkek és karcolatok* [Articles and sketches], in Gyula Bisztray and István Király, eds., *Mikszáth Kálmán összes művei* [Collected Works of Kálmán Mikszáth], vol. 64 (Budapest: Akadémiai Kiadó, 1974), XIV: 188–190.

7   *Ibid.*, p. 191. Mikszáth thought little of the substance and delivery of Istóczy's speech, an opinion that changed little in the course of time.

8   Istóczy, *Beszédei*, pp. 128–141.

9 Mikszáth, *Cikkek és karcolatok*, XIV:192–199. For additional information about Wahrmann, see Gyula Mérei, "Wahrmann Mór," in *Évkönyv* (1943), pp. 313–343; Ujvári, *Magyar zsidó lexikon*, s.v. "Wahrmann Mór."

10 Bosnyák, *Istóczy*, p. 49.

11 Mikszáth, *Cikkek és karcolatok*, XIV:193.

12 Kubinszky, *Politikai antiszemitizmus*, p. 140.

13 Bosnyák, *Istóczy*, p. 49.

14 Mikszáth, *Cikkek és karcolatok*, XIV:195.

15 *Magyar antiszemitapárt*, p. 8.

16 *Ibid.*, p. 7.

17 Kubinszky, *Politikai antiszemitizmus*, p. 140. Istóczy's inflammatory speech, provocation of Wahrmann and removal from the Liberal Party were not transformed into the ingredients of a heroic myth. The *Pesti Napló*, a popular daily, which was, according to József Bary (*Tiszaeszlári bűnper*, pp. 383–384), the investigative magistrate at Tiszaeszlár, a paragon of journalistic virtues—an endorsement the publishers of other contemporary newspapers would have found disquieting—offered the following commentary in its late edition of the eventful day: "We cannot regard the fact that Istóczy, the party which provoked the incident, suffers from a mental condition that borders on insanity, a mitigating circumstance. His feverish delusions and constant, unrelenting, intense hatred have reached a pitch where reason is unable to control impulse and the person is no longer the master of his will." Quoted in Kubinszky, *Politikai antiszemitizmus*, p. 140.

18 Handler, *Tiszaeszlár*, pp. 68–83.

19 Bary (*Tiszaeszlári bűnper*, pp. 378–404), provided a lengthy, useful, albeit venomous, account of the journalistic ballyhoo that engulfed the circumstances surrounding the discovery of the "Csonkafüzes corpse," named after the grove near Tiszaeszár where it was sighted, and the subsequent autopsies.

20 Representing right-wing factions of the Independence Party, Géza Polónyi (1848–1920) would subsequently acquire a reputation as a legal reformer and cap his political career as minister of justice (1906–1907). See Kenyeres, *Magyar életrajzi lexikon*, s.v. "Polónyi Géza."

21 Quoted in Kubinszky, *Politikai antiszemitizmus*, p. 141.

22 P. G. J. Pulzer, *The Rise of Political Anti-Semitism in Germany and Austria* (New York: John Wiley & Sons, 1964), p. 95. Hereafter cited as *Political Anti-Semitism.*

23 Quoted in Bosnyák, *Istóczy*, p. 51.

[24] For additional details on the evolution of modern German anti–Semitism, see Pulzer, *Political Anti–Semitism,* pp. 76–101.

[25] *Ibid.,* p. 103.

[26] *Manifest an die Regierungen und Völker der durch das Judenthum gefährdeten christlichen Staaten laut Beschlusses der ersten internationalen anti–jüdischen Kongress zu Dresden am 11. u. 12 September 1882* (Chemnitz: n. p., 1882).

[27] Quoted in Kubinszky, *Politikai antiszemitizmus,* pp. 254–255.

[28] *Ibid.,* pp. 146–147. In his speeches and writings, Istóczy often stressed his commitment to the maintenance of law and order and his belief that the goals of political anti–Semitism should be achieved by peaceful and lawful means. In the Diet facing censure and even expulsion, he could hardly do otherwise. However, Bosnyák's portrayal of the returning anti–Semitic leaders as the apostles of nonviolence who "everywhere attempted to caution the masses to order and calm, repeatedly stressing that only by legislative means could the Jewish Question be solved" (*Istóczy,* p. 53) is to legitimize deceit and misinformation. The tone of the *12 Röpirat*–led, anti–Semitic publications, to which new magazines of crude humor lent an additional cutting edge, was increasingly inflammatory. Many anti–Semitic pamphlets openly incited violence. Offensive cartoons inspired hate–filled sneers, not laughter.

Notes to Chapter IX

[1] Istóczy was thriving in the receptive climate created by the least educated, most isolated and superstitious segments of Hungary's rural population. He simply ignored those on whom the charge of ritual murder had no effect or denounced them for having allowed the Jews to dupe them. Still, an incident, involving Ónody, caused considerable dismay even in the ranks of the anti–Semites. In the summer of 1882, a certain Lipnitzki, the editor of *Politik,* a Prague daily, whose report on the Tiszaeszlár case had appeared in a Polish newspaper, visted Ónody in Tiszaeszlár. Ónody's hopes of spreading the charge of ritual murder abroad were dashed when Lipnitzki informed him that he had concluded that the anti–Semites were responsible for the disappearance and murder of Eszter Solymosi. See Kubinszky, *Politikai antiszemitizmus,* p. 97.

[2] Szatmári, *Húsz esztendő,* p. 32.

[3] A member of the Independence Party and one of Kossuth's staunchest admirers, Mezei's lifelong interests included the establishment of an independent Hungarian army, public education,

and the legalization of marriages between Christians and Jews. See Ujvári, *Magyar zsidó lexikon*, s.v. "Mezei Ernő."

4 Mikszáth, *Cikkek és karcolatok*, XIV:369–370. According to Szatmári (*Húsz esztendő*, p. 33), Mezei's speech, which was as eloquent as it was emotional, had a curious reception. Speakers were accustomed to being interrupted by catcalls, whistling and other more conventional expressions of support or disapproval. "No audible support for Mezei came," noted Szatmári, "either from the right side or the left." Mezei's principal informant was probably Miksa Szabolcsi, the journalist–sleuth of the Tiszaeszlár case, in whose *Egyenlőség* Mezei had written many articles. See Ujvári, *Magyar zsidó lexikon* s.v. "Mezei Ernő."

5 "The smartest man in the country," as Mikszáth called him (*Cikkek és karcolatok* XIV:174), Eötvös was a consummate anecdotalist who would sit down to a tableful of anti–Semites and leave them dazzled philosemites (*Ibid.*, p. 176). He may also have been the most calculating. Convinced that the inconsistencies which he had detected in the report of the Tiszaeszlár medical authorities were based on an inexpert autopsy and a flawed interpretation of the findings, Eötvös took a quick course in anatomy and pathology from an internationally known surgeon–professor on the Faculty of Medicine at the University of Budapest. He also wrote an autopsy report to his mentor and another prominent pathologist. The large number of errors made in observation and interpretation by the Tiszaeszlár doctors, the two experts concluded, justified Eötvös's request for a new autopsy. Thus was undermined the credibility of the medical evidence with which Bary hoped to irrefutably prove the guilt of the accused Jews. With underhanded ingenuity, Eötvös wasted no time in summarizing the findings and conclusions of his experts: he signed the document as Dr. Glaudius and had it printed and distributed among the sensation–hungry journalists. See Eötvös, *Nagy Per*, 3:168–175. However, Bary (*Tiszaeszlári bűnper*, p. 583) remained undaunted. He interpreted the substance of Eötvös's report differently, believing that it corroborated the findings and conclusions of the court–appointed medical examiners.

6 Kubinszky, *Politikai antiszemitizmus*, p. 148. At the first meeting of the League, the 363 participants ratified a program to "prevent the complete Judaization of our society and effect the eventual departure of Jews from the Christian nations." The editor of the local anti–Semitic weekly, the *Népjog*, was Károly Szalay. His brother, Imre, a parliamentary representative, had left the Independence Party and become one of Istóczy's lieu-

tenants.

7 Handler, *Tiszaeszlár*, pp. 94–103.

8 Ujvári, *Magyar zsidó lexikon*, s.v. "Kecskemét."

9 Kubinszky, *Politikai antiszemitizmus*, pp. 148–150.

10 Szatmári, *Húsz esztendő*, p. 34.

11 Zala had the dubious distinction of being second only to Somogy in the tally of counties (Kubinszky, *Politikai antiszemitizmus*, pp. 127–128) where anti–Jewish demonstrations had taken place. Tapolca was among the thirteen towns listed in Zala.

12 Bosnyák, *Istóczy*, p. 54. Although Jews had lived in Tapolca since the early eighteenth century, their community was formally established in 1813. It was another forty years until the first permanent rabbi, Ábrahám Neuhaus, was hired. Neuhaus remained rabbi of Tapolca's Jews until his death in 1881. He fought as a guardsman in the 1848 Revolution and was the chaplain of Jewish guardsmen in the revolutionary army. He was also a tireless proponent of Magyarization, delivering his sermons in Hungarian in the impressive synagogue which was completed, largely due to his efforts, in 1860, and making Hungarian the official language of instruction in the community school in 1860. See Ujvári, *Magyar zsidó lexikon*, s.v. "Neuhaus Ábrahám" and "Tapolca."

13 Istóczy, *Beszédei*, pp. 142–149. Despite Istóczy's claim that he no longer was the sole champion of anti–Semitism in the Diet (*ibid.*, p. 142) and his sarcastic, vindictive observation that the revelation of the Jewish threat no longer was "Istóczy's obsession" or "Istóczyism," but a conscious realization among all segments of the Christian Hungarian people (*Ibid.*, p. 146), the text of Istóczy's motion was signed—inexplicably—by only eight of the sixteen anti–Semitic representatives.

14 *Ibid.*, p. 150.

15 The son of a well–known pharmacist and botanist, Tamás Nendtvich (1782–1858), whose extensive collection of herbs and butterflies was the prize of the southwestern city of Pécs where he lived much of his life, Károly Nendtvich (1811–1892) was one of the founders of the modern school of natural science in Hungary. He was also a learned and indefatigable proponent of industrial technology. As punishment for his friendship with Lajos Kossuth and participation in the 1848 Revolution, he was tried and removed from his University position. Later he was pardoned and allowed to return to academic life. He was appointed dean of Budapest Politechnic in 1873. Following a distinguished career as a teacher and author of a number of well–received scientific works, Nendtvich retired in 1881. Although his political career was of

short duration (1873–1877), Nendtvich was not a negligible political presence. His anti–Semitic writings were numerous, earning
him praise both in Hungary and abroad. See Kenyeres, *Magyar életrajzi lexikon,* s.v. "Nendtvich Tamás" and "Nendtvich
Károly." In addition to his association with Kossuth and his
scholarly reputation, Nendtvich, a native of Pécs, located a mere
50 kilometers to the south of Szakcs, was considered an expert
of sorts on local affairs.

[16] Kubinszky, *Politikai antiszemitizmus,* pp. 151–152. Although
the election in Szakcs was the first in which a bona fide anti–
Semitic candidate was fielded, that small town offered no hope
to the anti–Semitic movement. Nor could it compete with Rum,
Istóczy's own stamping ground. Following his reelection in 1881,
Istóczy paid a fitting tribute to his supporters without whose
persistent and uncritical devotion his political career and perhaps even his entire movement might not have existed. "Let the
district of Rum remain anti–Semitism's impenetrable fortress of
rock off whose bastion the heavy shells of plutocracy bounce
harmlessly and whose foundations the cannons of Semitism try
to shake in vain." Quoted in Bosnyák, *Istóczy,* p. 38.

[17] Kubinszky, *Politikai antiszemitizmus,* pp. 187–188.

[18] *Az 1881 évi szeptember hó 24-en kihirdetett országgyűlés nyomta-
tványai. Képviselőház-irományok.* [Publications of the Diet Convened on 24 September 1881. House of Deputies—documents],
vol. 14 (Budapest: Képviselőház, 1881–1884), pp. 148–149.

[19] *Ibid.,* p. 149.

[20] Quoted in Kubinszky, *Politikai antiszemitizmus,* p. 153.

[21] Vadnay was one of the few of Istóczy's early supporters to work
his way back to political respectability. Mór Szatmári (1856–
1931), the prominent Jewish publicist who was a representative
in the Diet (1901–1910) and an acute and outspoken observer of
politics and politicians, noted that "Vadnay's anti–Semitism fell
on his young, green years." He praised Vadnay for his tireless
efforts while *főispán* [lord lieutenant] of Csongrád County to im-
prove the conditions of agricultural laborers. *Húsz esztendő,* p.
35.

[22] *Ibid,* p. 36.

[23] By expanding the rationale of such conclusions, the logic of which
was clear only to him, Istóczy triumphantly declared that the verdict had legitimized anti–Semitism and given a political stamp
of approval to the existence and platform of the National Anti–
Semitic Party. See Kubinszky, *Politikai antiszemitizmus,* pp.
153–154.

Notes to Chapter X

[1] József Bary, the investigating magistrate, was the principal proponent of the murder theory. However, he rejected both Istóczy's rationale and the anti–Semitic contention of the proven certainty of a ritual murder. See *Tiszaeszlári bűnper*, p. 805.

[2] Handler, *Tiszaeszlár*, pp. 153–154. Bary was unmoved by Ónody's antics—he recalled the incident in a brief, dispassionate account (*Tiszaeszlári bűnper*, p. 814)—and concluded that Ónody's presence was an irritant and an impediment to justice. Ónody was not Istóczy's lone man in attendance. Sensing defeat and out of contempt for the prosecutors, Károly Szalay, one of Istóczy's earliest supporters and himself a representative in the Diet, became the private attorney for Mrs. Solymosi, the mother of the dead girl. He was allowed to make a summation in which he argued passionately that a ritual murder had indeed occurred. The spectators frequently interrupted his speech with loud cheers. See Handler, *Tiszaeszlár*, pp. 159–160.

[3] *Ibid.*, pp. 157–172. Three of the legal experts in the Tiszaeszlár case, Sándor Kozma, Bernát Friedmann and Sándor Funták, had participated a decade earlier in Hungary's first judicial prosecution of the leaders of the workers' movement and, except for one, won verdicts of not guilty for their clients. Edit S. Vincze chronicles the circumstances and details of the trial in *A hűtlenségi per (1871–1872)* [The disloyalty case] (Budapest: Kossuth, 1971).

[4] For the text of the verdict, see Eötvös, *Nagy per*, 3:223–250.

[5] Fayer, *A magyar bűnvádi eljárás a mai érvényében*, p. 233.

[6] *Tiszaeszlári bűnper*, p. 841.

[7] *Ibid*, pp. 840–841.

[8] Bosnyák, *Istóczy*, p. 62.

[9] Handler, *Tiszaeszlár*, pp. 176–177. The ferocity of the disturbances caught even the anti–Semitic agitators by surprise. The clerical *Magyar Állam*, a consistent critic of the government on the Jewish Question, and other anti–Semitic publications called for immediate, severe measures to end the violence and punish the perpetrators. See Bary, *Tiszaeszlári bűnper*, p. 841. For a detailed description of the disturbances, see Kubinszky, *Politikai antiszemitizmus*, pp. 105–130; Idem, "Adalékok az 1883 évi antiszemita zavargásokhoz" [Addenda to the 1883 anti–Semitic disturbances] in *Századok* (1968), pp. 158–177. Although the anti–Semitic leaders did not seek an active role in leading the

demonstrators (*Ibid.*, p. 130), the numerous rapidly spreading, persistent documented acts of violence were indicative of the careful planning and inflammatory agitation of the most prominent anti–Semitic activists. The speeches and articles of Istóczy, Simonyi, and Verhovay were the sparks that ignited the tinderbox of suppressed hatred and frustration.

10 Although the preparatory groundwork began before the news of the disappearance of the young Tiszaeszlár girl attracted national attention, no acceptable piece of documentary evidence supports the contention of Zoltán Bosnyák (*Istóczy*, p. 62) that "Istóczy tried to keep his movement independent of the Nyíregyháza trials." In fact, the available evidence suggests a conclusion to the contrary.

11 *12 Röpirat*, 15 August 1883.

12 Bosnyák, *Istóczy*, p. 64.

13 On 15 October 1944, Admiral Miklós Horthy announced on Hungarian Radio that he would request a cease–fire from the Allies and ordered the Hungarian army to stop fighting. However, shortly after his announcement, military units of the extreme right–wing Arrow–Cross Party, supported by the Germans, carried out a coup and deposed Horthy. The Germans took him into protective custody. With that, the bloodiest final chapter in the tribulations of Hungarian Jewry—in Budapest's crowded ghetto, in particular—began. One of the acknowledged ideological forefathers of the Arrow–Cross movement, according to party theoreticians, was Győző Istóczy. See Lajos Marschalkó, *Országhódítók* [Nation conquerors] (Munich: Mikes Kelemen Kör, 1975), pp. 41–51.

14 Quoted in Gyula Mezei, *Magyar politikai pártprogrammok (1867–1914)* [Programs of Hungarian political parties] (Budapest: G. Ranschburg, 1934), pp. 313–314.

15 According to Bosnyák (*Istóczy*, p. 65), the new party faced two major problems: the lack of an official organ and the lack of funds. Neither, however, may be considered a debilitating handicap. Istóczy's *12 Röpirat*, Verhovay's *Függetlenség* and Simonyi's *Westungarischer Grenzbote* had already become effective disseminators of the doctrines of political anti–Semitism. Except for the early lean years of his career and after his retirement from politics, Istóczy rarely, if ever, blamed setbacks or failures on financial hardship.

16 Kubinszky, *Politikai antiszemitizmus*, pp. 159–161; Bosnyák (*Istóczy*, p. 65) admits that the handling of the donations was not done carefully and conscientiously. Yet he, like Istóczy, had

no qualms about adopting the skewed reasoning of men blinded by hatred and fanaticism. The real culprits, Bosnyák concluded, were the revengeful Jews who had been conspiring to ruin the Verhovays' reputation and destroy the *Függetlenség*.

[17] Mór Szatmári, the sharp-eyed and rapier-penned journalist turned politician provides an insightful account of the *Függetlenség* affair and a probing analysis of Gyula Verhovay's rollercoaster career in *Húsz esztendő*, pp. 40-53.

[18] Venetianer, *Magyar zsidóság*, p. 101.

[19] Szatmári, *Húsz esztendő*, p. 32.

[20] Quoted in *Ibid.*, p. 33.

[21] Quoted in Kubinszky, *Politikai antiszemitizmus*, p. 170.

[22] *Ibid*, pp.170-177; Szatmári, *Húsz esztendő*, pp. 33-34.

[23] *Emlékiratfélék*, p. 33.

[24] Eötvös, *Nagy per*, 2:94-101.

[25] *Emlékiratfélék*, p. 34.

[26] *Beszédei*, pp. 151-156.

[27] Mór Szatmári (*Húsz esztendő*, pp. 46-51) provides a colorful and detailed account of the debate over the so-called "Jew Bill."

[28] *Beszédei*, pp. 157-160.

[29] A seasoned and patient politician who had fended off many an ill-tempered attack with the agility and aplomb of a skilled fencer, Tisza did not appear to be overly concerned by the latest anti-Semitic offensive. He had learned to deal with the ourbursts of Istóczy and like-minded representatives during the preceding nine years. He was, however, severely tested in the course of the debates of the "Jew Bill." Károly Eötvös and Ottó Herman, two of the luminaries of the Independence Party, accused Tisza of contributing to the anti-Semitic agitation by insisting on the passage of the bill. See Szatmári, *Húsz esztendő*, p. 50.

[30] *Ibid.*, p. 51.

[31] Kubinszky, *Politikai antiszemitizmus*, pp. 188-190.

[32] The anti-Semites interpreted Hoitsy's presence as a well-designed provocation. A man of impressive intellectual credentials—in addition to possessing political and journalistic talents he was a trained astronomer and a certified teacher—Pál Hoitsy (1850-1927) bravely, albeit unsuccessfully, challenged Istóczy in the 1878 campaign in the district of Rum, the then still lone anti-Semitic politicians' lion's den. (*Ibid.*, p. 33). Prónay (1856- ?), the representative of the city of Vác, was a member of the inner sanctum of the Independence Party. Even though a politician of ubiquitous presence, his career contributed but a faint brush-stroke to the post-*Ausgleich* political landscape of Hungary.

[33] Szatmári, Húsz esztendő, pp. 42–46 and 54–58; Kubinszky, Politikai antiszemitizmus, pp. 191–194.

[34] György Széll, a one–term Independence Party representative of the town of Makó who ran on the anti–Semitic ticket, was associated with more disturbances than any other anti–Semitic candidate. Ironically, he was defeated in a bid to win reelection by an embarrassingly wide margin. See Kubinszky, Politikai antiszemitizmus, p. 211.

[35] Notwithstanding earlier promises to represent the National Anti–Semitic Party, a number of candidates had an inexplicable change of heart and withdrew. See Kubinszky, Ibid., p. 258, n. 24.

[36] The cause of political anti–Semitism suffered a further setback as each unsuccessful candidate was removed from the slate of fifty–five. One loss was particularly painful and embarrassing. Campaigning with all the psychological and emotional benefits that the backdrop of Tiszaeszlár provided, József Bary, the investigating magistrate who had attained a national reputation, ran as an anti–Semitic candidate in the district of Tiszalök. His defeat by the candidates of both the Liberal Party and the Moderate Opposition Party was clear proof of the weak appeal of the anti–Semitic premise and the fickle political utility of Tiszaeszlár which not even a well–known personality and native son, such as Bary, could reverse. On the other hand, the no less surprising failures of Helfy, Eötvös and Ernő Mezey to win reelection caused a triumphant uproar in anti–Semitic circles.

[37] The Liberal candidates were greatly aided by an unusually candid and pragmatic party platform and its successful presentation by the leaders of the party. Tisza sidestepped the Jewish Question, an all too frequently recurring theme, and stressed the importance of parliamentary reforms, including the reduction of the power and influence of the Upper House and the extension of the representatives' terms in the Diet to five years. Trefort denounced anti–Semitism, yet frankly admitted the existence of the Jewish Question. He called on the wealthiest and most cultured Jews to take an active role in removing those Jewish customs which kept Jews on the periphery of Christian society. See Szatmári, Húsz esztendő, p. 59.

[38] For accounts of the 1884 elections, see Szatmári, Húsz esztendő, pp. 51–59; Kubinszky, Politikai antiszemitizmus, pp. 194–212; Venetianer, Magyar zsidóság, pp. 357–358; and Bosnyák, Istóczy, pp. 70–72.

Notes to Chapter XI

[1] *Húsz esztendő*, p. 60.

[2] *Istóczy*, p. 71.

[3] Except for Simonyi who delivered his speeches with the expertise of a seasoned veteran, the lengthy and often confused oratorical feats alternately humored, bored and outraged the Liberal–controlled Diet. Judit Kubinszky (*Politikai antiszemitizmus*, pp. 214–218) provides a useful account the lackluster performances of the newly–elected anti–Semitic representatives and the many examples of the party's lack of discipline.

[4] Bosnyák, *Istóczy*, p. 71.

[5] Istóczy eventually decided not to attend the congress. See Kubinszky, *Politikai antiszemitizmus*, pp. 220-221.

[6] Iván Simonyi, representing the National Anti–Semitic Party, was elected co–chairman of the congress (*Ibid.*, p. 221). One of the featured speakers was an Istóczy loyalist: Dr. Ferenc Komlóssy. A priest turned politician, he won the election in the district of Verbó, Nyitra County. An inept orator, Komlóssy's rambling speech in the Diet in the course of the review of the official party responses to the address from the throne helped undermine the credibility of the National Anti–Semitic Party *Ibid.*, p. 215; Pulzer, *Political Anti–Semitism*, p. 111).

[7] Kubinszky, *Politikai antiszemitizmus*, p. 221.

[8] Bosnyák, *Istóczy*, p. 71.

[9] *Ibid.*, p. 72.

[10] Istóczy, *Magyar antiszemitapárt*, p. 8.

[11] For a useful list of Jewish contributions to Hungarian jurisprudence, see Venetianer, *Magyar zsidóság*, pp. 397–401.

[12] *Emlékiratfélék*, p. 37.

[13] Supra, pp. 100–101.

[14] Kubinsky, *Politikai antiszemitizmus*, pp. 221–222.

[15] *Istóczy*, p. 73.

[16] *Ibid.*, p. 74. The most frequently heard anti–Semitic representatives in the 1884 session of the Diet were Istóczy, Gábor Andreánszky, Ignác Zimándi, József Veres, and Géza Rácz. No trace of a conspicuously sharp or enduring strain of anti–Semitism was detectable in Zalaegerszeg. The Jewish community came into existence in the middle of the eighteenth century. Its members eventually accounted for over 10 percent of the population. See Ujvári, *Magyar zsidó lexikon*, s.v. "Zalaegerszeg."

[17] Istóczy, *Beszédei*, p. 161–164.

[18] *Ibid.*, pp. 165–168.

[19] An unswervingly conservative member of the Liberal Party and elected into the Diet nine times, Szapáry (1832–1905) served consecutively in three governments as minister of interior, labor, commerce, and agriculture. He was appointed prime minister in 1890. See Kenyeres, *Magyar életrajzi lexikon* s.v. "Szapáry Gyula."

[20] For the complete text of the stock exchange tax motion sponsored by the anti-Semites, see Istóczy, *Beszédei*, pp. 169–191. The reports of the economic and financial committees, issued in May and June respectively, advised against a full debate on the motion (*Ibid.*, pp. 191–195).

[21] *Ibid.*, pp. 196–202.

[22] *Ibid.*, pp. 203–218.

[23] *Magyar antiszemitapárt*, p. 8.

[24] *Ibid.*, pp. 8–9.

[25] Bosnyák, *Istóczy*, p. 75.

[26] Although Venetianer (*Magyar zsidóság*, p. 363) questioned the restraining influence of the cardinal's effort—many priests defied him and put their pulpits in the service of anti-Semitic agitation—Haynald's words weighed heavily on the conscience of many a politically active Catholic on the eve of the 1887 elections.

[27] Quoted in Bosnyák, *Istóczy*, p. 75.

[28] Molnár et al., *Magyarország története*, 2:128.

[29] Bosnyák, *Istóczy*, p. 75.

[30] Istóczy, *Magyar antiszemitapárt*, pp. 9–10.

[31] Of the eleven anti-Semitic representatives only Ferenc Komlóssy and Andor Vadnay made speeches on the floor of the Diet. See Bosnyák, *Istóczy*, p. 75. However, Komlóssy was an ineffective politician and an uninspiring speaker, whereas the articulate Vadnay was nearing the end of his brief career as an anti-Semitic spokesman.

[32] *Ibid.*

[33] Molnár et al., *Magyarország története*, 2:129–130. The crafty Tisza, however, managed to ease the heavy burden of ignominy and exited with a rousing, patriotic finale.

[34] Istóczy, *Beszédei*, pp. 219–223.

[35] *Ibid.*, pp. 224–248.

[36] Molnár et al., *Magyarország története*, 2:130–141.

[37] In light of the joint sponsorship the style in the motion was surprisingly innocuous. It demonstrated the enervated state to which the anti-Semitic remnant had sunk. Istóczy's signature was followed only by those of József Veres, János Kudlik, Péter

Detrich, Ferenc Komlóssy, Géza Ónody, and Imre Szalay. See Istóczy, *Beszédei*, p. 267.

38 *Ibid.*, pp. 249–353.
39 *Ibid.*, pp. 354–385.
40 *Ibid.*, pp. 386–395.
41 *Ibid.*, pp. 396–408.
42 *Húsz esztendő*, p. 60. Szatmári's view, however, was not shared by Adolph August, one of Istóczy's earliest detractors. August was so offended by the speeches of "Hungary's Cassandra" in 1875 that he published an emotional point–by–point refutation of the anti–Semitic rationale. See *Istóczy und die Juden* (Budapest: Grill, 1876).
43 Istóczy's self–pity deepened considerably with his decision to stop the publication of the *12 Röpirat*. After twelve years of fluctuating success—more often than not teetering on the edge of insolvency—the number of subscribers to the anti–Semitic monthly shrank to a mere fifty. He retained another monthly, *Joqi és Közgazdasági Útmutató* [Legal and administrative guide], but renamed it *Jogi Tanácsadó* [Legal counsel] in 1893. See *Emlékiratfélék*, p. 37.
44 Molnár et al., *Magyarország története* 2:144–151.
45 Istóczy, *Emlékiratfélék*, p. 36.
46 Istóczy, *Magyar antiszemitapárt*, p. 11.

Notes to Chapter XII

1 Quoted in Venetianer, *Magyar zsidóság*, p. 446.
2 *Ibid.*
3 Mór Szatmári ("Zsidók a magyar publicisztikában" [Jews in Hungarian journalism] in *Évkönyv* (1885), pp. 171–178, and Zoltán Bosnyák (*Harc a zsidó sajtó ellen!* [Fight against the Jewish press] (Budapest: János Held, 1938), evaluate the presence of Jews in the Hungarian press and its consequences, arriving at predictably contradictory conclusions.
4 Istóczy may have misunderstood the difference between a professing and practicing anti–Semite in his search for a permanent basis of livelihood. Whereas anti–Semitism was successfully harnessed as a convenient vehicle for many a political and literary career (see Zoltán Bosnyák, *Szembe Judeával!* [Let's Face Judea] (Budapest: Centrum, 1943)), practicing it did not yield a sufficient income for even its most prominent practitioner.
5 *Emlékiratfélék*, pp. 37–39.
6 *Ibid.*, p. 37.

7 *Ibid.*, p. 42.
8 *Ibid.*, p. 44.
9 *Ibid.*, pp. 46–47.
10 *Ibid.*, pp. 45–46.
11 *Ibid.*, pp. 48–49.
12 *Ibid.*, pp. 50–55.
13 Bosnyák, *Istóczy*, p. 82.
14 *Ibid.*, p. 83.

Notes to Chapter XIII

1 Istóczy, *Emlékiratfélék* pp. 56–61.
2 Istóczy, p. 3.
3 Ujvári, *Magyar zsidó lexikon*, s.v. "Világháború" [world war]; Bertalan Édelstein, "Az 5677 év [The year 5677], in *Évkönyv* (1918), pp. 303–305. Formed soon after World War I ended, the Committee of the Hungarian Jewish War Archives collected numerous valuable data in an attempt to make public a convincing record of Jewish contributions to the war effort. However, when its work—fragmentary and at times erroneous—was published, it only added fuel to the anti-Semitic bonfire.
4 The written responses of the participants were reprinted in a 165-page booklet, *A Huszadik Század körkérdései* [Public opinion poll of the Huszadik Század] (Budapest: Huszadik Század, 1917). It is interesting to note that half a century after the emancipation of the Jews in Hungary, arguments proving the existence of the Jewish Question retained a ring of validity. One of the more thoroughly researched and objectively written studies of that sensitive subject is *A zsidó kérdés Magyarországon* [The Jewish Question in Hungary] (Budapest: Aigner, 1882). Its author, Ödön Farkas, presented his views with unusual frankness.
5 József Révay's *Gömbös Gyula élete és politikája* [The Life and politics of Gyula Gömbös] (Budapest: Franklin, 1934) remains a useful biographical work.
6 Marschalkó, *Országhódítók*, pp. 194–195.
7 The post-war spokesmen for the Hungarist Movement in exile have disassociated themselves—the Arrow-Cross Party took a similar position during the last months of World War II in Hungary (October 1944–April 1945)—from the rabble of Budapest's population who, they claim, were uncontrollable and solely responsible for the atrocities committed against the Jews of the capital. See Kálmán Koós, *Voltunk, vagyunk, leszünk* [We were, we are, we will be] (Buenos Aires: Hungarista Mozgalom, 1960),

pp. 303–322 and Ferenc Fiala, *Zavaros évek* [Troubled years] (Munich: Mikes Kelemen Kör, 1976), pp. 137–147. However, documents, eyewitness accounts, and scholarly works attesting to the fate of the Hungarian Jews have identified by name the actual planners and executors of the atrocities and established grounds for their moral and legal culpability. Many civilian and military representatives of the various governments appointed by regent Horthy and Szálasi's Arrow–Cross Party—some were executed or jailed in Hungary or tried in absentia shortly after the war, others managed to escape retribution by settling in safe western havens—were proven guilty of some of the most heinous crimes committed during the war.

8 Paul Lendvai, *Anti-Semitism Without Jews* (New York: Doubleday, 1971), pp. 306–307.

9 *Ibid.*, p. 317.

10 "A vidéki zsidóság" [Provincial Jewry] in Endre Sós, ed., *Új Élet Naptár* (Budapest: Magyar Izraeliták Országos Képviselete, 1959), p. 147.

11 "Az ortodoxia a felszabadulás után" [The orthodoxy after the liberation], in *Új Élet Naptár*, p. 161.

12 "Adalékok a hajdúvárosok zsidóságának történetéhez," p. 122. Additional data are available in Harsányi's subsequent studies of other communities, such as "A nagykállói zsidóság történetéhez" [To the history of the Nagykalló Jewry] in *Évkönyv* (1971–72), pp. 145–154; "A nyíregyházi zsidók történetéhez" [To the history of the Jews of Nyíregyháza], in *Évkönyv* (1973–74), pp. 74–89; "A büdszentmihályi hitközség története" [History of the (Jewish) community of Büdszentmihály], in *Évkönyv* (1975–76), pp. 140–164.

13 *Országhódítók*, p. 195.

14 *Zavaros évek*, p. 143.

15 In *Világhódítók* [World conquerors] (Munich: József Süli, 1958), Marschalkó traces and identifies, albeit without a single document corroborating his conclusions, the various manifestations of the harmful influence of international Jewry.

16 *Magyar antiszemitapárt*, p. 14.

17 *Emlékiratfélék*, pp. 62–63.

18 *Ibid.*, pp. 14–16.

19 *Ibid.*, p. 21.

20 *Ibid.* p. 15.

21 Quoted in Marschalkó, *Országhódítók*, p. 194.

22 *Ibid.*, pp. 194–195.

23 To date, the only study of the first eighteen years of Herzl's life is Andrew Handler, *Dori: The Life and Times of Theodor Herzl in Budapest, 1860–1878* (University, Alabama: University of Alabama Press, 1983). Hereafter cited as *Dori.*

24 *The Complete Diaries of Theodor Herzl*, Ralphael Patai, ed., Hary Zohn, trans. 5 vols. (New York: Herzl Press, 1960), 1:v. Hereafter cited as *Diaries.*

25 *Ibid.*

26 *Ibid.*, 1:4.

27 *Ibid.*, 1:40.

28 Handler, *Dori*, pp. 26–27.

29 *Ibid.*, pp. 32 and 34.

30 For additional details of Herzl's earliest literary works, see Handler, *Dori*, pp. 58–86.

31 The eight years Herzl spent as a student in the two schools are discussed in full in *Ibid.* pp. 87–105.

32 Theodor Herzl, "Autobiography" in *Zionist Writings*, Harry Zohn, trans., 2 vols. (New York: Herzl Press, 1973), 1:15.

33 An aspiring actress, Pauline Herzl was taken ill with typhus and died at age nineteen on 7 February 1878. See Handler, *Dori*, pp. 97–99.

34 He grew up in a house where the language of conversation was Latin. As an adult he was a zealous proponent of physical fitness, habitually swimming in the Danube even in the winter. His antics caused people to shake their heads upon seeing him. They called him "crazy Simonyi." Klaus Schickert provides a detailed characterization of the life and politics of Simonyi in his *Die Judenfrage in Ungarn* (Essen: Essen Verlanganstalt, 1937), pp. 123–129.

35 Herzl, *Diaries*, 1:306.

36 *Ibid.*, 1:317.

Bibliography

Acsády, Ignác. "A zsidók a magyarság multjában" [Jews in the Hungarians' past], in *Évkönyv*, edited by József Bánóczi, pp. 7–20, (Budapest: Izraelita Magyar Irodalmi Társulat, 1902).

A Huszadik Század körkérdései [Public Opinion Poll of the *Huszadik Század*] (Budapest: Huszadik Század, 1917).

Andics, Erzsébet. *A magyarországi munkásmozgalom az 1848–1849-es forradalomtól az 1917 Nagy Októberi Szocialista Forradalomig* [The Hungarian Workers' Movement from the Revolution of 1848–1849 to the Great October Socialist Revolution of 1917] (Budapest: Szikra, 1956).

August, Adolph. *Istóczy und die Juden* (Budapest: Grill, 1876).

Az 1881. évi szeptember hó 24-én kihirdetett országgyűlés nyomatatványai. Képviselőház-irományok [Publications of the Diet convened on 24 September 1881. House of Deputies—Documents], vol. 14 (Budapest: Képviselőház, 1881–1884).

Balassa, Józef. "A magyar zsidó dialectus" [Hungarian–Jewish dialect], in *Évkönyv*, edited by Vilmos Bacher and József Bánóczi, pp. 114–117, (Budapest: Izraelita Magyar Irodalmi Társulat, 1898).

Barany, George. "Magyar Jew or Jewish Magyar" (To the Question of Jewish Assimilation in Hungary). In *Canadian–American Slavic Studies* (Spring 1974): 1–44.

Bary, József. *A tiszaeszlári bűnper. Bary József vizsgálóbíró emlékiratai* [The Criminal Case of Tiszaeszlár. The Memoirs of Investigating Magistrate Józef Bary], 2nd ed. (Budapest: Magyar Élet Kiadása, 1941).

Berend, Iván T., and Miklós Szuhay. *A tőkésgazdaság története Magyarországon 1848–1944* [History of Capitalist Economy in Hungary] (Budapest: Kossuth, 1978).

_____, and G. Ránki. *Hungary, A Century of Economic Development* (London: David & Charles, 1974).

Bernát, Tivadar and Mihály Viszkey. *Budapest társadalmának és gazdaságának száz éve (1872/3–1972)* [A Hundred Years of Budapest's Society and Economy] (Budapest: Kossuth, 1972).

Bernstein, Béla. *A zsidók története Szombathelyen 1687–1909* [History of the Jews in Szombathely] (Budapest: n. p., 1914).

——. *Az 1848/49-iki magyar szabadságharc és a zsidók* [The 1848–49 Hungarian War of Independence and the Jews] (Budapest: Franklin, 1898).

Bertényi, Iván. *A magyar korona története* [History of the Hungarian Crown] (Budapest: Kossuth, 1980).

Bogdán, István. *Régi magyar mulatságok* [Old Hungarian Pastimes] (Budapest: Magvető, 1978).

Bosnyák, Zoltán. *Harc a zsidó sajtó ellen!* [Fight Against the Jewish Press!] (Budapest: János Held, 1938).

——, *Istóczy Győző élete és küzdelmei* [The Life and Battles of Győző Istóczy] (Budapest: Könyv és Lapkiadó Részvénytársaság, 1940).

——. *Szembe Judeával!* [Let's Face Judea!] (Budapest: Centrum 1943).

Büchler, Sándor. "A magyar nyelv terjeszkedése a zsidók közt" [The spread of the Hungarian language among the Jews], in *Évkönyv*, edited by József Bánóczi, pp. 259–264, (Budapest: Izraelita Magyar Irodalmi Társulat, 1905).

——. "Zsidók a magyar egyetemen" [Jews in the Hungarian university], in *Évkönyv*, edited by Vilmos Bacher and József Bánóczi, pp. 168–172, (Budapest: Izraelita Magyar Irodalmi Társulat, 1897).

Csillag, István. "Hirschler Ignác ifjúkori arcképéhez" [To the portrait of the young Ignác Hirschler], in *Évkönyv*, edited by Sándor Scheiber, pp. 92–100, (Budapest: Magyar Izraeliták Országos Képviselete, 1979/80).

Csizmadia, Andor. *A magyar választási rendszer 1848/1849-ben* [The Hungarian Election System in 1848–1849] (Budapest: Közgazdasági és Jogi Könyvkiadó, 1963).

Czigány, Lóránt. *The Oxford History of Hungarian Literature* (Oxford: Clarendon Press, 1984).

Diószegi, István. *Nemzet, dinasztia, külpolitika* [Nation, Dynasty, Foreign Policy] (Budapest: Magvető, 1979).

Dobos, Ilona. *Tarcal története a szóhagyományban* [History of Tarcal in Oral Tradition] (Budapest: Akadémiai Kiadó, 1971).

Dóka, Klára. *A pest-budai céhes ipar válsága* [Crisis of the Guild Industry of Pest–Buda] (Budapest: Akadémiai Kiadó, 1979).

Du Mesnil–Marigny. *A zsidókról* [On the Jews], translated by Győző Istóczy (Budapest: Nándor Tettey & Co., 1875).

Eckhart, Ferencz. *A jog és államtudományi kar története, 1667–1935* [History of the Faculty of Law and Political Science] (Budapest: n. p., 1936).

Édelstein, Bertalan. "Az 5677 év" [The year 5677], in *Évkönyv*, edited by József Bánóczi, pp. 279–318 (Budapest: Izraelita Magyar Irodalmi Társulat, 1918).

Eisler, Mátyás. "Simon József," in *Évkönyv*, edited by József Bánóczi, pp. 226–237 (Budapest: Izraelita Magyar Irodalmi Társulat, 1916).

Eötvös, Károly. *A nagy per, mely ezer éve folyik s még sincs vége* [The Great Trial That Has Lasted for a Thousand Years and Still Is Not Over] (Budapest: Révai Testvérek, 1904).

Eperjessy, Kálmán. *A magyar falu története* [History of the Hungary Village] (Budapest: Gondolat, 1966).

Erőss, László. *A pesti vicc* [Pest joke] (Budapest: Gondolat, 1982).

Fabó, Bertalan. "A pozsonyi gyászos húsvét" [The mournful Easter of Pozsony], in *Évkönyv*, edited by József Bánóczi, pp. 276–280 (Budapest: Izraelita Magyar Irodalmi Társulat, 1913).

Farkas, Ödön. *A zsidó kérdés Magyarországon* [The Jewish Question in Hungary] (Budapest: Aigner, 1882).

Fayer, László. *A magyar bűnvádi eljárár mai érvényében* [Contemporary Hungarian Criminal Procedure] (Budapest: Franklin, 1887).

Felkai, László. *A munkásság művelődési törekvései a dualizmus korában* [The Cultural Endeavors of Workers in the Age of Dualism] (Budapest: Tankönyvkiadó, 1980).

Fiala, Ferenc. *Zavaros évek* [Troubled Years] (Munich: Mikes Kelemen Kör, 1976).

Flesch, Ármin. "A zsidó a magyar közmondásban" [The Jew in the Hungarian proverb], in *Évkönyv*, edited by József Bánóczi, pp. 176–194 (Budapest: Izraelita Magyar Irodalmi Társulat, 1908).

Fodor, F. and I. Vedres. *A közegészségtan és járványtan alapjai* [Foundations of Public Hygiene and Epidemiology] (Budapest: Medicina, 1975).

Gergely, András and Zoltán Szász. *Kiegyezés után* [After the Compromise] (Budapest: Gondolat, 1978).

Gracza, György. *Nevető Magyarország* [Laughing Hungary], 2 vols. (Budapest: Róbert Lampel, 1901).

Groszmann, Zsigmond. "Hirschler Ignác," in *Évkönyv*, edited by Samu Szemere, pp. 143–158 (Budapest: Izraelita Magyar Irodalmi Társulat, 1941).

———. "Meisel pesti főrabbi kora" [The times of Chief Rabbi Meisel of Pest], in *Évkönyv*, edited by Samu Szemere, pp. 100–113 (Budapest: Izraelita Magyar Irodalmi Társulat, 1933).

———. "Mezei Mór és kora" [Mór Mezei and his times], in *Évkönyv*, edited by Samu Szemere, pp. 197–208 (Budapest: Izraelita Magyar Irodalmi Társulat, 1936).

Grünwald, Fülöp. "A magyar zsidó mult historikusai" [Historians of the Hungarian–Jewish past], in *Évkönyv*, edited by Samu Szemere, pp. 208–222 (Budapest: Izraelita Magyar Irodalmi Társulat, 1934).

Halász, Geyza. *A Budapesten uralgott járványos betegségek történelme, különös tekintettel a cholerára* [History of contagious diseases prevailing in Budapest with special attention to cholera] (Budapest: Magyar Királyi Tudományos Egyetem Könyvtára, 1879).

Hanák Péter. "Polgárosodás és asszimiláció Magyarországon a XIX században" [Bourgeois status and assimilation in Hungary in the nineteenth century]. *Történelmi Szemle* (1974/4): 513–536.

————, ed., *Zsidókérdés, asszimiláció, antiszemitizmus* [The Jewish Question, Assimilation, Anti–Semitism] (Budapest: Gondolat, 1984).

Handler, Andrew. *Blood Libel at Tiszaeszlár* (Boulder: East European Monographs—New York: Columbia University Press, 1980).

————. *Dori: The Life and Times of Theodor Herzl in Budapest (1860–1878)* (University, Alabama: University of Alabama Press, 1983).

————, ed. and tr. *Rabbi Eizik. Hasidic Stories About the Zaddik of Kálló* (Cranbury, N.J.: Associated University Presses, 1978).

Harsányi, László. "A büdszentmihályi hitközség története" [History of the (Jewish) community of Büdszentmihály], in *Évkönyv*, edited by Sándor Scheiber, pp. 140–164 (Budapest: Magyar Izraeliták Országos Képviselete, 1975–76).

————. "Adalékok a hajdúvárosok zsidóságának történetéhez" [Addenda to the history of Jews in the haiduk towns], in *Évkönyv*, edited by Sándor Scheiber, pp. 116–165 (Budapest: Magyar Izrael- iták Országos Képviselete, 1970).

————. "A nagykállói zsidóság történetéhez" [To the history of the Nagykálló Jewry], in *Évkönyv*, edited by Sándor Scheiber, pp. 145–154 (Budapest: Magyar Izraeliták Országos Képviselete, 1971–72).

————. "A nyíregyházi zsidók történetéhez" [To the history of the Jews of Nyíregyháza], in *Évkönyv*, edited by Sándor Scheiber, pp. 74–89 (Budapest: Magyar Izraeliták Országos Képviselete, 1973–74).

Hegyi, Klára. *Egy világbirodalom végvidékén* [At the Borderland of a Vast Empire] (Budapest: Gondolat, 1976).

Herzl, Theodor. "Autobiography," in *Zionist Writings*, translated by Harry Zohn, 1:15–19, 2 vols. (New York: Herzl Press, 1973).

————. *The Complete Diaries of Theodor Herzl*, edited by Raphael Patai and translated by Harry Zohn, 5 vols (New York: Herzl

Press, 1960).

Hont, Ferenc, ed. *Magyar szinháztörténet* [History of the Hungarian Theater] (Budapest: Gondalat, 1962).

Ignotus, Paul. *Hungary* (London: Ernest Benn, 1972).

Istóczy, Győző. *A magyar antiszemitapárt megsemmisítése és ennek következményei* [Destruction of the Hungarian Anti-Semitic Party and Its Consequences] (Budapest: n. p., 1906).

———. *Emlékiratfélék és egyebek* [Memoirs of Sorts and Other Things] (Budapest: F. Buschmann, 1911).

———. *Istóczy Győző országgyűlési beszédei, indítványai és törvényjavaslatai, 1872-1896* [Győző Istóczy's Parliamentary Speeches, Resolutions and Bills] (Budapest: F. Buschmann, 1904).

———. *Manifest an die Regierungen und Völker der durch das Judenthum gefährdeten christlichen Staaten laut Beschlusses der ersten internationalen anti-jüdischen Kongress zu Dresden an 11. u. 12 September 1882* (Chemnitz, n. p., 1882).

———. *Statuten-Entwurf des Central-Vereins des Nightjuden-Bundes von Ungarn* (Berlin: n. p., 1880).

Kahn, Joseph. *An Illustrated Guide of Budapest* (Budapest: Légrády Bros., 1891).

Katzburg, Nathaniel. *Antishemiyuth be-Hungariah (1867-1918)* [Anti-Semitism in Hungary] (Tel-Aviv: Dvir, 1969).

Kenyeres, Ágnes, ed. *Magyar életrajzi lexikon* [Hungarian Biographical Lexicon], 3 vols. (Budapest: Akadémiai Kiadó, 1982).

Király, Béla K. *Ferenc Deák* (Boston: Twayne, 1975).

Kiss, György. *A budapesti várospolitika 1873-1944* [City Politics of Budapest], 2nd rev. ed. (Budapest: Közgazdasági és Jogi Könyvkiadó, 1958).

Kohn (Pap), Dávid. "Zsidó népmozgalmi statisztika" [Jewish demographical statistics], in *Évkönyv*, edited by Vilmos Bacher and Ferencz Mezey, pp. 35-47 (Budapest: Izraelita Magyar Irodalmi Társulat, 1895).

———. "Zsidók vándorlása" [Wanderings of Jews], in *Évkönyv*, edited by Vilmos Bacher and Ferencz Mezey, pp. 46-51 (Budapest: Izraelita Magyar Irodalmi Társulat, 1896).

———. "Zsidók vándorlása" [Wanderings of Jews], in *Évkönyv*, edited by József Bánczi, pp. 22-28 (Budapest: Izraelita Magyar Irodalmi Társulat, 1903).

Koós, Kálmán. *Voltunk vagyunk, leszünk* [We Were, We Are, We Will Be] (Buenos Aires: Hungarista Mozgalom, 1960).

Kővágó, László. *Nemzetiségek a mai Magyarországon* [Nationalities in Today's Hungary] (Budapest: Kossuth, 1981).

Kubinszky, Judit. "Adalékok az 1883 évi antiszemita zavargásokhoz" [Addenda to the 1883 anti–Semitic disturbances], *Századok* (1968): 158–177.

──────. *Politikai antiszemitizmus Magyarországon (1875–1890)* [Political Anti–Semitism in Hungary] (Budapest: Kossuth, 1976).

László, Ernő. "Hungarian Jewry: Settlement and Demography, 1735–38 to 1910," in *Hungarian–Jewish Studies,* edited by Randolph L. Braham, 3 vols. (New York: World Federation of Hungarian Jews, 1966–78), 1:61–136.

Lendvai, Paul. *Anti–Semitism Without Jews* (New York: Doubleday, 1971).

Listowel, Judith. *A Habsburg Tragedy Crown Prince Rudolf* (London: Ascent Books, 1978).

Luby, Margit. *A parasztélet rendje* [The Structure of Peasant Life] (Budapest: Centrum, 1935).

Makkai, János. *Urambátyám országa* [My Uncle's Country] (Budapest: Singer & Wolfner, 1945).

Marschalkó, Lajos. *Országhódítók* [Nation Conquerors] (Munich: Mikes Kelemen kör, 1975).

──────. *Világhódítók* [World Conquerors] (Munich: József Süli, 1958).

Marton, Ernest (Ernő). "The Family Tree of Hungarian Jewry," in *Hungarian–Jewish Studies,* edited by Randolph L. Braham, 3 vols. (New York: World Federation of Hungarian Jews, 1966–78) 1:1–59.

Mérei, Gyula. *Magyar politikai pártprogramok (1867–1914)* [Program of Hungarian Political Parties] (Budapest: G. Ranschburg, 1934).

──────. "Wahrmann Mór," in *Évkönyv,* edited by Samu Szemere, pp. 313–343 (Budapest: Izraelita Magyar Irodalmi Társulat, 1943).

Mikszáth, Kálmán. *Cikkek és karcolatok* [Articles and Sketches], vol. XIV, in *Mikszáth Kálmán összes művei* [Collected Works of Kálmán Mikszáth], edited by Gyula Bisztray and István Király (Budapest: Akadémiai Kiadó, 1974).

Molnár, Erik, Ervin Pamlényi, and György Székely, eds. *Magyaroszág története* [History of Hungary], 2 vols. (Budapest: Gondolat, 1967).

Nagy, József. "Falusi zsidó–élet Vasmegyében" [Rural Jewish life in Vas County], in *Évkönyv,* edited by József Bánóczi (Budapest: Izraelita Magyar Irodalmi Társulat, 1904).

Ortutay, Gyula. *Kis magyar néprajz* [Small Hungarian Ethnography] (Budapest: Gondolat, 1966).

Papp, Antal, ed. *Magyarország* [Hungary] (Budapest: Panoráma, n. d.).

Pulzer, P. G. J. *The Rise of Political Anti-Semitism in Germany and Austria* (New York: John Wiley & Sons, 1964).

Radó, István. "Zsidó vonatkozások Mikszáth műveiben" [References to Jews in Mikszáth's works], in *Évkönyv*, edited by József Bánóczi, pp. 166–195 (Budapest: Izraelita Magyar Irodalmi Társulat, 1913).

Révay, József. *Gömbös Gyula élete és politikája* [The Life and Politics of Gyula Gömbös] (Budapest: Franklin, 1934).

Sas, Andor. *A koronázó város* [Coronation City] (Bratislava: Madách, 1937).

Schickert, Klaus. *Die Judenfrage in Ungarn* (Essen: Essen Verlaganstalt, 1937).

Schindler, József. "Vidéki zsidóság" [Provincial Jewry], in *Új Élet Naptár*, edited by Endre Sós, pp. 147–155 (Budapest: Magyar Izraeliták Országos Képviselete, 1959).

Schück Jenő. "Az ortodoxia a felszabadulás után" [The orthodoxy after the liberation], in *Új Élet Naptár*, edited by Endre Sós, pp. 156–161 (Budapest: Magyar Izraeliták Országos Képviselete, 1959).

Simonyi, Iván. *Mentsük meg a magyar földbirtokot* [Let's Save the Hungarian Manor] (Pozsony and Lipcse: n. p., 1882).

_____. *Nemzeti tragikomédia* [National Tragicomedy] (Budapest: n. p., 1880).

Solymossy, László. *Hogyan épült Budapest? (1870–1930)* [How Was Budapest Built?] (Budapest: Fővárosi Közmunkák Tanácsa, 1931).

S. Vincze, Edit. *A hűtlenségi per 1871–1892* [The Disloyalty Case] (Budapest: Kossuth, 1971).

Szabad, György. *Forradalom és kiegyezés válaszútján (1860–61)* [At the Crossroads of Revolution and Compromise] (Budapest: Akadémiai Kiadó, 1967).

Szabó, László. *Magyarország földrajza* [The Geography of Hungary] (Budapest: Művelt Nép, 1954).

Száraz, György. *Egy előítélet nyomában* [In Pursuit of a Prejudice] (Budapest: Magvető, 1976).

Szatmári, Mór. *Húsz esztendő parlamenti viharai* [Paliamentary Storms of Twenty Years] (Budapest: Amicus, 1928).

_____. "Zsidók a magyar publicisztikában" [Jews in Hungarian Journalism], in *Évkönyv*, edited by Vilmos Bacher and Ferencz Mezey, pp. 171–178 (Budapest: Izraelita Magyar Irodalmi Társulat, 1895).

Széchy, János. *Az ittfelejtett nép* [People Left Here] (Budapest: Magyar Enciklopédisták Társasága, 1945).

Székely, Ferencz. "Számok és tanulságok" [Numbers and lessons], in *Évkönyv*, edited by József Bánóczi, pp. 43–49 (Budapest: Izraelita Magyar Irodalmi Társulat, 1900).

Tarr, László. *A delibábok országa* [The Country of Mirages] (Budapest: Magyar Helikon, 1976).

Tóth, Endre Mme. *Budapest enciklopédia* (Budapest: Corvina, 1981).

Ujvári, Péter, ed. *Magyar zsidó lexikon* [Hungarian Jewish Lexicon] (Budapest: Magyar Zsidó Lexikon, 1929).

Venetianer, Lajos. *A magyar zsidóság története* [History of Hungarian Jewry] (Budapest: n. p., 1922).

Verhovay, Gyula. *Az álarc korszaka* [Age of the Mask] (Budapest: F. Buschmann, 1889).

———. *Az ország urai* [Masters of the Country] (Budapest: F. Buschmann, 1890).

Vörös, Károly. *Egy világváros születése* [The Birth of a Metropolis] (Budapest: Kossuth, 1973).

Zay, Count Miklós. "Zsidók a társadalomban" [Jews in society]. *Huszadik Század* (July–December 1903): 948–968.

Zsoldos, Jenő. "Két elfelejtett Mikszath karcolat" [Two forgotten Mikszáth sketches], in *Évkönyv*, edited by Sándor Scheiber, pp. 166–206 (Budapest: Magyar Izraeliták Országos Képviselete, 1970).

———. *Magyar irodalom és zsidóság* [Hungarian Literature and Jewry] (Budapest: Országos Izraelita Tanítóegyesület, 1943).

Index